Advances in Computation: Theory and Practice
Volume 6

WEAK INTELLIGENCE:

Through the Principle and Paradox of Multiple Knowledge

Advances in Computation: Theory and Practice

Lee Keener, Editor-in-chief
Marcin Paprzycki (Editor)

Weak Intelligence: Through the Principle and Paradox of Multiple Knowledge
Matjaz Gams
ISBN 1-56072-898-1

Parallel Program Development for Cluster Computing: Methodology, Tools and Integrated Environments
José C. Cunha, Peter Kacsuk and Stephen C. Winter
ISBN 1-56072-865-5

Structured Matrices: Recent Advances and Applications
Dario Andrea Bini, Eugene Tyrtyshnikov and Plamen Yalamov
ISBN 1-56072-890-6

Recent Trends in Numerical Analysis
Donato Trigiante
ISBN 1-56072-885-X

High Performance Algorithms for Structured Matrix Problems
Peter Arbenz, Marcin Paprzycki, Ahmed Sameh and Vivek Sarin
ISBN 1-56072-594-X

Advances in the Theory of Computation: Theory and Practice
Volume 6

WEAK INTELLIGENCE:

Through the Principle and Paradox of Multiple Knowledge

MATJAZ GAMS

Nova Science Publishers, Inc.
Huntington, New York

Library of Congress Cataloging-in-Publication Data
Weak Intelligence: Through the Principle and Paradox of Multiple Knowledge / Matjaz Gams.
p. cm.
Includes bibliographical references and index.
ISBN 1-56072-898-1
1. Artificial Intelligence. I. Title.
Q335.G354 2001
006.3--dc21 2001018736

227 Main Street, Suite 100
Huntington, New York 11743
Tele. 631-424-6682 Fax 631-425-5933
e-mail: Novascience@earthlink.net
Web Site: http://www.nexusworld.com/nova

Printed in the United States of America

To all the universes we leave in
and to all our dearest

Contents

Preface

From 1930 until recent years, computer scientists and practitioners utilised single models, in principle executable on any Turing machine. For those unaware of Turing machines – it is a very simple machine with a couple of operations, a sort of an abstract primitive digital computer. Given sufficient time or speed of the primitive operations, it can simulate computing of any existing or future (similarly designed, digital or analog or of any today known) computer.

It was also thought that the human brain corresponds to a very complex machine, and that it is in principle executable on sufficiently fast digital computers with huge memory capacities. Now we know of several indications that **intelligence cannot be achieved on digital computers with classical approaches** – e.g., as claimed by Wilkes (1992) that no computer intelligence has been produced in the last 40 years despite efforts of the brightest computer scientists, by Penrose (1989; 1994) and his "seeing" the truth of Gödel's theorem which no Turing machine can produce, by Edelman (1992) and his returning the mind back into nature, by Searle (1982) with the Chinese-room thought experiment, by Winograd and Flores (1986) and Dreyfus (1979), and in particular by Wegner (1997).

There have been many discussions regarding **the nature of intelligence** (Dreyfus 1979; Edelman 1992; Hauser, Rapaport 1993; Minsky 1991a; 1991b; Penrose 1989; 1990; 1994; Schank 1991; Searle 1990; Sloman 1992; Wilkes 1992; Winograd, Flores 1986). Two extremes regarding artificial intelligence (AI) wash ashore: some say that even simple machines like thermostats or calculators have (a certain amount of) intelligence, and others say that even passing the Turing test does not suffice to be admitted as intelligent.

The first approach is often denoted as **strong artificial intelligence** (strong AI), "functionalism" or "operationalism", and claims that performance of the human brain can be simulated by a Turing machine with an appropriate algorithm. This group has very prominent representatives, and is close to formal sciences. It still dominates AI research despite heavy attacks from cognitive science and partially from **weak AI**. The milestone of this research direction is the Church-Turing thesis claiming that everything that can be described as an effective procedure can be simulated by and computed on a Turing machine. Furthermore, it has been shown that anything more powerful than a Turing machine, i.e. being able to solve problems which are theoretically impossible to compute by a Turing machine, is itself of a different nature – close to "not computable" or "unsolvable" in the usual meaning of human words.

On the other hand, the idea that the human brain is nothing else but a machine was often disputed by philosophers and other members of cognitive disciplines. Philosophy is one of the main competing sciences when modelling and automating human performance is in question. Philosophy builds from observing the performance of humans. From that view, there are so great differences between humans and computers (and also between animals and computers), and so little success in achieving true artificial intelligence, that empirical results so far are more in favour of those who see that there must be something wrong in representing humans as formal algorithmic machines. There are even those who think that the mind is outside the laws of this world.

New, weak AI is opened to new ideas from different areas. Relying on old positions has obviously not been fruithfull, therefore, this is a way to open space for new comprehensions. The term "weak AI" was coined by John Searle, and is very similar to "cognitive-sciences AI". This direction accepts that the human brain/mind is the only intelligent system according to our knowledge, and that we have to introduce new approaches in order to achieve intelligence on computers.

Traditional or **classical AI** implicitly or explicitly incorporates strong AI and parts of strong-weak AI. It is based on general computational concepts involving the kinds of data structures, and the properties of the control strategies used by systems solving intelligent tasks, e.g., intelligent data retrieval systems, natural language processing, learning, machine vision, automatic programming, logic programming, game playing. It is concerned with writing programs which solve tasks requiring human intelligence, e.g., playing chess, symbolic integration of complex expressions, automatic writing computer programs. It was thought that "such systems possess some degree of artificial intelligence" (Nilsson 1980). And that "AI has also embraced the larger scientific goal of constructing an information-processing theory of intelligence. If such a *science of intelligence* could be developed, it could guide the design of intelligent machines as well as explicate intelligent behaviour as it occurs in humans and other animals". The proposed approach was based on formal models and logic. It is interesting to compare these positions in one of the basic AI textbooks for graduate students with what we think today – around a decade later, which amounts to 20% of computer history. In the words of Penrose (1990) when describing traditional AI: "in the nature of this activity, however, that although there is much of it going on, I have been unable to perceive any fundamental new principles that have emerged." Indeed, a substantial part of traditional AI seems to be following decades old directions without incorporating or generating substantially different new general theories.

Several AI communities simply avoid this dilemma by statements like: "Please do not discuss or write about themata such as 'Can computers think'." Their argumentation is that discussions about principles of intelligence are unproductive since no new discovery has been made in this area in the last 50 years. In addition, there are several other excluding viewpoints on AI; for example, one sees intelligence as a Boolean category – it is either achieved (at human level; often subjectively judged) or not, and the other as a measurable quantity (on a scale from 0 upwards; rather objective). It is like the often quoted analogy (e.g., Churchland and Churchland 1990): light can be seen either as a binary category (either you see it or not) or a natural measurable phenomenon.

How do we know that something is intelligent and conscious? The famous Turing test (Turing 1950; Michie 1993a) is – although a probabilistic detective test – a YES/NO test. There is no scale to obtain a measurable quantity. For the time being we do not have any reasonable definition of artificial intelligence (Winston 1992) nor any reasonable procedure for measuring it. Yet, we have no troubles with labelling humans as more or less intelligent by applying IQ tests or common sense. We can rather easily sort animal species according to intelligence, or even different sorts of dogs, and specific individual dogs inside the same species.

For a start we shall accept Penrose's and Edelman's position that **whatever intelligence and consciousness is, our common sense supported by scientific opinions will recognise it**. Unfortunately for classical AI, today it is commonly accepted that existing computer systems are not intelligent and that they remain just quick calculating and information-processing machines. Even programs that are capable of performing intelligent tasks better than humans – e.g., computer chess – do not exhibit any intelligence or consciousness. At the same time, general opinion seems inclined to accept certain aspects of intelligence and consciousness of animals, e.g., chimpanzees, dogs and dolphins, although they cannot perform any of the symbolic tasks computers perform so well, e.g., algebra, data processing, reading or writing and storing huge amounts of digital data.

Whatever the case, one of basic questions – whether intelligence can be achieved on digital computers at all (Edelman 1992; Penrose 1989; 1994; Searle 1982; Wilkes 1992) – remains **one of the core AI questions with profound consequences for the human race**. All we have now are opinions and viewpoints – for example, some believe that human-level knowledge is going to be achieved on computers in a couple of years (Lenat 1989) while others say that knowledge is not a substance that can be stored in computers (Clancey 1989).

It is not to say that classical AI has not achieved important advances. For example, expert systems (Feigenbaum 1985; Harmon *et al.* 1988) and neural networks have raised great expectations, and had substantial commercial success (Rosenblat 1962; Soucek and Soucek 1988). It is only a false impression that the most successful AI programs are those playing chess. In fact, chess programs were hot stuff around ten to fifteen years ago. Today, they are regarded as classical computer programs, by-products of AI research. Indeed, this is the destiny of all AI achievements. Many challenges were given to AI as test beds, with chess being one of the examples. It was claimed that playing chess at the levels of human masters would certainly be beyond the reach of digital computers and if achieved, such programs could be accepted as intelligent. Today, that has been achieved, but we know that these programs are not intelligent, and it is commonly seen as not being true AI anymore.

This is **the story of real successes of AI** – not in the sense of achieving true intelligence, but in the sense of influencing classical progress of digital computers. What about WYSIWYG first implemented in Apples and now predominant on PC's? Hasn't it been researched at Palo Alto and at that time seen as AI research – how children communicate with machines? Hasn't that influenced visiting Jobs and created one of revolutions in computer industry? What about Smalltalk, the first successful object-oriented language, which was developed in the AI community? What about MACSYMA, the pioneering symbolic-processing system eventually leading to Mathematica and other successful mathematical packages? What about the AI technique "propagation of constraints"? That has been implemented in spreadsheets as claimed by Winston, former president of American AI Society. The influence might be indeed an indirect one, but who can claim that other achievements of computer science or science in general had more direct implications? Science is destined to run one step in front of applications.

However, no major step has been taken towards true intelligent behaviour of computer systems. Even systems rating highest in Turing tests (Epstein 1992) were simple action–pattern systems, scoring highest when they successfully misspelled a couple of words. Serious criticism has emerged once again, this time in serious scientific magazines (Wilkes 1992): "we take a working hypothesis that intelligent behaviour in Turing's sense is outside the range of the digital computer." Critics include most prominent researchers from computer science, philosophy and physics alike. Indeed, if computer intelligence were a single category, the constant growth of computer power would have to cause the growth of computer intelligence, however far from the human level. Furthermore, AI projects like the Fifth generation project (CACM-36-3 1993) and the CYC project (Stefik, Smoliar 1993) have not produced anything acceptable as intelligent or conscious despite huge efforts and substantial financing for over 10 years.

Therefore, **it is not very likely that we shall achieve true artificial intelligence with existing formalistic approaches** given however fast computers. It is either the case that human-level intelligence cannot be achieved on digital computers at all, or it can be achieved in a different way. The latter was already proposed by several researchers (e.g., Hendler *et al.* 1991), and it was claimed that (Minsky 1991a): "the future work of mind design will not be much like what we do today".

History teaches as that counter examples often result in new theories. The Michelson-Morley experiment has shown that light travels with the same speed in any direction – contradictory to Newton's model of the world. However, it took two decades before Einstein in 1905 provided a principle, which is now known as the law of relativity. Similarly, Heisenberg's new theory was introduced because at that time physicists were not able to design good models at the level of atomic particles with existing approaches. Heisenberg proposed his theory as the principle of uncertainty because at that time nobody knew how to formally prove it. Similarly, **AI needs new principles to explain the lack of intelligence in digital computers.**

Since new AI opposes the core of not only the predominant AI but also some interpretations of postulates of computer science in general, it is of no great surprise that it has been successfully suppressed until recent years. For example, the ideas of Winograd and Flores (1986), Dreyfus (1979) or Searle (1982) were more or less rejected in the natural- and engineering-sciences community. But the discussion is becoming less and less one-sided in recent years.

One of the first new theories about intelligence gaining world-wide attention was a non-computational hypothesis based on quantum physics. The special December issue of the "Behavioral and Brain Sciences" journal (Penrose 1990) was devoted to replies of different researchers. Comments by thirty-seven reviewers from several disciplines were followed by the author's unrepentant response. Both his books (1989, 1994) were accompanied by heated debates through Internet. Many papers in the "Journal of Consciousness Studies" were also devoted to analyses of Penrose's ideas. The journal started in 1994 with Penrose as one of the editors. Today, debates about Penrose seem outdated, but they mark the end of the old-minded AI period.

The author, an Oxford professor Roger Penrose is one of the most famous mathematical physicists with several discoveries from physics (e.g., regarding black holes with Hawking) and mathematics (e.g., how to tile a plane non-periodically with only two shapes). He has written his first book *"The Emperors New Mind: Concerning Computers, Minds, and the Laws of Physics"* (1989) because he was astonished by a TV debate with strong-AI supporters on BBC. The title of the book alludes to the emperor's invisible dress – everybody admires it, yet there is nothing to be seen. According to Martin Gardner's forward, Penrose is "the child sitting in the third row, a distance back from the leaders of AI, who dares to suggest that the emperors of strong AI have no clothes."

Replies from classical AI in correlation with formal scientific movement were uprising. In 1994, Joseph R. Abrahamson in his article "Mind, Evolution, and Computers" describes Penrose (despite admitting that he is one of the world's most eminent physicists) as one of those "who in the name of any one of a number of gods want to destroy rationality and science. It is important to be particularly aware when one of our attempts, in however subtle a manor, to suggest this magic should supplant or even be used to embellish reason and logic."

Based on old literature citations in Penrose's book, the predominantly strong AI community harshly attacked Penrose because of his obvious lack of knowledge of current AI activities. Even more, Penrose's arguments remain debatable even inside weak AI community.

Yet, the criticism by classical AI failed. Angell (1993) points out that symbolic approaches lack true understanding: "As if every word were not a pocket into which now this, now that, now several things at once have been put!" In a reply to Abrahamson's critique, Cronin (1994) writes: (old) "AI community has become an arcane, closed-minded, and theoretically incestuous field of computer science." Such words certainly did not encourage friendship between the two antagonising communities.

Abrahamson (1994b) in a reply to Cronin softens his criteria. Scientists should be open to all new ideas, and new ideas should be strictly verified before fully accepted. This seems to be the turning point of accepting weak AI as science as long as it accepts basic scientific verification. It also means denotes a certain split between serious weak-AI researchers accepting scientific approaches and alternative movements. But the difference in directions between strong and weak AI remains basically unchanged and the core of this book.

New theories are often accepted with a large dose of skepticism and resistance. For example, quantum physics was not accepted for a substantial period of time, and Einstein was one of prominent opponents. Today we accept quantum theory for granted. In analogy, current criticism should be regarded primarily as means of forcing proponents of new AI ideas to provide more formal and unrefutable laws.

Rather than being a mystic, Penrose accepts all natural laws and proposes another physical law concerned with events at the border of quantum and classical physical theory. This new theory is supposed to provide an explanation why quantum effects which supposedly take place in the human brain, have greater computational power and enable common-sense semantic reasoning which cannot be simulated by formal machines like the Turing machine or digital computers. In fact, Penrose has presented another quite strong indication that humans posses at least different kinds of thinking that Turing machines.

There are **several other well-established researchers in weak AI** representing the major human factor why this new wave of weak AI was not rejected as before:

- Francis Crick is probably one of the most well-deserved researchers for introducing consciousness as a legitimate subject of science. He shared a Nobel Prize for the discovery of DNA's structure in 1953. As a neuroscientist, he wants to study consciousness through the brain's internal structure.

- Another Nobel Prize winner is Gerald M. Edelman. He shared the prize in 1972 for research on antibodies. He is the author of Neural Darwinism, a theory promoting competition between groups of neurons as the basis of awareness and consciousness.

- Brian D. Josephson won his Nobel Prize in 1973 for a special quantum effect. He proposes a unified field theory encapsulating mystical and psychic experiences.

- Maurice W. Wilkes is the first person ever earning money for AI-related events. In the 1992 paper he presents an opinion that intelligence may be out of reach of digital computers.

Suddenly, at least part of criticism of strong AI is getting accepted. E.g., in Sloman's opinion (1992) excessively strong versions of AI attacked by Penrose and Searle are not worth defending or attacking being obviously wrong. If even some practitioners in AI believe in the extreme strong or strong-strong thesis, it is the reason for criticising them, not AI. In any field there are the "naive, ill-informed, over-enthusiastic".

Old knowledge and habits don't fade away easily. Students in computer sciences, mathematics and similar natural sciences get acquainted with the Church theses and Turing machines. After a while, technical details fade away, and we are left with a frame in our memory stating that practically everything reasonable is also executable by a Turing machine. Nobody has thought us of overabstractions of the Turing machine or substantial differences between formal sciences and real world. Hopefully, some day students will have better lectures than that. This book is certainly an attempt to recondition the observed discrepancies.

Sloman's most important new ideas are based on parallel architectures of intelligent systems. In his viewpoint of an intelligent system, it is not important *what* it does but *how* it does it. The internal structure/architecture is more important than the performance rate. The idea is primarily based on the **coexistence of mutually cooperating processes.**

Similar approach was proposed before, e.g., by Minsky (1991a): "In the early days of AI, students would ask, 'What is the best way to represent knowledge' and I usually answered that we did not yet know. But now I would give a different reply: To solve all but the simplest problems, we'll need to use several different representations. This is because each particular kind of data-structure has its own virtues and deficiencies, and none by itself can be adequate for all the different functions involved with what we call 'common sense". This resembles a modified strong-AI idea that only very complex computer systems with parallel architectures and real-world sensors can obtain intelligence (Abrahamson 1994a).

Gerald Edelman (1992) has similar but more biology-oriented ideas about multiplicity in the human brains. In the human brain there are groups of neurons that compete with each other. In this way, population thinking emerges representing the basis of evolution.

Although new ideas about intelligence are sometimes speculative and not easily accepted by scientific audience, they seem to have a common background. In this book, an attempt was made **to identify and incorporate the common denominator into a technical principle.** According to this viewpoint, future generation intelligent computer systems will substantially differ from existing systems in a way indicated by Brooks (1991); Edelman (1992); Kitano (1993); Gams, Krizman (1991); Minsky (1987); Penrose (1989; 1994); Sloman (1992) and Soucek

(1992) (And several others that should be mentioned if there were enough space and time. My sincere apologies to all of them).

We propose **multiplicity** as one of the properties which are essential for achieving artificial intelligence (Gams *et al.* 1991; Gams, Krizman 1991). **Multiple systems consist of subsystems which contribute their opinion from semantically different points of view** when a conclusion is to be made (see Figure 1). In this book, we provide many indications that in comparison to single models, multiple models enable important new super-set properties necessary for computer intelligence. (Related terms are multiple knowledge, multidimensionality, multistrategy, hybrid systems, multiple-agent systems, integrated systems.

Where does the multiplicity come from? We provide a possible physical background for the multiple theory of intelligence – the many-worlds model of our universe (Dewitt 1973). In this physical meta-theory, the basic quantum mechanical principle, called the superposition principle, can be applied also at the classical level. It introduces coexistence of alternative (multiple) universes.

If our working hypothesis proves to be valid, several profound consequences can be derived. For example, one-model systems could be regularly replaced by multi-model systems in research and engineering alike. Furthermore, new theories might provide better understanding of intelligence, and better chances to design truly intelligent artificial systems.

The consequences of the principle of multiple knowledge should not be taken too light. For example, if we combine solutions from several models (each model corresponding to a text on a paper sheet in Figure 1), an enormous number of possible combinations emerges and thus better adaptivity to real-life circumstances. If we combine different words from 5 paper sheets into one paper sheet, we get 10^{300} possibilities. Compare this to 10^{80} to 10^{120} as the number of all atomic particles in our universe. The only system that effectively uses and is capable to cope with such a computationally explosive approach are the brains and the mind combined. It also means that the two are enormously more complicated that thought before. Counting the number of neurons in the brains is like counting words in the 5 paper sheets in Figure 1. These numbers are enormously smaller than numbers of all possible dynamic either text or neuron combinations.

How does the proposed approach differ from those previously published? First, instead of Penrose's "oneness" of the human brain, consciousness, and our physical universe, it proposes their multiplicity or "manyness". Unlike Edelman, who practically eliminates anything nonbiological, the introduced principle of multiple knowledge encapsulates any intelligent system, as long as it follows the proposed directions. Instead of Sloman's engineering theories of parallel architectures and coexisting processes, we try to pin out the essential property of this phenomenon: different processes or agents have to have **semantically different points of view regarding the same problem.** In principle, parallelism itself does not mean much more than an implementation detail, although very important for engineering

Figure 1: The first impression of multiple knowledge. One-level knowledge (system, model) can be represented by text on one paper sheet. The first approximation of multiple knowledge is represented as a couple of paper sheets. Information from these multiple sheets should be properly combined in time and space, e.g., into one dynamic text on one sheet, in order to obtain more flexible and generally better real-world performance. This is a precondition for real-life intelligence.

purposes. Similarly, just combining two different approaches, e.g., classical and connectionist models (Boden 1991; Minsky 1991a; 1991b) represents just a little more complicated classical approach. In recent years these hybrid multiple approach is gaining popularity, but without a general argumentation or a principle that is introduced in this book.

Many publications indicate that there is something wrong with the Turing machine when applied to real-life and the human brain. In this book, it has been clearly and even formally proven where the difference comes from and why it is essential. In short – the principle of multiple knowledge is essential only for the real world we live in (or for a combination of many worlds where worlds such as ours are essential), and it is useless in an average single world where formal random worlds are as possible as real worlds.

Second, we try to incorporate interesting parts of previously known ideas, enhance and formalise them in a technical form as a language-independent cybernetical principle. The principle offers several noteworthy consequences, which can be – along with the principle – tested and verified empirically and formally. Time will tell whether our principle is scientifically and technically sufficiently defined at syntactic and semantic level. If not, upgraded ideas will emerge.

Third, the book tends to analyse currently relevant theses about key computing concepts – e.g., the Church thesis, Turing machines, Occam's Razor. If proposed modifications are valid, possible consequences are profound. Accepting the principle of multiple knowledge means substantially influencing further computer research and technology. The technical question addressed by the book is how to design a model of the problem domain in order to perform well in future tasks, i.e., how to represent knowledge in complex real-life domains.

The fourth difference is in the attitude towards current hard formal sciences and strong AI. While we agree with Penrose and Sloman that strong AI cannot achieve human-level intelligence, old knowledge is not going to fade away. Newton's physics has not faded away after quantum physics was discovered. Turing machines and the Church theses are going to remain among the most important concepts for formal domains even after new theses and principles about true intelligence will be fully discovered. This book is not an attack on the old knowledge, but an attempt to put it in the right environment where it is perfectly valid.

Fifth, AI, biology, physics, etc., are treated as independent and on equal rights in this book. While Penrose or Edelman rightly criticise old AI, they hardly mention weak AI, and even when they do, a great dose of misunderstanding and underestimation is present. For example, on the cover pages of "The Shadows of the Mind" (Penrose 1994), one can read that "he mounts an even more powerful attack on artificial intelligence". Which AI – strong or weak or both? No wonder that Edelman and Penrose eliminate each others ideas quite profoundly.

In reality, highly interdisciplinary weak AI embraces both Edelman's and Penrose's ideas as interesting scientific hypotheses about intelligence and the mind. **AI**

combined with all interdisciplinary sciences is the science whose predominant goal is to design intelligent artificial systems. (Or at least it should be). To achieve this, all related knowledge is welcome, be it from biology, chemistry, physics or psychology. By definition, weak AI encapsulates biological machines as well, which are definitively intelligent.

In past, many sciences had their wrong turns and needed a little help from related fields. For AI – less than 45-years old scientific discipline – a bit of sympathy and fairness is needed as much as friendly help.

This is what this book is about. As an upgrade of many previous Ideas, e.g., Collins (1996) uses a term "polymorphic actions", a rather simple cybernetical principle called "the principle of multiple knowledge" is proposed. It enables an important improvement in analysing and understanding minds and computers. Very good indications can be presented that the principle is valid, even a near-formal proof. Therefore, this book proves that **there must be something very special in our heads**, and one property of that "special" is becoming evident.

Arguably, the major attack on strong AI came from Wegner's paper in "Communications of the ACM" in 1997: "Why Interaction is More Powerful Than ALgorithms". Wegner shows that universal Turing machines are less powerful than the interaction Turing machines, i.e. machines that dynamically gather information in iteraction with other actors in the environment. This publication did not stirr major public attention, at least not compared to the uproar following Penroses' books. Yet, it is the formal proof that the Church-Turing thesis needs modifications. So in a way, the old strong-weak AI account is settled: **universal Turing machines on itself are not suficient to achieve intelligence.**

Edelman (1992) says that we are facing a major scientific crises in formal sciences. Many of the old truths are not eternal as seen a couple of years ago. Lots of new hypotheses are generated, many of them wrong and many of them approaching correct new ideas. New knowledge will significantly increase our knowledge about ourselves and the world we live in. Hopefully, this book will enable a step ahead towards scientific explanation of **the greatest mystery of our times** – the human brain and the mind.

Chapter 1

Artificial Intelligence

In this section we present current mainstreams, a short history of artificial intelligence, current, past and future trends and problems. Different, often critical viewpoints on AI are presented.

1.1 Artificial Intelligence Directions

Basically, there are three AI mainstreams:

1. **Classical, formal, strong**
   Maybe we should distinguish between classical and strong AI, however, distinctions between the basic three directions presented here are the major one. Classical AI represents a large majority of current AI events and establishments, e.g., conferences, magazines, etc. Although most current AI activities fall in this category, it is not as overwhelming as it used to be. Many well-known researchers provide valid arguments that this line is recently not progressing quickly and is not producing great new ideas.

2. **Cognitive, interdisciplinary, new, weak**
   This direction deals with consciousness, human properties, qualia (In short, qualia is what is left after one eliminates ration and logic from humans. What is left are feelings, subjective values, beliefs etc.). AI researchers in this category search for new comprehensions listening to philosophers, physicists, psychologist, evolutionists, and other scientists dealing with humans and live beings. The idea is that computers are either essentially different or even in principle inferior to humans, therefore, we have to learn from our nature, from the human brain and mind to make new discoveries that will enable creating better and maybe intelligent computers. This new stream has got some place under predominantly formal science politics only lately and is still fighting for recognition. It is open to new ideas, very wide and sometimes boundary or

even beyond that. Therefore, one should be at least a little cautious if expecting that all ideas here are pure gold. On the other hand, it is the most intellectually exciting, challenging and risky direction at the same time. The weak AI stream is very popular especially in USA and some Western countries while the rest of the world is following slowly. Trends are highly positive, results mixed.

3. **Invisible, design-oriented, engineering**
The emphasis is on systems that work in real-life applications. This direction is constantly progressing in recent years. Terms like intelligent systems and intelligent agents indicate that intelligence here is treated in the sense of making systems more flexible and user-friendly, not aiming at passing the Turing test.

1.2 History of Artificial Intelligence

To understand current trends in artificial intelligence, a short history of AI can be of great help (Michalski, Tecuci 1993b). Here we try to present AI history in 5-years intervals starting in 1955. AI history often starts with the Darthmouth conference in 1956 (Copeland 1993) where McCarthy organised the first AI conference.

Others propose Turing's "Computing Machinery and Intelligence" in 1950 for the beginning of AI. Another common milestone is the paper by McCulloch and Pitts published in 1943. However, these papers are probably not enough to encapsulate active AI research. For example, after the Darthmoutn conference artificial intelligence laboratories were established at a number of universities: Carnegie Mellon (Newell, Simon), Stanford (McCarthy), MIT (Marvin Minsky), Edinburgh (Donald Michie following Alan Turing).

Similarly, although Charles Babbage designed Difference Engine, a mechanical computer with a method for programming the machine, already in 1830s, it does not represent the start of computing. Electronic computing started around the Second World War, and AI followed gradually. Whatever the case, exact dating is always debatable while a general time span and directions are less questionable.

In AI history, there are ever recurring waves of overenthusiasm and overscepticism:

Early Enthusiasm or Tabula Rasa Craze (1955-1965)

The first AI era was impressed by the fact that human brains are several orders of magnitude slower that computers in transmission as well as in coupling speed. Therefore, making a copy of the human brain on a computer would have to result in something ingeniously better. Three subjects were predominant:

- learning without knowledge,

- neural modeling (self-organizing systems and decision space techniques), and
- evolutionary learning.

Dark Ages (1965-1975)

In the second epoch it became clear that the first approach yielded no fruitful results. There were strong indications that the proposed methods were unable to make further progress beyond solving a limited number of simple tasks. After funds for artificial intelligence research were deeply cut worldwide, new approaches were searched for. This era recognized that

- to acquire knowledge one needs knowledge, and
- initiated symbolic concept acquisition.

Renaissance (1975-1980)

Research in artificial intelligence continued despite cuts in funding, since it is a subject that will probably challenge human interest forever. Taking modest aims more appropriate to the level of current technology and knowledge sometimes produced even better results than expected. The characteristics are:

- exploration of different strategies,
- knowledge-intensive approaches,
- successful applications, and
- conferences and workshops worldwide.

AI Boom (1980-1990)

Artificial intelligence R&D produced a number of commercial booms such as expert systems. Literature, conferences, funds and related events have been growing exponentially for a few years. "Superprojects" like the CYC project and the Fifth Generation project were in full progress approaching final stages. Artificial intelligence was reaching maturity as indicated by:

- experimental comparisons of AI methods and systems,
- revival of non-symbolic methods such as neural networks and evolutionary computing,
- technology-based fields gained attention – agents and memory-based reasoning,
- computational learning theory,

- integrated and multistrategy systems, and
- emphasis on practical applications.

However, no generally accepted intelligent (i.e. "truly" intelligent) system was in sight.

New AI Winter (1990-1995)

Major AI projects like the Fifth Generation project or the CYC project have not resulted in intelligent or commercially successful products. Overexpectations backfired again and criticism emerged with two basic claims:

- There are several indications that intelligence cannot be easily achieved on digital computers with existing approaches and methodologies.
- Today's computers as well as existing approaches basically do not differ much from those of 30 years ago (apart from being faster and having better storing capacities) and, therefore, are very unlikely to approach not only human-level but also any level of intelligence established by biological intelligent systems.

Note that here are at least two different opinions: some say that computers are already intelligent and others say that none computer/machine is ever going to be intelligent. Our opinion is a common-sense one and close to the one presented by Penrose in 1990: we **humans would recognise true intelligence**

although different from the one we possess. There is no major reason why other beings/machines would not become intelligent, as long as they have fulfilled necessary preconditions. After all, a human is a special kind of a biological/chemical ... machine and being at the same time.

Possible consequences of these debates are profound: for example, if computers cannot think, then quests for true intelligence on computers are as unrealistic as searching for perpetuum mobile. Another possible implication is as follows: if computers can nevertheless think and if the brightest minds have not been able to achieve intelligence in over 30 years on the best computers available, then they must have been trying in the wrong directions.

Funds for science in general, and AI in particular in this period are decreasing as a long-term trend.

Engineering AI, Weak AI and Agents (1995-...)

Engineering or invisible AI produces working systems, although it has disappeared from the first pages of semi-scientific journals with titles such as "Artificial intelligence is changing the world". One important milestone is IBM's Deep Blue program defeating world champion Kasparov in 1997. Less noticed by public, software engineers are adding model-based diagnoses, rule-based modules and intelligent-interface agents on top of their conventional systems. AI techniques get invisibly inter-woven with other approaches inside working systems. Intelligent systems, agents and the Internet are top success stories. Humans are overloaded and lost in the world of information overload. They desperately need intelligent assistants, even when it comes to dealing with operating systems and Office applications. Wizards, Office assistants and other programs help humans avoid problems with rigid formal computer systems and increase productivity. It is not top AI formal science, but it works.

At the same time, **bold new ideas are emerging, challenging the fundamentals of computer science as well as science in general** – the Turing machine paradigm, Gödel's theorem and Church's thesis.

The First Dawn Approaching? (20XX-...)

Humans are intelligent, and there is no principal reason why we wouldn't be able to design intelligent being and machines in reasonable future. Currently there seem to be more unsolved questions than lights at the end of the tunnel, but no doubt this will change.

1.3 Where's the AI?

Thinking about the definition of AI, one should ask "Where's the AI?" (Schank 1991). There seem to be at least four prevailing answers to that question.

The **first view** sees AI as something magic that emerges out of a computationally effective computer system after you put in it enough things.

Indeed, it is still often acclaimed that neural networks mimic the behavior of human brains. That is rather surprising since what they do at present is to mimic a numeric filter at best able to tune predefined parameters. Not surprisingly, computationally more diverse and structurally more complex statistical methods often achieve better classification accuracy. This approach has already contributed to the first dark age at the beginning of AI and is still present in many subfields of AI. On the other hand, one should not underestimate the advantages of neural networks such as flexibility and robustness. And in addition, humans undoubtedly possess neural networks. But there is no magic in current artificial neural networks. The "magic" is in the neural networks of humans.

The **second view** sees AI as a superb inference engine and therefore resembles knowledge engineering. What one has to do is to find an expert, encode his/hers knowledge into lists of rules, add an inference engine with appropriate interface and there you are. This has led many people to think that AI means rule-based expert systems, and then they thought they understand them as well as AI. And since they have also learned the limitations of rule-based systems, they also think that is the limitation of AI, not just of one component of AI (Hayes-Roth, Fikes

1991). While connectionism as well as knowledge engineering and inference engines are important parts of AI research and applications, labeling it intelligent or as AI itself is misleading (Schank 1991).

The **third view** maintains that, if no machine ever did it before, it must be AI. For example, years ago research in computer chess was one of the central themata in AI. People thought that computer programs playing chess well would certainly have to be intelligent. Now, nearly everybody agrees that these programs do not have any deep intelligence at all. Luckily, there are several explanations of this contradiction. For one thing, this viewpoint seems to confuse getting a machine to do something intelligent with getting it to be a model of human intelligence. More important, if you define AI in that way – to be one of frontiers of computer science, once the area that you are looking at is understood, then it is no longer at the frontiers of computer science and therefore no longer AI, and so it is a no-win kind of ever-repeating situation.

The **forth viewpoint** sees intelligence in learning, in improving performance on the basis of experience when acting in dynamic environment. Since there is no computer program changing its performance on the basis of true learning, there is no true AI. This holds for classical programs as well as for most of the machine learning programs. A typical machine learning program gets fed by data and performs some kind of capturing properties of data into a compressed form. Intelligent agents on the Internet are essentially more advances since they gather information from unexpected sources/actors through the Internet. However, even they do not perform true learning in the sense biological being do.

So, where is the intelligence in computer programs? As mentioned earlier, many difficult problems which had long been thought to require real intelligence, have been solved by rather unintelligent methods. Intensifying this argument, even superb intelligent behavior does not guarantee that real intelligence and understanding have been achieved. For example, Searle (1982) has constructed a hypothetical Chinese room in which a group of workers performs intelligent translation between two natural languages (English-Chinese) and each of them performs only a subpart of the whole process on the basis of a predefined procedure. Although such a Chinese room could behave seemingly intelligently and even pass the Turing test, the room (and nobody inside it) does not understand the whole process and there is no real intelligence at all.

After a decade of quite intensive debates this paradox still represents a philosophical question: Is performance, i.e. a mechanistic approach really sufficient? From a practical point of view, most things in our world work in the mechanistic mode. Of course, there are paradoxes and unsolved questions (e.g. are there other civilizations or is there only ours?) but people have successfully lived with them. Not to mention that other approaches based on ideology or spiritism have not yielded similarly good results.

Since strong AI relies on the mechanistic viewpoint, and mechanism is prevailing in the developed countries in general, strong AI could be seen as the correct orientation. However, there are at least two arguments corrupting the strong-AI image and the formalistic scientific approach:

- If intelligence (in computers) were simple, fast and powerful computers would have facilitated it a long time ago. Indeed, for so many times humans thought they are approaching the secret of human intelligence, and they were disappointed for so many times that it is hard to believe that it won't happen again. Understandably, some are a little pessimistic about possibility of reaching it at all, e.g., Angell (1993): "the closer we look at knowledge, intelligence or wisdom, the less we understand them". Yet, we must try again and again in different ways, and to learn through mistakes.

- Many of the old AI ideas have produced much more optimism than real improvements. Actually, there is no sign that we are indeed approaching true computer intelligence.

Serious scientists like Searle (1982) claim that digital machines cannot be intelligent as biological beings since they are essentially different. Some disagree. For example, (Hayes *et al.* 1992) claims that no proof is given for such claims.

Two compromising arguments seem plausible:

- Real human intelligence is very complex. If it were simple enough for us to understand it, than we would be too simple to perceive that.

- Intelligence may be an emerging property of very complex information machines or beings controlling real-world environments. There does not have to be any deeper motive or principle behind it. This approach is very close to "artificial life" or "evolutionary computing" where computational models share many characteristics with biological computation (Brooks 1991).

There are additional thoughts about intelligence:

- Intelligence is in size. It is hard to expect a small program to display intelligence. Intelligence is neither simple nor easy understandable.

- Intelligence is in complexity and heterogeneity. This area is sometimes related to multi-strategy learning (Michalski & Tecuci 1993), multiple-knowledge approach (Gams *et al.* 1991) and multi-agents (Minsky 1987).

- Intelligence is in the ability to perform well real-life tasks which require the use of knowledge. Without knowledge and without dynamic relation to the real world there seem to be no chance for machines to become intelligent.

Any of these single items is not enough for intelligence, but they already exclude majority of classical AI project as candidates for achieving intelligence. For example, Mathematica, a program for symbolic computing, is regarded as unintelligent as a numeric library. But only fifteen years ago, programs performing symbolic integration were regarded as the most interesting AI programs.

Furthermore, there are several aspects of intelligence each of which can be compared if not measured on a scale. For example, motional intelligence can be quite high in many animals. In another aspect, AI research can well be at the frontiers of computer science while AI applications fell into an application area years away from new theoretical achievements. AI applications do not have to be intelligent, they have to be related to AI research similar to other science/application relations.

In AI like in all sciences there are two major groups: **scruffies** and **neats.** Scruffies want their systems to work well under real-life circumstances without paying too much attention to great ideas. They are often called engineers, practitioners, craftsmen etc. Neats prefer ideas over anything else. It is not really important that an idea is implementable in reality, sometimes it is even better if it is not. Neats are also termed as poets or theoreticians. Remember the prehistoric story how many teeth does a horse have? Neats open books and argue about different sources. Scruffies open horses' heads. On the other hand, neats write down equations such as $E = mc^2$.

Another story explaining relations between scruffies and neats goes like this: In order to discover America, scruffies organised the project, gathered the stuff, money, ships. But to go searching for America, neats had the major role making scientific guesses about a continent far, far West. Of course, they thought that there is India – a rich country worthy establishing a trade route.

The problem in AI is that especially in the past, scruffies were bluffed away even at events where they should have the primary role. For example, look at many AI-application events. It is not so rare that a substantial part of participants, board members, contributors and editors have not produced any workable system in their whole life. This debate was very alive already in mid-80s when the logistic and probabilistic schools have clashed over the appropriate directions using terms such as "the logic mafia, the formal straighthacked" (Neufeld 1994).

Most reasonable people admit that both scruffies and neats are essential in various scientific and engineering disciplines. The problem in AI and science in general is that neats have taken an unproportional percentage of the field setting their own criteria. Why haven't discoverers of turbine, computer or the Internet got Nobel prizes? Haven't they moved our knowledge ahead and positively affected the way we live?

In short, while agitated debates about AI raise interest and in both ways affect funds, what really matters is what works and which new discoveries are produced. **"It is not that AI needs definitions; it is more that AI needs substance"** (Schank 1991). Although general artificial intelligence has not yet been achieved, we know more and more about it. Some basic facts, legends and myths about AI (Fox 1990; Mettrey 1992; Gams 1993) will be represented in the following subsections.

1.3.1 Facts

The first AI concept is search. Most difficult problems involve choosing between alternative solutions and evaluation processes in which the best solution is found. This basic search schema may not be immediately observed in diverse subareas of AI such as intelligent agents, scheduling, games, learning or expert systems. Novice readers in AI might get distressed by different terminology and diverse techniques. However, even one of the oldest definitions of AI promotes it as **a fight against combinatorial explosion.**

The search methods mentioned here should not be identified with pure algorithmic search techniques such as depth-first-search. Rather, we denote search as a general method for finding appropriate solutions from many possible. Humans apply much more diverse search techniques and approaches than computers. Typically, computer systems apply just one search technique or in the best case a couple of predefined search methods. Humans dynamically try different search methods, and modify and create new ones if necessary.

While faster computers certainly help, simple search techniques cannot ever deal with the exponential growth rate of the number of possibilities in a search tree. For example, in a single factory having 85 orders, 10 operations, and only one substitutional machine, one could create over 10^{880} alternative schedules (Fox 1990). Obviously, the key question is how to reduce search space.

The second AI concept is knowledge representation. It is not that the knowledge representation concept is second to search; it is one of the two major. Knowledge is probably even more important than search in biological systems. In real life, response to a specific pattern is usually prestored – learned through experience. This resembles the fourth viewpoint on AI presented earlier; even more the memory-based approach. But from a practical point of view, computers as well as AI are more successful in search than in knowledge representation.

Although there are many techniques from semantic nets to frames, the most successful AI applications currently are intelligent systems and intelligent agents, and in not so distant years expert systems and neural networks. At times, it was thought that the expert-systems or neural-networks approach enables a uniform solution to knowledge representation problems. It has led to overenthusiasm and overselling the technological possibilities. Now we know that each approach has its own deficiencies. For example, expert systems are appropriate only when problems are relatively small and stable or can be decomposed into such subproblems, meaning that experts agree with each other upon a proposed knowledge base. Different studies, e.g., (Keyes 1989), report that when coping with more difficult real-life tasks, problems may arise due to the following reasons:

- there is no single compact body of encodable knowledge,
- there is no static knowledge, independent of time, related events and environments.

- there is no perfect single algorithm for utilizing the existing knowledge.

It is surprising that artificial intelligence literature until recent years rarely mentioned the use of multiple, contradictory and redundant knowledge to increase performance. A keyword search of 50,000 abstracts from artificial intelligence literature performed several years ago (Clark 1990) indicated that only a few referred explicitly to this problem. But the power of human thinking is not in reproducing clear-cut formal numerical or logical solutions – rather, it is the power of computer systems. Humans perform well in real-life messy situations dealing with multiple possibilities and multiple solutions.

Some well known artificial intelligence systems like DENDRAL, MYCIN, PROSPECTOR and DIPMETER already allow the use of multiple knowledge to a certain degree in terms of overlapping rules or knowledge bases, combining evidence, etc. However, multiple knowledge is not explicitly treated as in some recent systems.

New approaches based on multiple knowledge have been introduced recently in several areas such as hybrid intelligent systems, knowledge acquisition and learning. In qualitative modeling (Leitch *et al.* 1990) and second generation expert systems (Steels & Van de Velde 1985), the multiplicity is manifested as the combination of qualitative and quantitative models. In knowledge acquisition, different views of experts sometimes result in the construction of multiple knowledge bases (Boose *et al.* 1989; Clark 1990). There has been an explosion of multi-strategy learning in the machine learning ares in recent years (ICML 1999).

The main problem, how to represent different kinds of knowledge, complex and heterogeneous knowledge, and combine them into one system, has not been solved yet. Sure, successful combining brings better results, but these combining methods are only computer meta-methods performing as formal algorithms. As a consequence, successful learning from interactions with the environment has not been, and quite probably cannot be achieved without successful use of massive multiple knowledge.

AI copes with the search combinatoric explosion by using knowledge. The use of knowledge enables successful pruning of a search tree. For example, in an expert system OPEX (Gams *et al.* 1986; Sluga *et al.* 1988) for generating appropriate machining operation sequences, there are three levels of rules:

(a) Rules for applying basic machining operation. Example:

operation drilling : if
    gdb:fc is-a-cylinder-in and
    gdb:dc included interval(3,40) and
    gdb:lc/max(gdb:dc) = 10 and
    gdb:nc subset interval(11,12)
then
    fc := is-a blank and dc := 0 and nc := undefined

(b) Rules that define various possibilities of linking basic machining operations within an individual feature. Example:

from boring to drilling if true end.
(c) Rules for combining operation sequences that define which operation sequences should be adopted for a combination of features. Example:
combination drilling and drilling if true end.

The task of OPEX is to design operation sequences for a machine and a specified part, and sort them according to predefined criteria. Naive combining of operations quickly leads to a combinatorial explosion, but through smarter selection of possibilities, i.e. by utilising domain knowledge to control search, the combinatorics is reduced to a feasible level.

As indicated by previous example, AI enhances search by reformulating problems, through the use of opportunism, heuristics, and by abstraction and differentiation of quantitative or qualitative models. These are techniques behind the general principle of using knowledge to control search. Thus, the use of knowledge can greatly improve performance. In these days, one of the most modern techniques based on similar ideas is *Constrained Logic Programming* (CLP). It is claimed (Wallace 1996) that CLP is in recent years the most successful general method for solving real-world scheduling problems.

AI systems can increase productivity. Various reports estimated the number of AI systems regularly in use a couple of years ago to around 3000. Some of them were already in use for more than 10 years. These days, some AI systems on the Internet are used by millions of people per day. Other AI systems are sold in several 10.000 copies daily – such an example is Office Assistant. Some even say that AI is becoming mainstream at least (Hedberg 1998). (Even our small AI group can report around fifty small-scale applications (Urbancic *et al.* 1991). For example, a hybrid intelligent system controls emulsion quality in a factory which produces 100.000 tons of steel per year (Gams *et al.* 1993; 1996; 1997). This AI application (Karba 1994) is among the biggest in Central and Eastern Europe. It was in use for 7 years at the Acroni Iron and Steel Works Jesenice. It is the last in a row of a couple of implemented expert systems in this firm (Karba, Gams 1991). Another example – Hungarian Prolog was sold in over 1500 copies to over 25 countries. These examples show that AI applications have found their roots in countries all over the world.)

The main problem with such reports is where to put borders between AI and non-AI applications. For example, is a Prolog interpreter an AI application or not? Clearly, there is no intelligence in it. On the other hand, Prolog (Bratko 1986) as well as Lisp (Winston 1992) and many other products were designed as a tool or as a by-product of AI research. Maybe, they should be included as AI applications as well as neural networks. In this viewpoint, marketplace AI-software packages fall into at least four major categories: programming languages and tools, programming environments, problem-solving shells (for a class of problems), and application shells (specialised for a given domain). Major AI market trends correspond to the changes in computer generations, from programming to tools and information activities.

Currently, intelligent agents and systems, data mining and intelligent information activities are the dominant AI market areas.

AI should incorporate and copy knowledge from related disciplines like biology and neurosciences. Since the only known truly intelligent system is the human brain, we should study, copy and learn from it as much as possible. Our evolutionary roots and analyses of other species and forms of life are helpful as well. This is the major weak-AI direction.

1.3.2 Legends

AI systems are easy to build. Indeed, under specific conditions, improvements in speed and productivity are significant when using AI systems. For example, having stored a history of events, it is possible to design an expert system with the use of inductive learning tools in a couple of days (Michie 1991, 1993b). On the other hand, there are problems which take more or even much more time than by classical methods.

Specifications and prototyping largely enhance productivity. This is partially true. If the problem fits an application shell, knowledge gathered from experts can be put into a system quickly and then tested. Rapid prototyping elicits the requirements and specifications of software for ill-defined problems; in recent years it has been included in software development approaches as another example of AI product finishing in classical computer science and applications. But the limitations of the methodology and conditions for successfulness have also become known.

AI systems are easily verified and maintained. Since AI systems rely on knowledge instead of formulae, e.g., expert knowledge in expert systems, it is often propagated that these systems are highly understandable and, therefore, easy to be verified and maintained. For example, expert systems provide explanation possibilities as a sort of rule tracker instead of 'trace' or 'spy' in conventional programming languages. Practical experience has shown that while it is an important improvement over classical methods, verification and maintenance remain time-consuming phases.

1.3.3 Myths

Artificial intelligence approach does not need conventional program engineering and management techniques. This incorrect belief is still quite common due in part to academic ignorance of the requirements for building production level systems.

Systems working on simple examples can easily be upgraded to full-scale real-life systems. On the contrary is well known in AI circles as the **scaling problem.** For example, performing speech understanding for a small vocabulary of, say 50 words, differs greatly from the same task with thousands of words. Similarly, many problems are difficult only because of their size. The myth of simple scaling is still very alive mainly due to the academic approach where it is most important that the idea is fresh and attractive (working on a simple, carefully designed problem). Literature reviews in AI show that about half of all publications clearly belong to this category and only half of the systems actually work on non-extreme-toy problems. In the worst scenario, some subareas of AI have for years attracted interest and funds without actually producing a program working on a realistic problem. There seem to be certain similarities to fashion movements in which a new direction promoted by famous people attracts global interest. After a critical mass is obtained, the movement can sustain for several years without any realistic verification. The problem is similar in several other sciences. The fast-food-generation science tends to produce famous writers instead of famous scientists, researchers, engineers or inventors. However slowly, in AI it is changing in favor of more strict verification of results. For example, there are several projects which for years have evaluated different methods (Brazdil *et al.* 1994).

Small systems can exhibit full-scale human intelligence. In serious AI circles it is known that it is not possible to simulate full-scale human intelligence without huge and complex systems and that searching for a genuine simple intelligent algorithm is similar to searching for perpetuum mobile.

If we have an expert, then we can create an expert system. Obviously, a lot more is needed; first of all a feasibility study.

AI does not need business motivation to produce valuable results. Several studies have shown that those initiated by management have much better chance of returning profit compared to those initiated by academic stuff.

AI tools can enable novices to develop complex AI systems. Inexperience and lack of skill cannot be compensated in any field.

AI systems consist of AI systems. Typically, in AI systems there is much more than that, including lots of classical programming.

AI systems perform as specialised, stand-alone programs. Actually, they access databases, conventional programming languages, operating systems etc.

All AI tools are the same. There are different categories and different systems, thousands of them..

All AI systems are either rule-based or neural-networks based. Many AI systems are of this kind, but there is much more.

AI systems do not make mistakes. In real life there is no such thing.

AI replaces conventional approaches. Rather, they can both be useful depending on conditions, and are often combined together.

AI knowledge engineering is all we need to know about AI. The more you know the better. Again, AI consists of many diverse subareas.

AI tools are good only for AI applications. AI software supports qualitative and quantitative reasoning equally well.

Exhaustive search can provide solutions. Yes, for toy problems.

Tools equally support various approaches, e.g. forward and backward chaining of rules. Tools are typically more appropriate for specific types of problems. There is no "golden bullet".

The more general the tool the better. Task specific tools are usually more productive but on a more narrow area.

There exist universal algorithms for specific subareas such as learning. In an overgeneralised theory, not working in practice.

Several subareas of AI have good theoretical foundations. No true intelligence has it so far. Of course this does not mean that we should not use mathematics and statistics. On the contrary, statistical theory usually based on Bayesian or minimal-encoding theories are of greatest help in realistic applications. It has been shown by a paper "Learning from Examples – a Uniform View" (Gams *et al.* 1991) that AI methods are very similar to statistics and that general schemata can be constructed encapsulating AI and statistical methods with variations regarding implementation details. The problem in strong AI is that fancy new theories are usually useless not only for achieving true intelligence but also for making useful applications that work in real life. Relying on abstract formal mechanisms and theories when trying to achieve true intelligence has simply been fruitless so far. The time has come for other approaches.

In recent years, main AI results are based on integration with classical computing such as low-level-intelligent agents, intelligent assisting systems introducing some additional features such as flexibility to classical systems, or expert-copying expert information systems.

From the designer point of view, AI systems can work well under favorable conditions, and are neither panaceas nor research curiosities. AI is not (just) art or fashion, it is first of all a scientific and an engineering discipline. At present, AI can importantly improve productivity and enhance the application areas of computers. As all other technologies, **AI must be used with a certain precaution and especially when circumstances are favorable.** More knowledge about AI in general as well as knowing about common legends and myths about AI may improve the success rate and extend the number of AI applications.

To achieve true intelligence, the engineering and weak AI seem to be the more promising of the three directions mentioned earlier.

1.3.4 Interdisciplinary AI

There are several antagonisms such as the strong versus weak AI or symbolic versus connectionism or symbolic versus numeric. Bickhard and Terveen (1996) intensively criticize the symbolic approach and instead propose interactivism. Pfeifer and Scheier (1999) speak about new AI, cognitive-science intelligence. Some other seemingly contradictory viewpoints on AI are represented in (Gams, Paprzycki, Wu 1997; Ratsch, Richter, Stamatescu 1998; Boden 1996). Here we represent the following components of intelligence:

Symbolic formal intelligence. Typical property of this kind is measured by in the past so famous IQ tests or recently in other formal tests similar to solving mathematical problems. It is funny to notice that computers often solve formal problems that are used for rating humans as intelligent (e.g. IQ tests) quite well while failing miserably in other tasks we often find self-understanding like common-sense or vision. Other high mental abilities like creativity, intuition, social intelligence, value intelligence and consciousness are typically not measured and are often even not directly tested or trained in the whole education process.

Intuitive and creative thinking. In schools, we often get a set of all possible questions in preparation of exams. In several cases, literature is not allowed during the actual test. As if we don't have books and computers when doing anything relevant in our later life. Who measures intuition and creativity? But these properties are essential in real life. Computers are very good at remembering large amounts of data, they are excellent at quick computing. For humans, intuitivity and creativity are often more important than pure formal intelligence. But our formal education system hardly recognizes that. Some even say that intuition and creativity can not be taught and learned. If that is so, then this is another confirmation that there is an essential difference between formal and other key human properties. One can be learned and others are of different nature. No wonder that strong AI neglects these areas.

Social and emotional intelligence. These two types of intelligence are among essential properties displayed in human societies. Some say that they are related to politics, others say that they are related to personal happiness, and still others say that they are related to successful organization of human grouping of any kind. Indeed, stand-alone computers seem to be dumb by a pure fact that they don't communicate with others. Intelligent agents are again quite extraordinary, since one of their essential property is capability to exhibit limited social performances.

Integration of rational, emotional, sensory ... and motoric intelligence. The true power of humans is in integration of various, multiple sources of information and action. It seems that humans are capable of integrating all these subsystems into something substantially stronger than when these separate standalone systems were just put together. Nobody knows how we do it, but this must be one of the great mysterious powers of the human mind.

1.4 Storage/Memory vs. Processing/Thinking

How much storage/memory and how much processing/thinking should one apply to get best results?

To understand this, let us study Figure 1.2 (Similar figures have been published before, e.g., in (Nilsson 1980).). There, the cost of two approaches, one using algorithms (processing) and the other data (memory) is presented. For example, if all is known, then the cheapest way is to use memory. All knowledge can be memorized

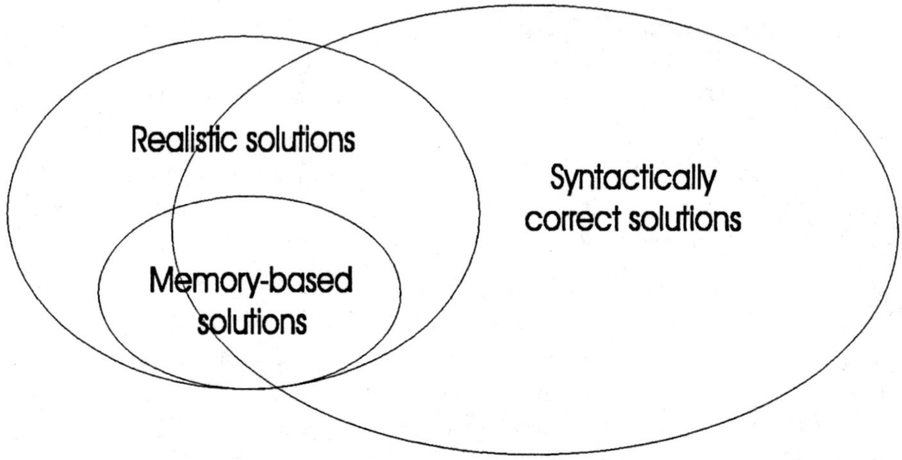

Figure 1.1: Spaces of solutions.

and directly used upon demand. The same tasks can be solved through processing, however, it is much more expensive.

In reality, optimal solutions/programs consist of a proportional amount of data/memory and a proportional amount of thinking/computing/program code. When designing a program, this corresponds to the cost of computer memory (hardware) and the cost of coding = the cost of a programmer (human). Here comes the main advantage of the memory-oriented approach – in the last 20 years human programmers produce basically the same amount of program lines per hour while the primary memory capacity of PC grew from 4 KB in 1980 to 8 MB in 1990, and are around 1 GB in 2000. This progress constantly and substantially moves the optimal approach towards using more memory and less code. And due to the enormous computer progress, most of "normal" human-computer communication, e.g., communication with an application package or operating system, can easily be captured in the primary memory of personal computers with response time well below one second.

The basic idea of using extensive memory is not new – it is the so called **memory-based approach** (Stanfil, Waltz 1986; Nagao 1984) which builds on memory as the foundation of intelligence. Past experience is stored as large numbers of specific events. New situations are first handled by recalling and comparing with previous events, and then performing similar or modified reactions.

One of the main advantages of the memory-based approach is that the space of all realistic solutions is substantially smaller than the space of all syntactically correct solutions. Furthermore, some realistic solutions in complex communication environments are very difficult and some impossible to capture with formal rules or syntax. These relations are presented in Figure 1.1. A typical problem domain of

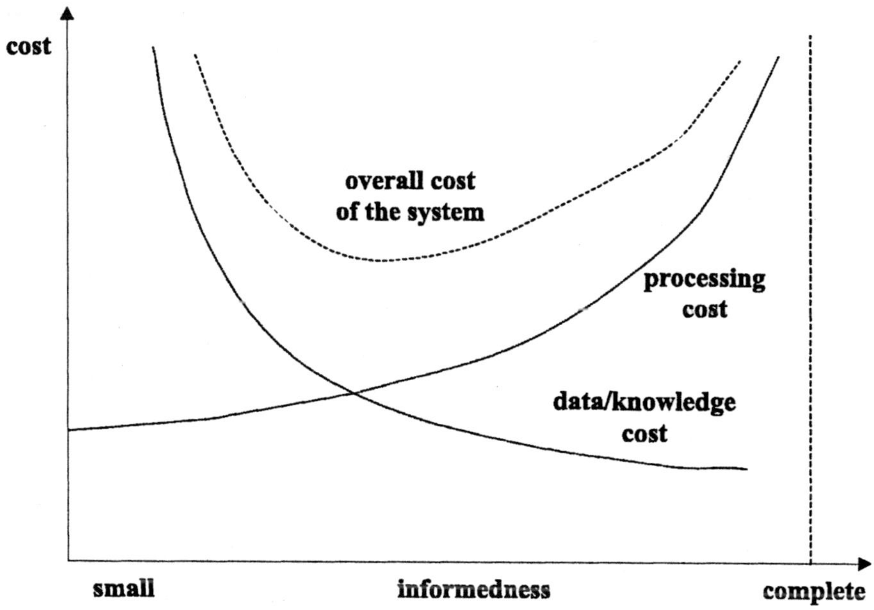

Figure 1.2: Processing vs. memory.

this kind is translation or communication between humans in general.

In this way, **old AI approaches with new hardware can produce good results**. The last statement is probably **the motto of the engineering AI**.

Figure 1.2 indicates why implemented systems rely on memory as well as on processing. The difference between classical and memory-based approaches is in the share of the whole system devoted to memory as presented in Figure 1.3.

One of the major hardware-oriented AI suggestions is that AI as well as computer science and engineering are much more dependent on the development of computer hardware that generally recognized. Bare computer power has already beaten the best human chess player. It means that even classical methods can be successfully implemented for certain complex tasks if computers are fast enough. On the other hand, there are tasks which are extremely difficult for specific computer architectures. Several other authors have also highlighted the importance of combining AI with software engineering (Drescher 1991; Kitano 1993).

1.5 Problems With Formalistic AI

When observing various AI publications, a typical paper consists of a couple of logical/numerical functions describing the essential contribution of the paper. The obvious question is – **are numerical functions really related to true, e.g., human-level intelligence?** Are humans really using numeric functions in their

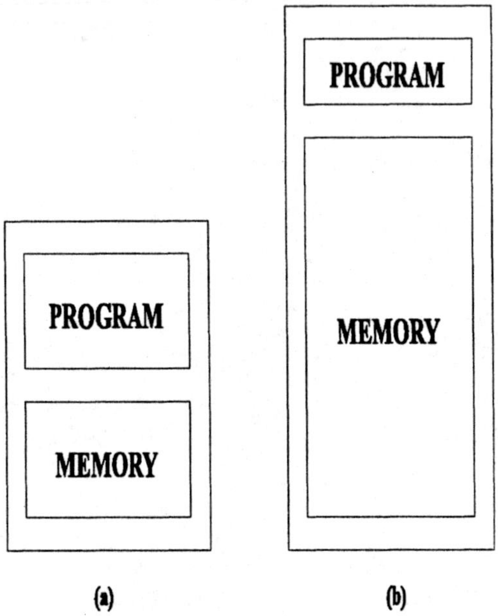

Figure 1.3: The ratio between memory and program code in the rule-based (a), and in the memory-based (b) approach.

every-day life or when being creative? A related question is if the refereeing process is indeed oriented towards filtering through original perspective ideas or is it oriented towards technically correct papers full of fancy formal derivations dealing with very limited technical problems?

It might seem that the formalistic strong AI has distanced not only from true AI but from applications as well. The main reason is simple – formal criteria are not fit for engineering applications. And if you want to have many publications, you simply cannot spend too much time with systems working in real-life circumstances. You have to publish, publish, publish.

There might be several other reasons why most of the papers are seemingly unrelated to real world. Since scientific motto in general is search for excellence, it is hard to find methods mature enough to be tested in real-life environments and at the same time so intellectually new and attractive to pass the refereeing procedure. At several conferences, remarks of participants working on real-life problems often indicated that one of the key assumptions enabling a new (although not verified) idea was related to the absence of real-life circumstances.

Another reason might be the **"publish or perish" frenzy** (or similar – citation frenzy). It seems that certain circles in modern science have accepted that all that counts is the number of publications, and related reputation inside closed circles. In return, this criterion has forced scientists to devote most of their energy to publications and meetings, and not to genuine scientific research. Often one can observe two researchers or two groups pursuing similar ideas and implementing similar systems. Quite often, the one designing better and more innovative systems publishes less. As a consequence, their work is less appreciated in scientific terms, and their scientific careers downgraded.

There are many questions regarding the refereeing process. John Koza (1995), one of best-known researchers in genetic algorithms, was one of the brave enough to present his story about papers rejected at specific conferences and magazines, and accepted elsewhere. In the abstract he writes: "The story here is about the systematic abuse of the peer review process and of unethical behavior, intellectual dishonesty, scientific misconduct, and – there is really no other word for it – corruption." In 68 pages he presents communication in relation to submitted papers and the refereeing process. Putting harsh words aside, the problem is very real and many scientists are aware of it. The last page of Koza's booklet is a copy of the paper "Ethics and Peer Review" by D. Goodstein (1995). Goodstein reports that majority of asked young researchers agreed that some kind of misconduct is rampant in all fields of science. Since scientific movement is these days mainly constrained by the number of research posts and the amount of funds available, intensive competition has replaced joined intellectual efforts directed towards new discoveries. In recent years, the scientific contest for new discoveries has been constantly changing into a political or managerial fight for influence and money. This probably irreversible change is not only going to cause more scientific fraud, but also other forms of misconduct.

Some of the scientists say that probably some errors were made, however, there is no refereeing process without errors. But carefully reading Koza's comments, there are simply too many too severe mistakes that can be verified. When discussing with colleagues from different countries, many had the same opinion.

Many other scientists have expressed their concerns about politicizing science and making a fashion-business of it. **It is on scientists or even more on society to either continue with further "politisation" of science**, however small and subtle, or to return to searching for true comprehensions. But if one thinks that only AI researchers have troubles mainly because of the strong-weak antagonism, think about lawyers and their oath – science is still a little better off than some other professions.

1.5.1 Are Truths Formal?

Science and technology are well-deserved for the great success of human race – the number of people, their wealth and life-expectance is increasing. Yet, according to Edelman (1992), hard formal sciences are in crisis because they have not been able to explain the most important process of all – the process of consciousness and intelligence in the human mind.

According to Penrose (1989), scientists belong to three categories: **Platonists,**

formalists and intuitists. Platonists believe in the world of objective truths. Formalists believe in formal sciences, e.g., in mathematics. Intuitists rely on intuitive thinking. Strict formalists were ruled out around 1930 by the Gödel theorem. Current formalism is based on a postulate that anything including understanding and intelligence can be put into formal rules, e.g., mathematical formulae. Intuitism is based on a different kind of logic in which true and false statements are not exclusive. Unfortunately, this forbids many important mechanisms in formal thinking. According to Penrose, Platonism is the only alternative for true scientists. All truths exist in the abstract Platonistic world. Humans do not invent new truths but just discover those truths previously unknown to them.

Platonism relies on truths. What counts is which knowledge of all possible are we aware of and for how much have we moved the knowledge frontier ahead. Knowledge and commonsense evaluate the importance of new scientific achievements.

Another view is proposed by Edelman – Platonism and formalism have caused several problems in the mind research and science in general. **Taking the mind out of nature, i.e., out of biology, is simply wrong.** All that matters are human heads and bodies, not abstract external formalisms or objective truths. For example, in our heads there are subjective processes which are unrelated to Platonistic or formalistic truths.

Maybe, Platonism, formalism, intuitism and other approaches should be studied, used and integrated. Formalism is good for formal problems, Platonism for several scientific disciplines and appropriate philosophical relation to science in general, while nature dominates our real world. Isolated old truths are losing momentum.

There are other formal-science related problems. In relation to the predominant theme of this book – are computers substantially different than the minds – one should ask if school teaches appropriate knowledge in appropriate ways. Alan Cromer (1994) claims that the mind was not designed to study formal disciplines such as mathematics or physics: "science and objective thinking are unnatural activities". Cromer is not the only one claiming that **the mind is not hard wired for abstract, logical thinking.** Unlike Penrose, who sees direct links between minds and Platonistic truths, Cromer assumes that all humans have intuitive knowledge of how the world works. No formal formulae, no formal logic. Of course, formal sciences are very useful. But the idea that they are the most appropriate for all situations in the real world seems overstretched. Formal sciences have meaning only when combined with other relevant real-life knowledge.

Consider **how many human experts display formal computing when performing every-day operations.** Layers, politicians, doctors, managers, engineers? Consider for example Einstein or Edison. None of them was particularly good in school, none of them has published hundreds of formal papers full of equations. Both were extremely creative and productive in terms of real life and common sense, not in terms of the publish-frenziness.

Another global scientific problem is saturation. It is a natural phenomenon.

Consider a 100 m sprint. In latest years, records are improved by hundreds of seconds. No one dreams of a one-second improvement. Similar situations have been encountered in many scientific disciplines. Which is the most important scientific improvement in recent years? Isn't it the Internet? Or what about Nobel prizes? An average human certainly does not understand any explanation in recent scientific awards. Clean short scientific discoveries like Einstein's $E = mc^2$ are just not waiting around any more.

When no great new ideas are discovered in a particular subfield, scientists tend to evaluate their success not according to the prime production of important new ideas, but according to the second-order criteria such as the number of publications or the number of citations. Heads of scientific institutions or larger scientific groups tend to be coauthors of any publication that is published in their unit. You quote your friends and they quote you in return. You invite them to visit your institution and they invite you. No matter that some researchers have not produced any interesting new idea by themselves, had they achieved a proper leading position and got enough good young bright scientists, they will most often be coauthors of published papers and they will get the highest citation indexes. In this process of alienation, science is the one to loose. Fair to say, these problems can easily be solved. One just has to adapt the basic scientific and development criteria and apply it with common sense.

But, and really luckily but, **all scientific disciplines are not equally saturated or perspective. Human intelligence, understanding and consciousness are slowly getting ripe for the assault.** Artificial intelligence has enormous possibilities to proliferate. One might even say that, as long as we are going to live, there is going to be artificial intelligence and vice versa.

Kitano nicely summarizes problems with formal approaches in classical AI (1993). Complete, correct and consistent problem domains are categorized as toy domains unscalable not only to intelligent systems (black box in Figure 1.4), but also to real-world domains (gray box in Figure 1.4). Such domains have dominated in many research directions in AI. **Real-world domains are denoted as incomplete, incorrect, inconsistent, and are in addition characterized by human bias, tractability and economics.** In Kitano's opinion, AI research should be oriented towards real-world problems in order to design systems that pay-off and in time (maybe) become intelligent. Future computer projects can be characterized by massive computing, massive parallelism, massive data. Problems in real world differ quite a lot from formal or toy problems. Real-world domains are by definition very difficult to explain because simple ideas and simple algorithms do not work well in such circumstances. Massively parallel systems enable collaborative reasoning which enables use of redundant information. This idea is close to our principle of multiple knowledge.

One of the central Kitano's messages is that computer hardware should be fully exploited in order to produce helpful computer assistants. His proposition is already graphically presented in Figure 1.4: first we should design successful real-life intelli-

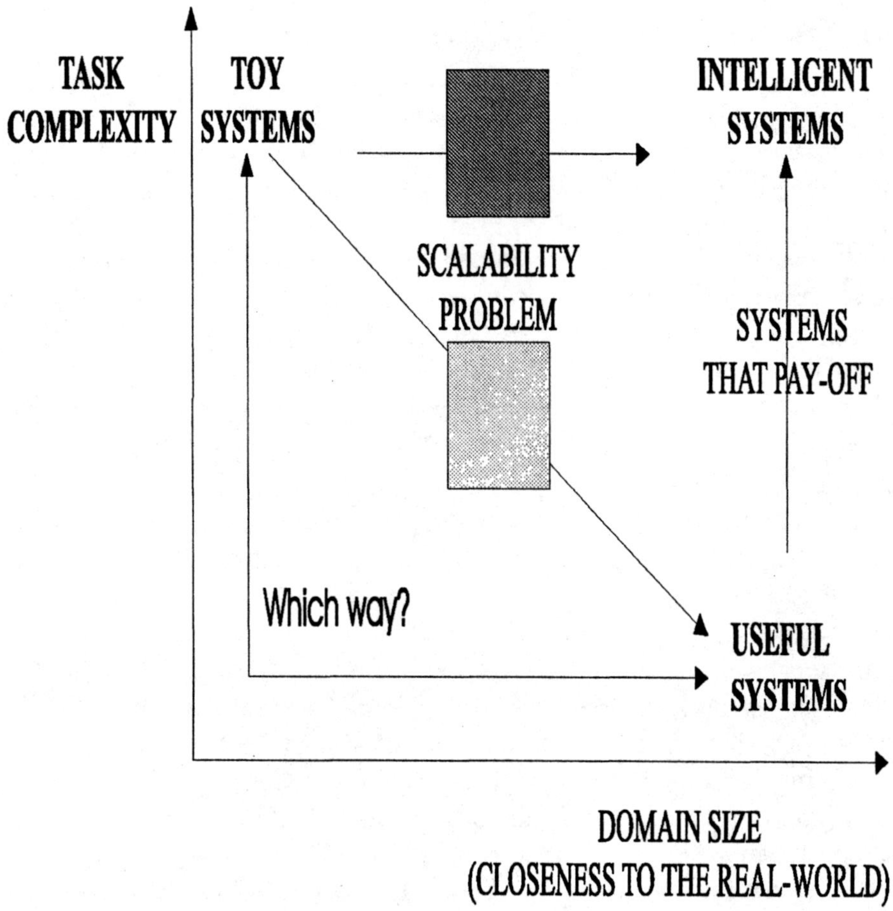

Figure 1.4: Modified Kitano's approaches for building intelligent systems.

gent applications. Then, in time and with additional features, these system will be ripe to the final assault on the human mind. Looking at what has happened since 1993, one might say that is exactly what is going on. No major new formal AI ideas, a great success in AI applications and a feeling, that cognitive AI is more and more perspective.

New AI may substantially influence science in general. Suppose that there is indeed important new knowledge hidden in our heads and not accessible by current formal techniques. That would be a huge success substantially enhancing our knowledge.

Not only that AI is waiting for its great discoveries, new computer systems are along the road. They will be much more friendly and helpful than the stupid boxes we lose time with today. **They will be our assistants and our friends** – at least for a while.

And to be fair, even at strong-AI-related conferences bold ideas emerge from time to time. Some successful, some not.

1.5.2 Minsky's Society of Minds vs Formal Oneness

Roger Minsky is one of the gurus, pioneers and grand old professors in artificial intelligence.

Minsky's book "The Society of Mind" was published in 1886. It was one of the first in the row of popular books written by serious scientists about artificial intelligence, the brain and the mind. Since then, there has been a surge of interest in models and architectures of mind in different scientific fields. **In recent years an intellectual stampede has emerged in which mainstream researchers jostle with philosophers, psychiatrists and scientists from other disciplines.** Debates, meetings, experimentations spark around. Among them the Tucson conferences "Towards a science of consciousness" in Arizona, USA.

Semi-scientific books are often written similar to scientific books, however, they usually apply less technical terms and mechanisms. Minsky's book is different even compared to an average semi-scientific book. It consists of a series of short one-page articles, or better say thoughts. These thoughts in a way represent a society of small ideas about the mind. This organization has numerous excursions along the way, sometimes a bit distressing. Dyer (1991) warns that the book is "not intended to serve as a format how to survey articles, term papers, or dissertations should be written". According to Reeke (1991): "This style is perhaps ideal for the reader brought up in the age of television, but it comes across to this reviewer as somewhat of a hodge-podge". But according to Isaac Asimov, it is "270 brilliantly original essays on ... how the mind works."

Minsky himself admits that he tried to write the story in a more traditional way, however, it never seemed to work. One could agree with Minsky that current knowledge about the mind cannot be polished in the form of a neatly straightened text. Furthermore, according to the principle (see Figure 1) no complex knowledge can be put on paper as a single-line story. Organization in the Minsky's book resembles to the "wise old-man's thinking" in the good and bad sense. The bad side is highlighted by Ginsberg (1991): "in abandoning the standard methods of scientific inquiry, Minsky has allowed himself to fall into the classic trap of speculative science" and later "an adventure in speculation, and not substantive science".

But as pointed out by Smoliar (1991), a stylistic spiritual ancestor, Wittgenstein's Philosophical Investigations (1974) similarly offered numbered paragraphs as individual atoms of insight. Also, Wittgenstein was one of the first to highlight the shortcomings of formal logic. The problems both authors face is how to combine relevant and deep thoughts together. None offer much help. It is simply on the reader to do it.

Minsky's main contributions are:

- reopening an interesting subject – the mind science in artificial intelligence
- criticism of formal logic and its role in AI
- representing the idea that the human mind and the brain are essentially multiple, that the mind can be represented as a society of agents.

There is an interesting scientific theory that as soon as somebody discovers a new idea or a pattern of behavior, others will do it even though there is no connection whatsoever. It is supposed to be valid for humans and for other beings. For example, Dennett (1991) says that "at any point there are multiple 'drafts' of narrative fragments at various stages of editing in various places in the brain". Ornstein (1991), Sloman (1992) and several others describe similar ideas sometimes even without quoting Minsky (see for example Ornstein 1991). But Minsky was surely among the first and among the most influential in AI community to start the new discussion about the brain and consciousness in AI.

Despite his criticism of formal logic, Minsky can be at times seen as a proponent of **functionalism**, i.e. strong AI, although he denies that (Minsky 1991b, p. 383). This functionalistic school anticipates that the relevant description of mental processes is not at the physical level, but at the level of formal functional states. Thinking is computing and its functional descriptions is independent of its physical realization. Therefore, symbolic description is the most appropriate to represent processes in our heads as well as in computers.

For example, Minsky writes: "the so-called problem of body and mind does not hold any mystery: Minds are simple what brains do". Therefore, it can be concluded that Minsky considers that the brain as a kind of computer. Our behavior is supposed to be determined by algorithms, and our free will is an illusion. In the 1994 Scientific American article Minsky proposes to prolong our lives by replacing body-parts including certain functions of the brain. First attempts in this way could include direct connections between the brains and computers. In this way, humans would not only prolong their life thus being able to work longer, they would also increase their mental capabilities.

According to Minsky, humans as a species have reached a plateau in intellectual development, e.g., hardware limitations. There is no sign that people are getting any smarter during the last centuries. When we find ways to replace every part of the body and brain, we shall reach a new evolutionary stage. We will become part humans and part machines, i.e. "our own mind-children". Says Moravec (1988): "We are very near to the time when virtually no essential human function, physical or mental, will lack an artificial counterpart." These new robots will inherit the Earth as our next-evolutionary-step children. No great ethnical questions for Minsky – he thinks that he could learn, discover, know much more if enough time and storage capacities were available to him.

However, as Reeke pointed out (1991), **maybe Minsky fails to notice that computers have difficulties with problems that people solve easy and vice versa because of his assumption that minds perform like computers.**

Dyer (1991) sees several schools of the mind/computer matter: "mind-is-logic", "mind-is-a-connectionist-network", "mind-is-conceptual-dependencies", "mind-is-rule chunking" and Minsky's "mind-is-a-society-of-agents" with affinity to connectionism and conceptual dependency theory.

Minsky briefly mentions other approaches just to dismiss them. In his opinion, philosophers are searching for the magical spark while there is nothing magic about human thought. In Minsky's words: "What magical trick makes us intelligent? The trick is that there is no trick". But human thought is so rich that every artificial system that we have ever built is missing hundreds of properties of intelligence and consciousness. No wonder all systems existing today cannot dream of passing the Turing test. Physicists, on the other side have explained physical science in terms of so few principles, and are trying to explain the brain in a similar way. But, according to Minsky, this approach does not work because the mind has enormous complexity. Simple ideas on itself are worthless when dealing with human thinking. Instead, the brain rarely uses a single representation (Minsky 1994). It "**always runs several scenarios in parallel so that multiple viewpoints are always available**", and later "In order to think effectively, you need multiple processes to help you describe, predict, explain, abstract and plan what your mind should do next." This is already very similar to our principle of multiple knowledge.

Minsky upgrades the old strong AI at least in two ways: by adding multiplicity in the sense of multiple agents, and by criticizing formal logic. Minsky sees logic as the way humans formalize thought that has already occurred by some other process. In this way, he opposes the formalistic approach which sees logic as fundamental for machines as well as for beings. For example, in natural language Minsky sees grammar as the servant of language, not the master. These views contradict formalistic approaches, e.g., to Chomsky's and Fodor's theories of language. Or as counter-attacked by Ginsberg (1991): "Good science, quite frequently, builds on good mathematics" and later that The Society of Mind "does not pretend to be good mathematics. My aim is to discuss the question of whether or not it is good science". Funny, Ginsberg later admits that logic and AI have achieved much less than expected.

Well, Minsky's book is really not science if science requires a strict line of formal mathematical derivations. Of course, accepting that equations are necessary for science also means that animal and human intelligence are not inside the reach of formalistic science. Luckily, this is only the old formalistic approach to science. New interdisciplinary views are much broader. But Minsky's book clearly is science if science is treated as a discipline promoting new knowledge. This brings up the question about the form of science. Is a great idea not published properly worthless? Is a weak idea excellently published really a major scientific achievement? Form or subject, that is the question.

Minsky's attack on logic seems to be justified in the sense of dismissing formalism and scienticism in general, and first of all – as the most appropriate tool for describing processes in human minds.

General attacks on logic as a scientific discipline are often overstretched. After all, Minsky had several interesting discoveries in the area of neural networks, but was also one of the most responsible for the first discouragement in neural networks. About thirty years ago Minsky and Papert showed that simple one-level neural networks (perceptrons) cannot solve some simple problems like the exclusive OR (Minsky, Papert 1969). It took two decades until connectionism revived. Minsky's criticism in formal logic as means for achieving true intelligence must be seen as an attempt to improve computer approaches in the multiple, agent directions, and not to abandon logic.

One of the central Minsky's contributions is proposing a large-scale model of the mind by introducing societies of agents consisting of several layers. The number of levels is not clear, and Minsky's ideas are represented in a recursive way – a society of agents at some level consists of a society of levels of agents one level below. In the multistrategy community, similar idea of combining several learning algorithms at different levels is often analysed in recent years. Our version of the general recursive integration schema is presented in (Karba et al. 1994).

The basic ingredient of society of agents is an agent. **An agent is a procedure having a certain amount of autonomy, devoted to a specific task.** Unlike isolated procedures, various agents cooperate and compete at different levels. Agents have substantially different properties, knowledge representations, they apply different approaches. Some agents remember everyday or other repetitious tasks. Frames are among essential parts of Minsky's organization.

Agents are usually simple, but because of their complex cooperation a complex behavior emerges. Several properties of this behavior such as intelligence and understanding seem magic, but according to Minsky there is no magic, no spark. In this way, advanced human properties are reduced to properties of complex mechanisms consisting of several layers of rather simple elements. Finally grained primitive elements are dumb and simple. The mind is therefore a society of small ideas. The brain is a complex structure of simple neurons. Similar approach has been introduced and analyzed by Hofstadter (1979) and Dennett (1981, 1990, 1991).

For new structures Minsky introduces new terms: nemes, paranomes, pronomes, polynemes, micronemes, isonomes, K-lines etc. Reeke (1991) sees these new terms as reinventing previous concepts. For example, an agent is a function, subroutine or module; a microneme is a microinstruction. It is not clear whether these new terms are necessary as Minsky proposes in his reply (1991) or we see another example of scientism, a disease with many faces that scientists find difficult to resist: Scientific ideas have to be packed in new aureole and new terms. On the other hand, denoting agents as just functions or procedures is not very sensible. Agents are a special kind of procedures and then it is quite reasonable to coin another term. But about all those "-nomes" and "-nemes" one might quite well go along with Reeke: "It is not clear whether the new terms are introduced deliberately to prod the reader into seeing well-known concepts in a new light, or whether Minsky has deliberately used them in his own thinking for so long that he is no longer aware of the need to point out their relationship to more familiar terms". Minsky perceives the last sentence as an insult.

Whatever the case, Minsky's ideas are of a great wise person with its pluses and minuses. Among minuses are too general descriptions of several key concepts, e.g., self-awareness or the brain research. For example, in the split-brain research page he writes that either one or the other hemisphere takes charge of a person. But in Minsky's defense, to capture main characteristics of such an enormously complex system like our brains it would take at least several billion kilometers of books. Therefore, a couple of nails in the wall called the brain is the best what one person can hope for in one book.

The Society of Mind is the first fundamental computer-science analyses of intelligence after Turing's "Computation Machinery and Intelligence" in 1950, as seen by Smoliar (1991). Turing had foreseen that intelligence could be reproduced by machines, even those capabilities seen as inherently human: "Be kind, resourceful, beautiful, friendly, have initiative, have a sense of humor, tell right from wrong, make mistakes, fall in love, enjoy strawberries and cream, make someone fall in love with it, learn from experience, use words properly, be the subject of its own thought, have as much diversity of behavior as a man, do something really new."

Today, these words on their own could be seen as the old-fashioned strong-AI optimism. But more justly, you can see that Turing had a vision that faded away with the formal strong-AI. It is the bold weak-AI ideas that are again taking the original position to study consciousness and to build truly intelligent machines. The main difference is that new AI relies not on classical algorithmic Turing machines, but on more complex machines, or at least on special types of Turing machines with additional properties.

Minsky had the spirit and guts to reapproach the basic concepts of intelligence on the broadest front, and not to stick to small technical improvements often unrelated to true intelligence. In that approach, he managed to write down several major thoughts we were not capable to formally define at that time or even now, yet we must see and feel that they are in the right direction.

1.6 Strong–AI Super–Projects

To evaluate successfulness of the strong-AI approach we examine the two major strong-AI projects, the Fifth Generation project and the CYC project.

1.6.1 The Fifth Generation

The FGCS project (Furukawa 1993; FGCS 1993) was the first research project in Japan to embrace international collaboration and exchange (around 100 scientists involved). It created a frenzy in the developed countries, fearing that Japan is going to take the lead in another central technological area – new generation computers. As a result, several other projects were started, based on logic programming (LP), the core of the FGCS project. The project was heavily based on logic programming to bridge the gap between applications and machines. Several (some concurrent) versions of Prolog (e.g. KL1) were designed to support different levels, from the user-interface to machine language. The profound effect of LP is obvious even today, as it remains one of the central areas of computer research despite serious criticism. However, the Fifth Generation project did not produce any major new scientific discovery nor market application.

The unsuccessful outcome raises ground for a crucial question: **Is logic appropriate for real-life tasks?** Obviously, it has several advantages, among them a very strict formal basis, and great expressive power. However, while it may be suitable for computers and formalists, it may not be so for humans and intelligent systems in general. Arno Penzias says: "Logic is cumbersome – that's why humans rarely use it." The logical approach effectively assumes that AI is a subset of logic and that intelligence and life can be captured in a global and consistent logic form. But one should be careful to distinguish between different kinds of logic. Fuzzy logic, logic of informal systems, and many-valued logic seem to differ from the logicism analyzed here. Logic in AI real-life applications (Bratko, Muggleton 1995) is another area that should not be identified with "pure" logic approach. According to logicism (Birnbaum 1992), knowledge representation is independent of its use – quite opposite to the new AI approach based on biological and cognitive sciences.

The progress in both logic programming and AI-based logic areas as well as in the pursuit of general-purpose parallel logic-based computers has been modest but certainly not null. Although the Fifth Generation has not been able to compete with commercial products, the rest of the world listened to it. Japan has afterwards launched the Sixth Generation project, based on real-life domains, neural networks, optical connections, and heavy parallelism. These results were much less publicized in USA and Europe, but again did not achieve any major breakthrough.

1.6.2 The CYC Project

The CYC project was started by Dough Lenat in 1984 as a ten-year project (Stefik, Smoliar 1993; Lenat, Guha 1990; Lenat 1995). Substantial funding was provided by a consortium of American companies. It was based on two premises:

- that the time has come to encode large chunks of knowledge into a meta-system encoding common-sense knowledge, and
- that explicitly represented large-scale knowledge will enable a new generation of AI systems.

This "knowledge is power" (the Renaissance-era slogan) approach claims that by using huge amounts of knowledge, performance and intelligence of new generation AI systems will increase substantially. The intention is to overcome one of the biggest obstacles of existing AI systems, their brittleness (dispersed isolated systems working only on carefully chosen narrow tasks).

The CYC project addresses the tremendous task of codifying a vast quantity of knowledge possessed by a typical human into a workable system. Lenat estimates (1995) that they have entered 10^6 general assertions into CYC's knowledge base, using a vocabulary with approximately 10^5 atomic terms. CYC is intended to give on-line sensible answers to all sensible queries, not just those anticipated at the time of knowledge entry. Lenat and Guha estimate that this will require at least ten million appropriately organized items of information, including rules and facts that describe concepts as abstract as causality and mass, as well as specific histographic facts. CYC includes a wide range of reasoning facilities, including general deduction and analogical inference. Reasoning is done through argumentation, through comparison of pro and con arguments.

CYC is the first project of its magnitude, and therefore represents a pioneering work. Several questions and problems were posed for the first time. The whole project had strong emphasis on pragmatism – to make something workable. There are four important design characteristics:

- the language is first-order predicate calculus with a series of second-order extensions
- frames are the normal (general) representation for propositions,
- nonmotononic inferences are made only when explicitly sanctioned by the user, and

- knowledge acquisition and inference involve different languages between which translation is automatic.

All knowledge in CYC is encoded in the form of logical sentences, and not in diagrams, procedures, semantic nets, or neural networks. The mechanism for managing uncertainty is not as common as Bayesian networks or reason maintenance systems. One of the interesting aspects in the CYC project is the distinction between epistemological and heuristic levels of representation. A user communicates with CYC in a high level epistemological language. CYC translates queries and assertions in this language into a lower-level heuristic notation, which provides a variety of specialized inference mechanisms corresponding to special syntactic forms.

According to the authors, success would be achieved if the system worked and was used by different institutions for further research and development of new (generation of) expert and knowledge-based systems. Authors of the project have also quite cleverly changed success criteria and basic aims a couple of times during the last ten years, obviously trying to please public interest and accommodate scientific remarks. One of these "commercial" moves was quite probably the astronomic price of the CYC system.

There have been several strange events related to the project from the start. For example, in the overview book by Lenat and Guha (1990), there are 22 publications, of which 7 were written by the head of the project (Lenat). In (Lenat 1995) there are only 9 publications, and only 4 of them were not (co)authored by Lenat. In addition, CYC's runtime behavior as well as the assessment of the program in (Lenat, Guha 1990) was far too brief to be convincing. Overall, the CYC project was a failure similar to the Fifth Generation project.

Reviewers of the project (Stefik, Smoliar 1993) generally claim that it has not succeeded to the point proclaimed by the authors. Lenat even claimed that machines will start learning by themselves when the CYC computer system becomes operational around 1994 (Lenat 1989). In 1995, it was becoming clear that nothing like that is going to happen. According to critics like Dreyfus (MTCM 1992), the CYC system is as dull as any other program. Since then there were no new positive news.

On the other hand, important new understandings were arrived at, some positive and some negative, which could be very useful for new projects. In Lenat's words (1995): (CYC) " is not a bump on a log. It saddens me how few software-related projects I can say that about these days." To a certain extend, CYC has shown that commonsense knowledge is essential for any intelligent program, and that brittle systems still dominating AI are not related to any true intelligence.

1.6.3 Strong–AI Dinosaurs?

The CYC and FGCS projects have addressed several fundamental questions and come with modest and in some areas even with reasonable success. CYC has managed to encode a huge amount of knowledge and the Fifth Generation project resulted in tens of working computer systems (software plus hardware). Implemented systems have worked better than commercial ones on specific tasks. Their apparent commercial failure lies in the fact that commercial computer products such as new PC's and workstations are not only more general and applicable than the products of these huge R&D projects, but also the pace of their progress was and still is faster.

Being a pioneer has its dangers, yet one has to do it if we are to get anywhere. After all, AI is constantly changing in search for true discoveries, and will continue to do so.

But in the eyes of public, both CYC and the Fifth Generation project have not fulfilled their promises. **The failure revived the old hypotheses that classical symbolic AI may not be able to achieve intelligence on digital computers.** Lenat himself proposed that the success or failure of the CYC project will give a good estimate whether the symbolic paradigm is flawed and if so, how (Copeland 1994). Bickhard and Terveen (1996) claim that "encodings is fatal for the further reaching programmatic aspirations of both Artificial Intelligence and Cognitive Science". Dreyfus (MTCM 1992) was more direct a long time ago: "(classical symbolic) AI is finished". In the words of Robert Kowalski when responding to the criticism of the Fifth Generation Project (FGCS 1993): "The field of AI, in particular, was notorious for raising great expectations and producing disappointing results".

It is **surprising that the whole AI took most of the blame**. There was no weak- or engineering-oriented AI. Logic programming (which is not AI at all) and strong AI were the dominant research directions in the mentioned superprojects, falsely perceived as the whole AI discipline.

Unlike previous statements that the failure of these major projects indicates that all symbolic approaches are insufficient to achieve true intelligence on computers, we apply a more modest conclusion: Strong-AI approaches based on symbols and the Turing machine seem to be incapable of achieving true intelligence. New approaches are necessary, but they might quite likely be based on some sort of symbol manipulation and some sort of Turing machines plus something else. In this book we propose multiplicity – one of those "something else". The subtitle analogy with dinosaurs lies in the fact that CYC and FGCS represent dominant approaches and achievements of their time, but their evolutionary line is a historic dead-end. "Hairy", weak AI systems married with agents on the Internet will probably supplement formal approaches or at least subsume them in an integrated approach.

It should be noted that CYC and FGCS are not the only major AI projects. Another example is SOAR, a general problem-solving and learning system based on symbolic production-systems methodology. SOAR has been published in tens of different publications (Laird et al. 1987; SOAR: An Architecture for General Intelligence). For years it has been one of the major AI projects with tens of research groups worldwide cooperating without major central funding. But after the death of Allen Newell, and combined with the period of the new dark AI age, the interest is somehow sadly fading away. Interesting, though, is that Franklin in his 1995 "Artificial Minds" book sees SOAR as "a prime candidate for the title of artificial mind". Similarly, several other books, e.g. "Fundamentals of the New Artificial Intelligence; Beyond Traditional Paradigms" by Munakata published in 1998 see new AI as the one consisting of neural networks, genetic algorithms and evolutionary computing, fuzzy systems, rough sets and chaos. This might seem as the Sixth Generation aspirations. But since there is pure absence of even an attempt to create true intelligence, the "engineering intelligent systems" term seems more appropriate. For example, Gootinalike and Treleaven edited the "Intelligent Systems for Finance and Business" book in 1996 with the following major areas: neural networks, genetic algorithms, fuzzy systems, expert systems, hybrid systems, and agents.

According to the argumentation presented here, older approaches based on predominantly strong-AI research directions could not produce truly intelligent systems at all since these attempts didn't fulfill even the basic preconditions for achieving intelligence. For example, the CYC and the Fifth Generation projects have adopted the computationally strong-AI approach instead of at least combining it with others, e.g. engineering or weak-AI. By disregarding the intelligent-systems and intelligent-agents approach on the Internet, these major projects have seriously hampered themselves in the sense of achieving commercial success. By disregarding the "new school of AI" these systems have distanced themselves from possibilities to achieve any real intelligence. These two consequences are nicely explained in Figure 1.4.

The new AI approach claims that to design an intelligent system, one has to give it properties of intelligent creatures: unity (i.e. multiple knowledge and multistrategy approach), intentionality, consciousness and autonomy along with generality and adaptability. However, doing this will be much more difficult than previously expected.

BRAINS VERSUS COMPUTERS

We shall analyze basic properties of computers and the brains to see if the two are reasonably similar or essentially different. If analyses show that the world of computers (i.e. Turing machines) is sufficiently similar to the mind-brain world, there is no reason to believe that Turing machines will have great problems to simulate any part of the world we live in including the brains. On the other hand, if there are substantial differences, then it is reasonable to expect serious problems in the strong-AI progress.

Chapter 2

Trends of Computer Progress

Several authors have tried to make unbiased analyses of computer history, their implications on every day life and prognoses of computer progress. Some of these authors belonged to industry, some are recognized scientists of different kinds – from sociologists to computer researchers. Most widely published and read opinions are mainly those belonging to popular or semi-scientific group. Publications of these kind often tend to exaggerate or even deformate certain facts in order to attract common reader. On the other hand, basic laws and trends presented in this section are were known for a long time in computer community. Still, it might be interesting to stress some light on the trends of computer progress regarding the differences between strong and weak AI approach.

2.1 Short History of Computing

The key difference between computers and, say, TV sets, is in ability to perform algorithms – definitions of procedures consisting of groups of commands in loops with branching conditions. Computers can be in principle of any physical realization as long as they are able to execute algorithms. Computers can be general or specific in the sense that the first are able to perform general algorithms, while others can perform algorithms only in a specific problem domains.

Similar to Deutch (1992), there are the following interesting milestones in computer history:

- 1834 – Charles Babbage designed the first mechanical machine able to execute algorithms. Although he never completed physical realization of the theoretically designed machine, now we can clearly see that he was the first to design a computer of any kind. Ada, Countess of Lovelace exchanged romantic mails with Babbage about how to control the designed machine. Ada is generally accepted as the first programmer in the world. By the way, she was a daughter of the famous poet Lord Byron.

Babbage died as a broken man. His ideas were not well accepted at that time and the government refused to fund his project. Many pioneers in computer science and informatics, and science in general shared his fate. It might not have always been the stupidity of governments, but some of them clearly were, e.g., the ideas of Nazi government to first produce more guns and bullets and win the war, and only after winning the war to produce advanced versions of Konrad Zuse's electromechanical computers. But in some cases the needs and market at the time were not ready to provide a breeding place for new scientific ideas. For Babbage, there were additional discussions about possibility to design a mechanical machine with existing technology having in mind problems with friction. But this argument was put aside with actual construction around century and a half later. So Babbage had an ingenious idea a long time ago while the government made an obvious error not supporting computer research. Similar situations can be observed with the introduction of information society - some national governments support is, some are indifferent.

- 1936 – Alan Turing, Alonzo Church, Emil Post and others, mainly mathematicians, defined two of the most fundamental scientific concepts of our time – the Turing-Church thesis about computatibility and the universal Turing machine. Church was mainly concerned with different types of functions and found that there is a class of functions that is computable in effective (procedural) way, and that there are functions that are not computable. Turing independently discovered a slightly different thesis – the class of functions that is computable is computable on Turing machines. Soon it was realized that this is actually the same concept in two slightly different forms. Another concept constructed by Turing alone was the Turing machine – a universal machine able to compute anything computable.

- 1941 – Konrad Zuse, a German, designed the first running general-purpose programmable computer. It was not a fully electronic machine since it used electromechanical relays as the basic unit. Due to the war efforts, these achievements were not further developed, and were recognized only recently.

- 1943 – Collosus, the special-pupose electronic computer for decoding codes became operational. Turing helped decode the Enigma code and helped win the war.

- 1945 – Eniac, the Electronic Numerical Integrator and Computer machine was the first general-purpose electronic machine. Unlike secret British Collosus, American Eniac attracted world-wide attention.

- 1951 – Mark I, the world's first commercially manufactured electronic computer with electronic stored-program was installed. A little later UNIVAC, the world's second commercially available machine became available in America.

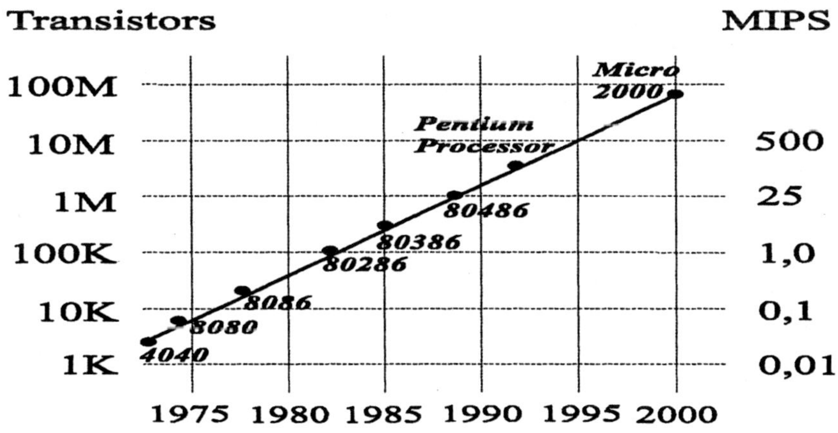

Figure 2.1: Plotting the number of transistors per chip versus time shows the Moore's law: every 1.5 to 2 years the integration density doubles.

Because of the war, the defence ministries were eager to order and buy these products, a little later science and other areas of human activities. Enormous progress followed with conceptually similar but technologically substantially improved machines.

- 1982 – Paul Benioff described a classical computer consisting of quantum components. The general idea is simple – since chip density constantly increases it will coon or later approach quantum dimensions and thus quantum processes.

- 1985 – David Deutch developed a quantum version of the Turing machine – the universal quantum machine. Instead of bits (0 or 1), these machines deal with linear superposition of atomic "bits". As in quantum physics, although it is impossible to set exact parameters of quantum particles such as position or the wavefunction, it is possible to compute well. This might sound weird for those not familiar with quantum physics, but is usually presented in high-schools all over the world without much problems. Deutch was attacked by critics that his models are irrelevant since there is no practical implementation of these ideas.

- 1993 and later – S. Lloyd, P. W. Shor, H. J. Kimble, D. J. Wineland and others further developed areas of applications of quantum computers and designed the first prototypes of quantum logic gates. These results are far from practical applicability, but present an important improvement over previously purely theoretical definitions.

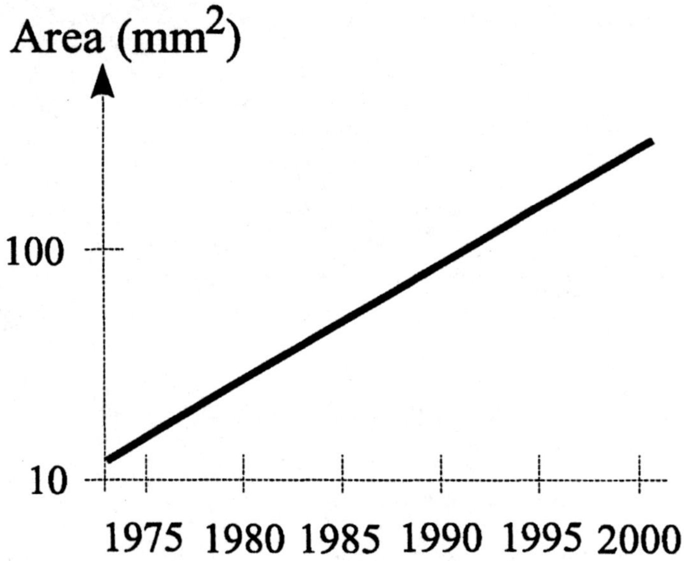

Figure 2.2: Die chip size versus time shows constant improvements.

2.2 Trends of Hardware Progress

The progress of microelectronics is the essence of computer progress in the last 40 years. An overview shows the following major indicators:

- performance (density, speed) steadily increases while
- costs (buying, operation, power) steadily decrease, and
- applications (penetration in new products) steadily increase.

Performance

Integration density. The number of transistors per chip has increased exponentially according to the Moore's law (Moore 1975) and has so far doubled every 1.5 years. The law can be observed from the line in Figure 2.1. Note that the Y scale is logarithmic. If shown on a linear scale one could see only the last couple of values due to the exponential growth. The increase has been faster for memories due to more regular and simpler structure while logic devices require longer design times due to more complex design.

Speed. Gate speed constantly increases as well. However, while gate delay progressively decreases, circuit access time does not increase proportionally due to more and more complicated circuits.

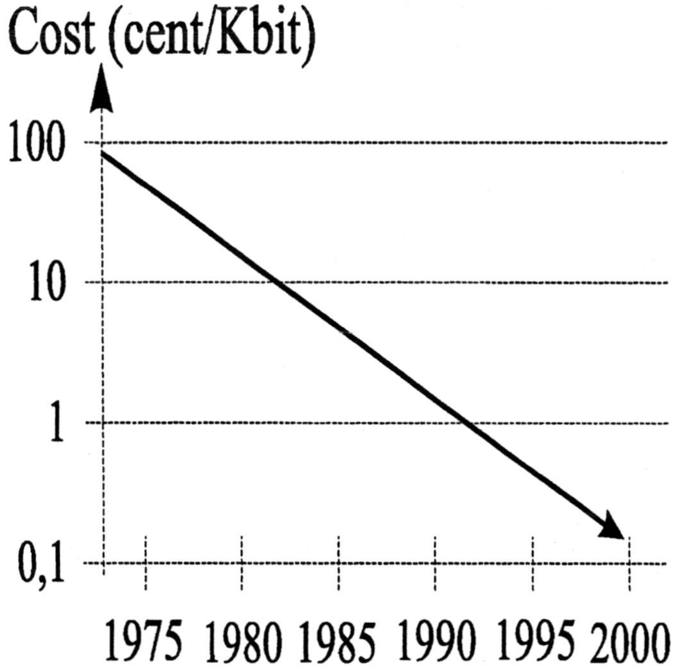

Figure 2.3: Cost per bit versus time for DRAM's.

Size. Growing density and speed are based on the reduction in feature size and the increase of die size (Figure 2.2). The growth was enabled by the ongoing progress in lithography and the improvements in the quality of materials.

Costs

The cost per bit exponentially decreases in the last 25 years (Figure 2.3; source ICE Report 1990). However, while the overall cost per bit decreases, process cost (i.e. production or equipment cost) actually increases and represents one of the biggest annoyances in future progress.

Applications

In recent years microelectronics has become a key component of all electronic equipment. Not only there is a constant grow in already established areas like computer applications, also, microelectronics have gained important new areas like video-recorders and CD's. The ratio between semiconductors and equipment sales is

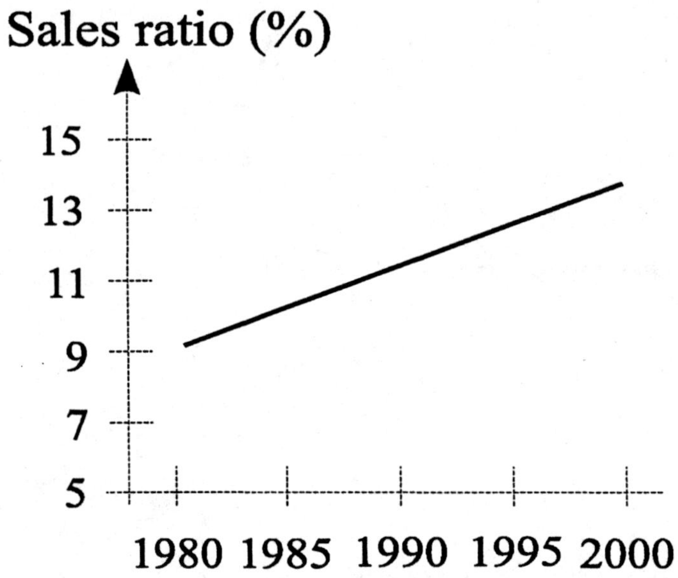

Figure 2.4: Ratio between semiconductors and equipment sales indicates an ongoing progress in semiconductor applications.

presented in Figure 2.4; (ICE Report 1990). The hypothetical crossing point is year 2150, when nearly all technical devices will be equipped by semiconductors (Of course, some products will never contain electronics – for example, a toilet paper.) This broader use brings development of new features like analogue circuitry or digitally controlled power capabilities and will effect everyday life in more or less every human activity, e.g. in smart houses or smart cars.

Evolution of the Basic Computer Component

A switch can be regarded as a basic computer component and by evidencing it's progress we can understand the basics of computer progress.

In Table 2.1 we see that roughly each 10 years a switch was produced in a different technology. In the first decade, electronic computers were based on electronic tubes, the next 10 years on transistors and somewhere around 1964 chips emerged as a new product integrating transistors into one integrated circuit. The following 10-year periods are based on new technologies that achieve higher and higher density of transistors: LSI - Large Scale Integration, VLSI – Very Large Scale Integration and finally ULSI – Ultra Large Scale Integration.

Due to the fact that the switch was each decade produced in a new technology, it became much smaller, faster, reliable and with longer exploration period. The

YEARS	SWITCH
10	tube
20	transistor
30	chip
40	LSI
50	VLSI
60	ULSI

Table 2.1: The progress of the basic component of computers - a switch – can be roughly grouped into six 10-year periods.

improvement of overall efficiency is especially noticeable when compared to the price of one switch. The next decade will see even faster and even more integrated chips with higher density.

The technological progress of the basic computer component largely influenced the progress of computer hardware, architecture, peripherals and also software.

Technological Limits

While general extrapolation shows no major obstacle for further development, the following issues can become critical in mid- or long-distance future:

- **Lithography.** In the last twenty years, the minimal feature size has been Substantially reduced. The progress has been achieved through advances in optical lithography and, most importantly, no real barrier is likely to appear in the next ten years.

- **Transistor architecture.** A recent critical point has been reached for MOS transistors with device lengths around 1.2 μ m due to the increase in power density. But new solutions happened as predicted at the level of the scaling rules and the reduction of the supply voltage around 2-3 V.

- **Interconnections** Since logic devices are becoming more and more complex, a certain limit of interconnections is becoming one of crucial factors. The solution could be the use of more metal levels, going from present two levels to three or more.

- **Defect density.** In the last twenty years the particle density in the production environment has been reduced by at least three orders of magnitude. While the production costs grow, the problem of defect density basically translates to the cost limitations.

- **Cost limitations.** The cost of semiconductor facilities steadily grows and, perhaps the darkest observation is that specific costs grow even faster. For example, the lithography costs versus feature size seems to be exponential.

2.3 Software Evolution

2.3.1 Software Generations

Software progress can be represented by the development of the basic unit of the programming or communicating language (see Table 2.2).

PERIOD	LOGICAL UNIT	TYPE OF LANGUAGE
1	010110100	machine language
2	LOAD B	assembly language
3	DO I=1,10	procedural high-level language (Fortran)
4	procedure invert(var A: arrT);	modular high-level language (Pascal, C)
5	data tasks	objects, programming tools spread-sheets and data bases programming environments (Delphi)
6	information tasks	Internet, intranet Java, intelligent agents

Table 2.2: Evolution of software through the progress of the basic unit of the programming language again enables structuring the history into 6 roughly equidistant 10-year periods.

First programmers had to code in sequences of 0's and 1's in machine code. This awful task was substituted by programming in simple commands that were still strongly hardware oriented – for example, LOAD B means that the value of B is loaded into a specialized register – accumulator. Already, these assembly languages represented a large step ahead. The next generation of procedural high level programming languages enabled even better programming in terms of statements. For example, the presented loop in Fortran in Table 2.2 means that the following statements are to be executed 10 times. These statements remained only slightly changed also in newer languages like Pascal, Modula and Ada, but they enabled new concepts – a subroutine, a process and a module together with structural programming. For a while, logic languages such as Prolog were seen as new hope. But the progress come through specialized tools such as those in Microsoft Windows and

Office. The next generation is represented by the information society with agents – intelligent assistants or secretaries through the Internet and intranet. Global information exchange through the Internet is becoming the dominant activity. Future software generation will quite probably look like an improved society of intelligent agents – systems performing intelligent assisting tasks (See Table 2.3).

GENERATION	DOMINANT ORIENTATION
1	hardware
2	software (programming languages)
3	tools and environments (data-bases)
4	information and data tools (Windows Office)
5	global-networks information exchange (Internet)
6	knowledge and intelligence (intelligent systems) ??

Table 2.3: Generations of human-computer relations. The sixth generation here is only a hypothesis.

Each new software generation was more adapted to the human way of communicating meaning more and more work for translation into machine code and execution was left to computers. While the price of computer work is exponentially declining, the price of human work remains more or less constant. Therefore, the technological progress of computer capabilities directly dictates more and more human-like communication. In fact, it urges for more and more intelligence in computers – a task software designers are still unable to provide realistically. Instead, they fake intelligence in intelligent systems and agents.

2.3.2 Distributed and Parallel Computing

In the next ten years, more and more attention will be devoted to distributed and parallel computing. However, classical Von Neumann computer architecture will probably remain dominant for at least 10 years since there are some difficult unsolved obstacles in parallel computing (Hertzberger 1991; Duby 1991). Specialized tricks like adding a couple of coprocessors or organizing a net of a couple coprocessors currently dominate.

Some areas of parallel computing will evolve naturally with growing computer, microelectronic and transmission performances. For example, visualization requires specialized processors and high speed communications requires quick accepting and storing large amounts of data. It is also quite likely that specialized artificial neural network processors will be used for pattern recognition tasks. Another successful area for parallelism are numerically intensive applications. Not surprisingly, since the parallelism in supercomputers, e.g., vectorization of applications was an essential step to improve processing speed. Different classes of parallelism are being identified: domain parallelism, where data structures are distributed among various processors; algorithmic parallelism, where the computer network is designed to match a particular algorithm and suitable code fragments and data flows are constructed; and task-parallelism, where a problem is divided into a large number of subproblems.

One of the fundamental problems is coordination and control of the communications among parallel fragments that comprise the task. One of the major bottlenecks in parallel computing is the lack of a coherent general model of describing and organizing a parallel computing process. There were some promising attempts, unfortunately without greater practical meaning. In one approach (Valiant 1990), the possibility was defined as an idealized parallel processor PRAM, similar to the Turing machine. It was also shown that under certain conditions, an algorithm runs P times faster on a parallel machine with P processors.

Therefore, at least theoretically it can be shown that parallel universality exists. On the other hand, practical solutions seem still quite far away as can be shown by a simple calculation: If only 1% of the whole process has to be solved in a sequential way, any parallel machine with any number of processors cannot achieve improvement by 100 times.

Also, in the area of distributed computing some of the problems might slow down the expected progress, maybe simply by the unwillingness of many user communities to fully exploit the new possibilities by paying the price of forgetting the old-style approach and corresponding knowledge and skills. In addition, several implications seem inevitable, e.g., the role of big computers will quite probably further decrease because of the cost-effectiveness and enormous computing power of personal computers based on one-chip improvements.

2.4 The Near Future

In the near future of around 10 years, given the large amount of investments in the field, given the strong interconnections between microelectronics and the bulk of electronic industry, and the existing R&D prototypes, no revolutionary change will take place. Performances, e.g., speed, complexity or feature size will continue to grow with exponential growth as they did so far. Technology will continue to change as rapid or even faster than today, therefore, due to the constant introduction of new approaches and the growth in performances, microelectronic industry behaves like a young and innovative industry. However, from the point of investment, growing manufacturing costs, and a decrease of the number of semiconductor companies, it appears a mature industry branch with all its pluses and minuses.

Besides microelectronics, several other areas like magnetic storage technology record important progress as well. Performances, such as density, access speed and transfer rates continue to improve. Also, optical storage will fully develop in parallel with magnetic storage.

What impacts will these computers performances provide? Certainly, several tasks will be done in other way than today. Disk sorting techniques will be less important due to a simple fact that most of the sorting will be performed in the main memory. Simple calculation shows than 10 years from now personal computers will have enough central memory to store (and sort) names and surnames of all people in an average country or store movies on a disk. Similarly, relational and object databases will benefit from those memory sizes while hierarchical systems will be in further decline. Large databases will influence every-day applications of artificial intelligence and knowledge-based systems.

User interface will be one of areas where additional speed and capacities will enable great improvements. High definition graphic interface for both input and output will become pervasive while speech will enable high quality output as well as reasonable input. Since around 1 GIPS is needed for high speech and graphics performance, high-performance PCs will be able to do it at professional level while low-price personal computers will have to be contented with reasonable compromises. The differences between expensive personal computers and workstations will practically disappear and categories of computers will be based primarily on price and purpose. On the other hand, several new peripheral devices will become available such as smart scanners, readers and general data collectors from instruments and sensors. Most important, these new products will be task-user oriented for specific profiles. In display technologies, cathode ray tubes are expected to remain most widely used with evolutionary improved resolution.

In operating systems, less time will be devoted to memory allocation and more to new functions like distributed services and data (Internet), symbolic data query, cooperative processing and fault detection and recovery. After all, with all information available from the Internet, who needs to buy all programs for himself and to store them on huge hard discs? Diskless computers or at least intranet and Internet-oriented personal computers are about to come. With Internet fully developed as the information highway, all information in the world will be at our fingertip.

Progress in communicational technologies is expected to grow even faster than in computer technologies. Performance such as bandwidth is growing as in other areas of computer progress. It will effect architecture as well as disk needs since new transmission techniques will enable terrabytes per second access rates. Due to the availability of many different kinds of data, standardization will become pervasive in about every domain of computer technologies and applications from hardware to software, communications and user interfaces. Yet, communication with computers will become much more human-like and application user-oriented since most of the users will basically have no technical knowledge about computing.

One of the main improvements will be more and more complex applications. Simulated models will replace experiments and enable efficient search for optimal solutions in many areas. Very large and complex data will enable access of all interesting data such as encyclopedic data bases or business history for specific branches. Multimedia will be part of every-day activities for everybody.

2.5 Trends of Computer Progress

To repeat, many trends of computer progress are very constant over the last 50 years, among them the density of components per one square millimetre. Each 10 years the density of components increases roughly 100 times.

Greater density enables other improvements, e.g. shorter connections, faster computing and as the final result computers become approximately million times more capable each 10 years. **This progress is beyond any comparison with other technologies** which are usually much more tided by natural limits. For example, in only a couple of years with such a tempo of progress we should get a super family car capable of reaching the speed of an airplane having the capacity of a cargo ship and costing about the same as family cars a couple of years ago. Obviously and unavoidably, car progress is limited by air friction, roads, human passengers and other natural limitations. Computer progress is not.

Considering the present state of computer technology we can see possible limits in chip capacity, computing speed, overheating of components, etc. But it was the same in the past and each computer was actually produced within the limits of existing computer technology. There were no reasonable unavoidable limitations for the progress of computers in the past and there are not in the near future. In fact, it has always turned out that **the cause of the limit was our knowledge or rather the lack of it!**

There are several promising possible break-throughs in the near future such as erasable optical disks, communications in natural language and through intelligent graphical interfaces; further away there could be superconductive quantum fully intelligent computers. And even when we reach the limits of these technologies, there are plenty of others. For example, when we reach the limits in computing or chips posed by the electron (e.g. the tunneling effect), we might try with photons.

2.6 Practical Implications of Computer Progress

Around a hundred years before Konrad Zuse constructed his first working computer based on relays (a little before World War II), Charles Babbage designed the first digital computer. None of these two machines resulted in market products. Not only Charles Babbage and Konrad Zuse, first constructors of electronic computer faced the same problems: while the idea seemed great, the time was not ripe yet. There was no commercial boom behind.

For a commercial success, much more than an interesting idea is needed. According to Robert Noyce (MTCM 1992), one of the inventors of the integrated circuits,

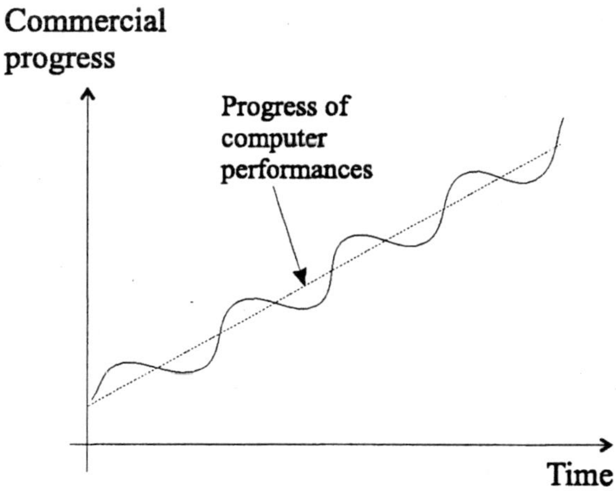

Figure 2.5: Commercial break-throughs in computer market follow technological advances in offer/supply/demand circles.

the following three conditions for success are necessary:

- a need that current technology does not sufficiently support,
- a theory or vision for a new technology that addresses the need, and
- the enabling technology that makes if possible to produce the theory.

Practical implications of computer progress are influenced by technological development, market characteristics and several other factors. Market break-throughs happen whenever a new and better type of computer product reaches market maturity. Whenever an advanced product reaches a preferable cost/benefit ratio, it causes great commercial attraction. All products of this type are bought by customers and offer/supply/demand ratio is preferable for any productionist capable of mastering new technology. The production grows very rapidly and gradually overfills the market – the supply becomes greater than the demand. A hard competition ruins many of the productionists but on the horizon there is another technological break-through which rolls the circle once again (see Figure 2.5).

A well-known example is a sequence of break-throughs of microcomputers: home computer (Spectrum, Commodore) with a boom in computer games and children education, personal computer (Apple, IBM PC) with a boom in small business and smaller tasks, current PC and workstation (SUN, HP) with more complex applications (Internet, communications, multimedia).

We can roughly estimate the importance of computers today. To replace the work of all computers today we would need something like 1000-10000 times more people than the whole human population. Despite the fact that not all of the work

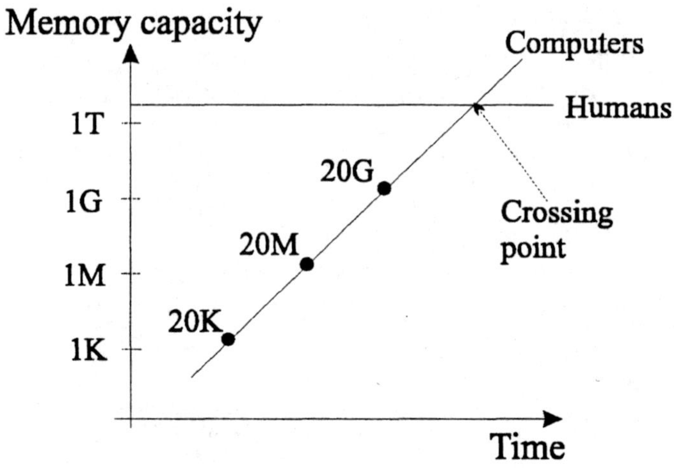

Figure 2.6: The progress in computer mass memory is constant and promises to reach capacity of people in the near future.

would have to be replaced by "brute" human work we can still claim that we would need more people for the replacement of all computers than for the replacement of all other machines! This tells us how vast is the amount of computer work, and its influence on our lives.

2.7 Mass Memory – a Possible Break-Through

First electronic computers were useful because they outperformed humans in speed and precision of numerical computing thus becoming valuable assistants. Similarly, important break-throughs happen when computers outperform people in other areas and so far there seems no end to this. The only question is when and in which area will it happen.

One of the important areas where capabilities of computers are approaching human performances is mass memory (see Figure 2.6). According to Moravec (1988), another is the processing power (see Figure 2.7).

The progress presented in Figure 2.6 is rather constant, and can be more effectively presented in Table 2.4. There, the possibility of another break-through is more evident.

To understand the importance of a qualitative leap ahead let us make a comparison with a car. If the first prototype of a car reaches only 8 meters/h and the second 8 km/h, we achieve a leap of 1000. Although this is a large jump ahead, these cars currently remain economically quite uninteresting. But one jump more by the factor of 1000 radically changes the commercial outcome: we have a car with the maximal speed of 8000 km/h and a clear market boom.

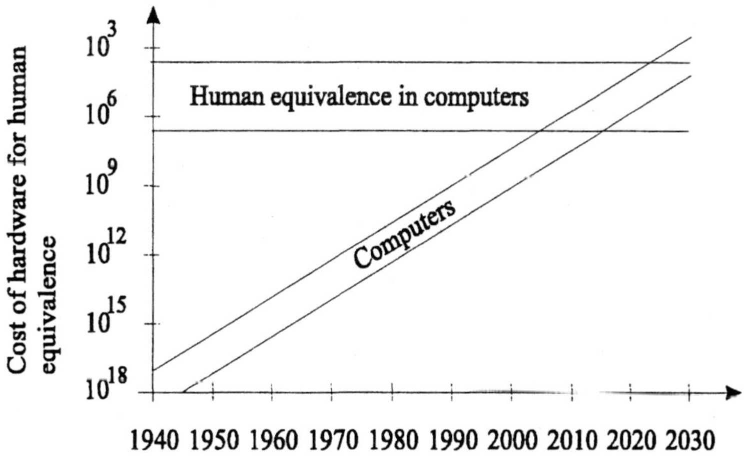

Figure 2.7: Moravec sees a break-through in computing power in a couple of decades.

TYPE	CAPACITY	LENGTH	TIME FOR TYPING
home c.	20 K	3 mm of books	0.002 years
old pers. c.	20 M	3 m of books	2 years
current pers. c.	20 G	3 km of books	2000 years

Table 2.4: Jumps in the capacity of mass memory from first reasonable home microcomputers to first reasonable IBM PC's and current personal microcomputers. Memory capacity of the computer is presented in the second column. In the third column we see the corresponding length of books on a book shell and in the last column years needed for typing that amount of information.

First home microcomputers had around 20 K memory. This amount of information is typed by a typist in 0.0002 years on a 3 mm thick book. Old personal computer had a 20 M disk which corresponded to 3 m of books and 2 years of typing. Current personal computers reach 20 G corresponding to 3 km of books and 2000 years of typing. This certainly represents an important break-through since one person needs for its work only about 100-200 M on a paper. The capacity of a human maximally reaches about 100000 G around the age of 50. These numbers are near the reach of new mainframe supercomputers soon, and PCs in not so distant future.

Note that one should be weary when using direct comparisons between humans and computers. If our principle of multiple knowledge holds, the human brain is able to combine its information into an enormous number of reasonable combinations while computers are currently not able to do it. Thus, the same amount of basic information is dynamically extended by several orders of magnitude in the human mind/brain while computers are currently not able to "extend-multiply" stored information.

Whatever the case, a potential break-through is emerging. It is not easy to predict which areas will it first influence. We will be able to store lots of films and lots of encyclopaedia on one disk. But how will it influence learning process and the access to (computer) libraries? Communications through picture and sound will become nearly natural and maybe even the rudimentals of the human recognizable artificial intelligence. We are able to see that something important is going to happen due to the growth of pure computer power, but are not able to see when and especially how it will happen. The basic reason is again lack of knowledge.

2.8 Exponential Growth Leads to Explosion

To understand why the growth of computer capabilities is unnatural, incomparable to progress in other technical disciplines, we have to understand the growth of numbers. Consider for example, three functions: $3n, n^2, 2^n$. These functions have values $3, 1, 2$ for $n = 1$; $6, 4, 4$ for $n = 2$ and $9, 9, 8$ for $n = 3$ as can be observed from Table 2.5. Nothing spectacular. But at $n = 100$ we get $300, 10000, 2^{100}$. Since 2^{20} is approximately 1000000, 2^{100} is close to 10^{30}. The 2^n function is exponential as are all functions of the $a^{f(n)}$ form.

n	$3n$	n^2	2^n
1	3	1	2
2	6	4	4
3	9	9	8
10	30	100	1024
100	300	10000	1267650600228229401496703205376

Table 2.5: **Exponential growth starts slowly and ends in an explosion.**

Since basic computer properties double faster than in two years (e.g., chip density), computer progress qualitatively corresponds to the most right column in Table 2.5. Where does it bring us to? Let us make another example. Suppose that we are breading new sorts of corn using three different methods. In the first year corn A grow by 3 mm, corn B by 1 mm, corn C by 2 mm. Further growth corresponds to the growth in the right three columns in Table 2.5. Of course, 1000 mm is 1 m and 1000000 mm is 1 km. In hundred years, corn A grows by 0.3 m, corn B by 10 m, and corn C by 10^{30} mm which is 10^{24} km. Compare the last number with 10^{23} km, the diameter of our known universe. A corn bigger than our universe? Obviously, nothing materialistic can cope with such exponential progress for a longer period of time, computers included. But so far and in the near future of, say 10 years, the computer growth is exponential and as mentioned, is referred to as the Moore law. This is something quite extraordinary compared to other scientific and technological disciplines.

Is exponential growth uncommon on Earth? Consider for example a nuclear bomb. The exponential growth of the chain reaction results in a huge explosion. If the armor is able to contain the process for a very small portion of a second, the explosion is a couple of times stronger. But there are many more examples of exponential growth – each species basically evolves by the exponential growth, be it humans, elephants or bacteria. Usually, each species is regulated by predators, parasites, diseases, lack of space and food. When a species is brought in an environment without usual decreasing factors, it explodes similar to the right row in Table 2.5. Rabbits in Australia are a good example of this kind. But it only means that there are lots of rabbits around for a while, because they meet their limits at upper levels, not at the level close to the start-up density. However, somewhere in the future there is a limit for rabbits, computers or humans.

What is the meaning of this for the human-computer relation? Say that we measure intelligence on some scale and that normal human performance is 100. Had computers been 10.000 times less intelligent than humans 40 years ago, they would reach an average human if their intelligence grew with the same speed as chip density. Since electronic computers emerged around World war II, this means that **by now computers should have to be several hundred times smarter than humans. There must be something wrong with this scenario** since true intelligence of computers is far beyond our level of recognition. Computing and storing powers of computers are growing exponentially while their intelligence is stagnating around zero. How can that be if intelligence is not something essentially different than advanced computing capabilities of computers?

2.9 Discussion

In the last half of this century, computers are probably the leading technological product influencing the human progress. Analyses of computer history show several distinctive laws indicating that

- computer progress is very constant over the last 50 years,
- this progress is at least one order of magnitude faster than progress in other sciences and technologies,
- there are no reasonable limits for this progress in near future (Baldi 1991; Hamilton 1999), and

- we can expect computers to greatly enhance their impact on our every-day life by becoming dominant over humans in several important characteristics such as mass memory.

Therefore, it is safe to conclude that speculations of either stagnation in computer industry or spectacular break-throughs in computer intelligence are as unsound as ever.

To repeat – **the scope of computer progress is beyond comparison with other sciences and technologies** alike and is still very far from the limits that could threaten to slow it down. Already, computer is the most important single machine invented by humans and it will tend to largely enhance its influence on every-day life by becoming dominant over people in more and more categories. But **since computer's intelligence is still around 0 while being able to perform calculations million times faster than humans, several essential human properties like true intelligence or consciousness have to be essentially different than computing.**

Chapter 3

The Brain

This decade is the decade of the brain. Maybe it should be the decade of the mind and the brain, because it is becoming evident and widely accepted that the two are connected in a way that truly understanding of what goes on in the brain demands understanding how the mind works, and vice versa (Mind and Brain, 1993). The times when Aristotle thought that the mind is related to the heart, or when Descartes thought that the mind is basically separated (yet combined) from the brain, are long gone. It is too easy to see that **the mind and the brain are closely related.** All we need is to take a small amount of chemicals and suddenly our mood changes, we start laughing, seeing hallucinations, become superactive, fall asleep or even lose consciousness and die.

But to understand brains, a short history of the Earth and human evolution might be welcome.

3.1 Our History and Future – the Human

3.1.1 From Apes to Humans

Most of the last 1000 years, people thought that we do not have common ancestors with apes. Just a decade ago, it was thought that humans separated from apes around 10 to 20 million years ago. Until recently, it was thought that a bipedal walking developed because climate changed and instead of tropical tree-rich surroundings, savannas prevailed. What is the point of climbing capabilities if there are no trees around? Walking freed hands and an evolutionary boost was on. Then, human ancestors slowly progressed into more and more upward and more and more intelligent creatures.

Nothing of this is seen as true these days. In recent years, science got an important new tool to rediscover the past. When the two cells merge to start a life of a new child, genetic crossover happens as when messing together two stacks of cards. There are over 10^{2000} chances from the start. These gene crossovers are

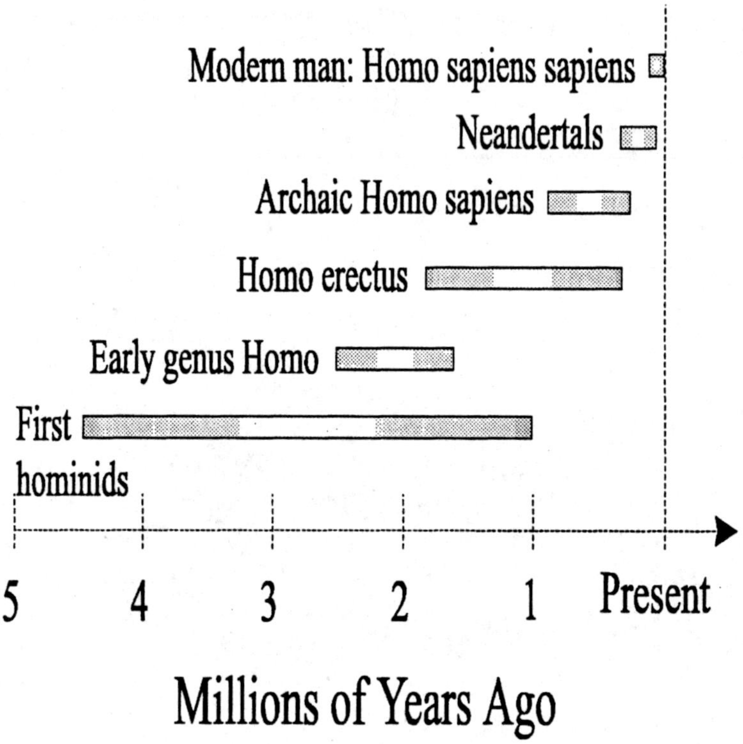

Figure 3.1: Human family tree.

something usual. More unusual are mutations, random changes in the genetic code - as if one card in a stack has changed due to some unknown error. Most of the changes are bad, but some are miraculous. Evolutionary more advanced offsprings have better chances to survive and to have more offsprings. Around 10 years ago scientists approximately mastered numeric chances in these processes. Then, they theoretically turned the clock backwards and calculated our history on the bases of genetic materials taken from people all over the world. Suddenly, they could calculate when humans separated from apes. It happened around 4-5 million years ago (see Figure 3.1). New discoveries of Australopithecus Ramidus, 4.4 million years old, in Northern Africa, probably indicate one of the missing links. Surprisingly, the discovered remains of Australopithecus Ramidus indicate that although living in a jungle, they occasionally or regularly used bipedal moving around. Instead of having great canines as baboons, they gained other evolutionary advantages. Regularly standing tall, though, has been reportedly developed much later, with Homo Erectus around 2 million years ago, as studies of the inner-ear bones indicate. The Australopithecus family was very likely not fully bipedal.

One of the essential questions is what is the nature of progress of intellectual

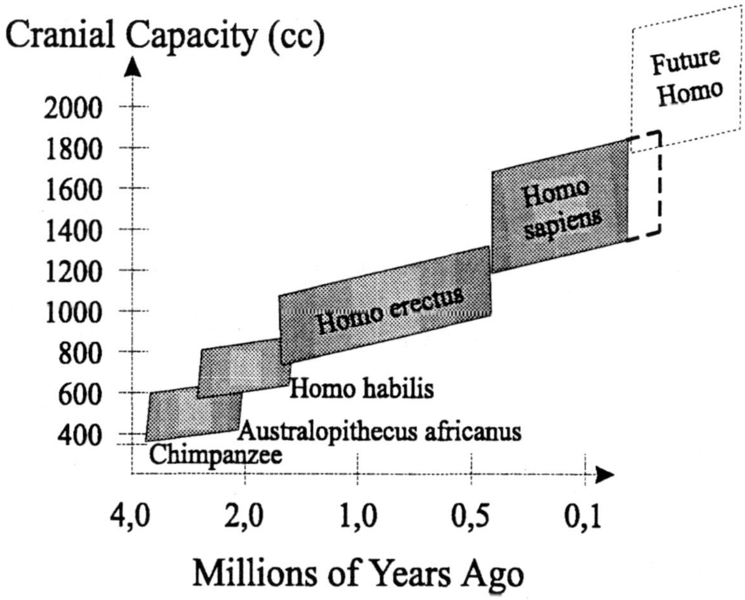

Figure 3.2: The growth of the human brain.

capabilities, what is its influence on the progress of human race and vice versa. The following conclusion can be drawn: **The progress of the human brain was more or less constant for longer periods followed by characteristic jumps ahead caused by mutations**(Figures 3.2).

Homo Erectus was one of the great genetic wonders, very probably – like all great changes – caused by a mutation. Homo Erectus emerged about 2 million years ago, eliminated all other versions of human ancestors including all Australopitecus human prototypes and Homo Habilis as well. Note that Australopitecus Robustus was more like a gorilla compared to a relatively fragile Homo Erectus. Yet, the later regularly walked straight and regularly used tools. Its brain capacity was substantially bigger (see Figure 3.2). Around a million years ago it conquered the whole world. Homo Erectus mastered fire and put on a street today (shaved and dressed properly), people would walk by without paying much attention to it.

Homo Erectus later evolved into Homo Sapiens. For a substantial time there were two versions of Homo Sapiens: Homo Sapiens Neanderthalensis and Homo Sapiens Sapiens. The later eliminated the first one entirely. Today, no genetic traces of any kind are found in Homo Sapiens (which now stands for Homo Sapiens Sapiens).

The last major change, caused by another mutation, happened around 100.000 years ago. From there on, we have no dramatic changes in our genetic material. Our brains are essentially like the brains of our ancestors of around 50-100.000 years ago. The evidence comes from multiple and mutually supporting sources. Be it types of bloods, be it language similarities, be it genetics, be it fossils, results are surprisingly similar. Especially interesting is the genetic evidence. The best known analyses come from the genetic material in placenta that is directly inherited through the maternal line – from mother to a woman child – because it is not affected by the crossover process. In this way, it is much easier to calculate the reverse process. The calculation shows that the new breed – our breed – started around 100 to 80.000 years ago in one person. (This is genetically very modern, but not exceptionally new. For example, the polar bear appeared roughly in the same time span.) It was a woman or a man, but that man if existed, passed his genetic advantage only to one woman child whose genetic material is traceable today. That child is the mother of all currently existing humans on Earth. No wonder it was called "Eve". There could first be a man etc. so the story can be more complicated. The trace method returned one woman.

Discovered around 10 years ago, genetic count-back substantially changed our view of human evolution. First a friendly conclusion: **We are genetically all very similar.** Our genetic material is ten times more similar to each other than that of one chimpanzee to the other chimpanzee because we are much younger species than chimpanzees with which we share 99% of the genetic code. The genetic variety in humans is met with those in just 55 chimpanzees. We are all very alike, be it black, yellow or white. Our first ancestor (Adam or Eve) was black. It came from Africa, as did Homo Erectus.

Then a more troublesome conclusion: **The new version of human eradicated all other coexisting versions of people on Earth.** No matter that several thousands of generations mated with the new subspecies, its new genetic material "eliminated" others out to the point that other forms are not tractable. Of course, there were some subvariations, those that explain why we are different today. But the general picture is clear. How did the elimination of other subspecies happen? Some of the conflicts were probably brutal. It is unlikely that the evolutionary advantage over the last human version one was based on physical strength. Rather, the improvement was in advanced performance, probably in better language-speech or better mental capabilities enabling better use of stored events for future planning. Another possibility is in advanced tools and weapons, e.g. bows and arrows over javelins. To use such technology, advanced brains are needed. Although it is not clearly known how it happened, the geographical progress of our ancestor is evident from different sources, be it fossils, blood types or language similarities. From Northern Africa, the new human moved to Asia, and then to Europe, America and so forth. And wherever it came previous very similar versions of humans existed, those whose genetic material differed only by 0.1 percent. Note that the whole Earth was conquered by humans roughly a million years ago.

A lesson learned from the past about future – **It is not a question if the next new version of a human will emerge – the question is when** (Figure 3.2). Since the last new version of humans emerged around 100.000 years ago and today people live in greater numbers, a simple calculation shows us that the time when the new human will emerge is statistically close. Maybe, the new human is already here among us. Note that while chimpanzees and gorillas survived, the too-close human-type competitors were all eliminated. It is also the case with computers – new generations of computers eliminate the previous ones, not the humans. It also means that **humans and computers are basically not competitors and that they will live together without major troubles** unlike in sci-fiction horror films. **They just live in too different habitats.** So, if there is a lesson from history, it says that the new superior genetic material will overwhelm in a rather mysterious random mutation process.

One might ask, what is the relation of the evolution of the human species and the brain compared to the major thesis of this book. But one might also – and maybe with better reason – ask what is the relation between computing machines and intelligence. After all, **only the human brains enable consciousness and intelligence**, while computers are only the best potential candidates! If we can't create intelligence on the basis of fast computing and algorithms, we might succeed by copying properties of the mind and the brain. This is one of the weak-AI postulates.

3.2 Brains and Minds

Until recent years, consciousness was a taboo concept in many fields of science, including psychology and artificial intelligence. The main reason was that no reasonable results were produced, and then, it was seen as a waste of money. Attempts to put the mind into equations were as fruitful as attempts to build beings (alive machines) from metals. Only recently, a scientific assault on consciousness was mounted in a collaboration among psychologists, neuroscientists and theorists. Their first idea was to explain consciousness on the basis of the firing of large sets of neurons.

So, how does the brain work? Where are the switches, connections, and modules? The first look shows nothing special – it weights about 1.5 to 2 kilograms and contains around 100 billion neurons. But the complexity of functions it performs indicates that it is something hardly comprehensible. **The human brain is a result of millions of years of evolution making unknown and incomprehensible steps.** There is no single plan, no single modular schema.

However, several things about the brain are known and our knowledge about the brain grows with an increasing speed. The brain consists of several parts (e.g., the left and right hemisphere connected by the corpus callosum; there are tens of other parts such as cerebellum, hypothalamus, hippocampus or spiral cord), and the basic cell (a neuron) (Figure 3.3) is well analyzed. One of the most mysterious part of the human brain is the cortex – the highly convoluted two millimeters thick surface of the cerebral hemispheres. The surface area of the cortex is around 1.5 m^2. It is the most modern part of the brain. Some parts of the brain are pretty ancient, especially those taking control of specific body functions. But it is evidently wrong to claim that the cortex is the part of the body responsible for the mind; **the mind emerges from collective activity of several brain regions of which some are connected to the body**; some even say that the body itself is involved in the mind as well. The mind itself depends on several functions – e.g., consciousness, moods, desires and subconsciousness.

The cerebral cortex can be further divided into several subareas, e.g., motor-control area, sensory area etc. Some actions (e.g. low-level vision) are well located in specific modules, others (typically learning, associations, memorizing, thinking) are dispersed over broader areas.

There are about thirty to fifty general types of neurons. Each neuron itself is quite likely unique from the point of its topographical structure. Therefore, a direct comparison with switches (i.e, transistors) in computers is not possible. A neuron can have a short connection only to its closest neighbors, or the connection is made to a region quite far away. Quite often, neurons are grouped together in columns or slabs that e.g., extend through the thickness of the cortex. A module could include more that 100.000 cells.

Much is known about the chemistry in the neuron, and about basic performance. For example, a signal in the axon is dissipated in one or two millimeters. Since some axons measure many centimeters in length, the signal must be frequently regenerated – similar to signals that travel through wires several hundred kilometers far. Another limitation is the rate at which action potentials can be generated – it is less than 2000 per second.

Some of the performances of neurons are ridiculously low compared to transistors or wires in computers. For example, a neuron can transmit 10 impulses per second. Only 30 bits per second can travel through information channels. Short memory has only 7 pointers. A simple mathematical operation takes us from a couple to hundreds of seconds. Computers can compute millions of such operations per second. While the speed of information in humans is comparable to the speed of sound, the same speed in computers is comparable to the speed of light. On the basis of these comparisons, fifty years ago it was assumed that only an appropriate mechanism has to be found and a sufficiently complex computer will outperform any human brain. As mentioned, this has let to the first dark age in AI history. It would be similarly naive to expect that a single mechanism could produce the mind. In this light it is hard to see how neural networks or quantum processes in synapses could be the only one responsible for such a complex system. No really complex system can be simply explained. Thoughts must depend on the cooperation of impulses conducted over many axons in parallel and over very complex connections. It has been discovered that even simple percepts are processed as different characteristics of the same event in parallel. It is still a mystery how neurons coordinate actions. However, specific oscillations of 30-70 (most often referred as 40) cycles per second

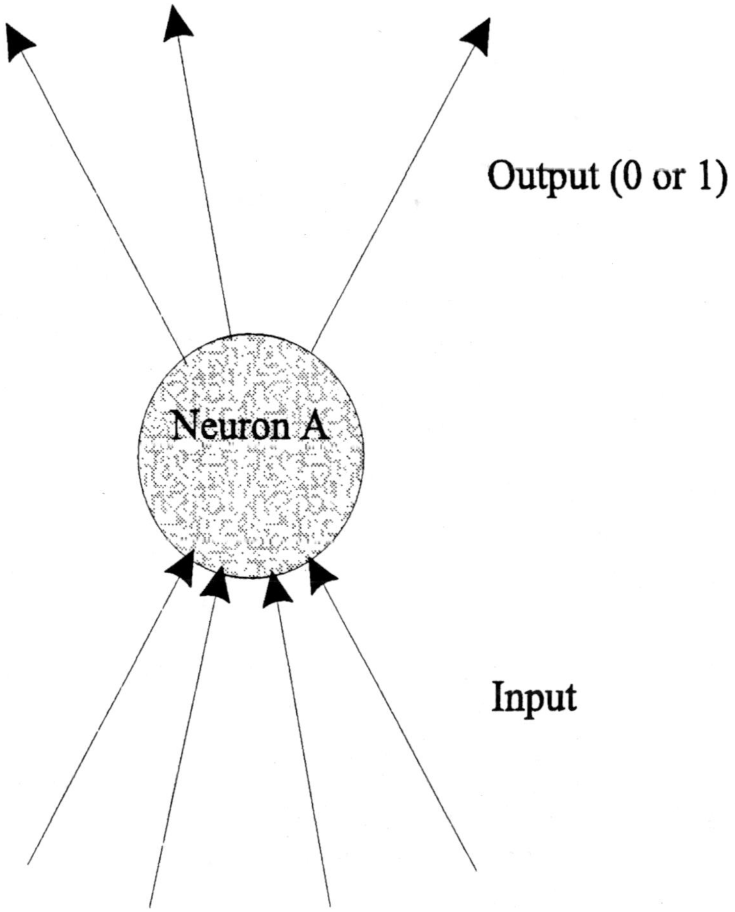

Figure 3.3: A neuron is a complex computer itself; it gets information from several neurons, integrates and modifies information, and submits results to other neurons. A neuron has only one axon that transmits information as a binary cable (yes, no). The axon of one neuron is connected to several hundred dendrites of other neurons enabling enormous connectibility - graphical representations like the one here are misleading. The contact between dendrites is made through synapses.

have been independently confirmed in neuron structures.

One of the major impulses for new discoveries in the brains are nondestructable scanning techniques. The two most often mentioned are positron emission tomography (PET) and magnetic resonance imaging (MRI). Other most common methods are superconducting quantum interference device (SQUID), single-photon emission computerized tomography (SPECT) and electroencephalogram (EEG).

3.2.1 The Developing and Aging Brain

The number of neurons increases practically only during embryonic life. It starts with merging of the two cells together. This is a miracle itself – there are 10^{2017} combinations when each of humans starts living. Compare this number with 10^{80} to 10^{120} as two approximations of the number of all atomic particles in our universe and see that for each human the universe is really inside of us; that **the universe outside is the smaller one**. No wonder that most of the neurons are connected with other neurons dealing with inside functions; only a small fraction of neurons is connected to outside-related sensors.

More than 100 billion neurons (among others) have to develop in 9 months. In that period, growth as well as wiring are determined mainly genetically. Many processes follow during the childhood and later to the final end. For example, the mass of the brain quadruples from the just born to the grown adult. Neurons grow in size, the number of axons and dendrites as well as connections increases and later decreases during different life stages. In the early period of a young child, the choices of particular connection targets are strongly stimulated by the outside world. Without a proper stimuli, children mentally and overall progress abnormally slow. Extra stimuli is useless, normal stimulation is sufficient.

Although in most instances the paths of axons grow along genetically preprogrammed lines, the final choice of connection is to a large extend left to the feed-back from the real-world. A competition between axons as well as between groups continues mostly throughout the whole life, although is the most active during fastest growth of fetus and child. Axons often fine-tune their connections.

At the age around 14, most of the brain is fully developed. Coupled with fast reflexes, this is roughly thr age of the best players of reflex-based computer games. More complex strategic games need decades of experience. Chess is best played by players 20 to 30 years old, and the ability to play brilliant chess decreases very slowly. Most of structural and chemical modifications in later stages become apparent in the fifties and sixties.

Every day we lose thousands of neurons, yet during years mental performances in healthy humans only slowly deteriorate. It seems that the brain compensates losses during years with other mechanisms. Some older adults quickly lose their minds, however, several studies show that the cause for that must be some kind of illness, be it of the brain or of the body. The leading causes in older population are Alzheimer disease, multiple strokes, Parkinson's disease or simply diabetes. These

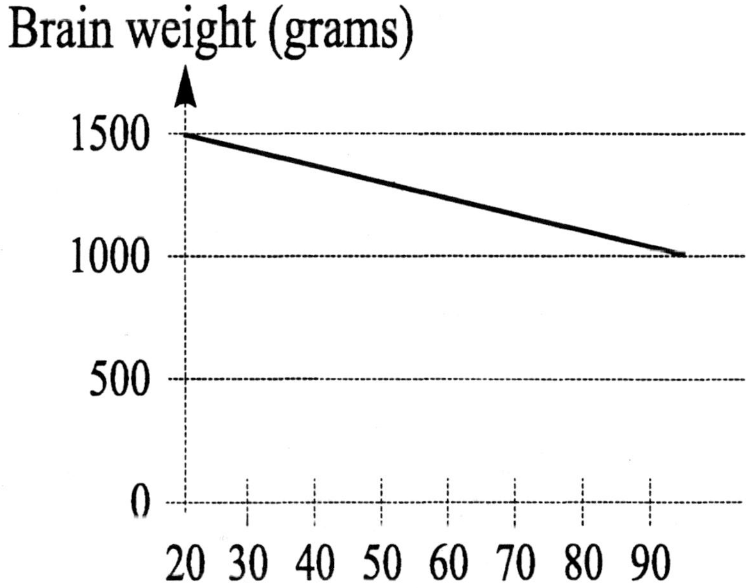

Figure 3.4: The number of neurons and the brain weight decreases during ages, however, most intellectual abilities only slowly decrease in healthy humans.

diseases cause destructive processes in the brain. While some parts of the brain usually without any special harm lose around 30 to 40 percent of the original number of neurons, some diseases decimate neurons to two thirds or more of the original numbers. Around that number, the loss significantly influences the performance of the brain to the point that it cannot perform normal functions any more. What happens with the brain when neurons continue vanishing? First, the brain weight decreases (Figure 3.4) from normal 1.5 kilograms to around 1 kg at ages over eighty. Second, plagues and tangles appear in the brains as useless fillers of once useful parts of the system. They appear in healthy aged adults, however in restricted areas and in limited percents. If the brain is riddled with senile plagues and neurofibrillary tangles, it is a sure sign of Alzheimer's disease. The problem with "holes" in the brain tissue is evident also in aging monkeys, dogs and other animals. The process, though, should not be messed with the "mad cows" disease which similarly causes degeneration of the brain tissue riddling it with holes. The nature of the process is different.

The good news about aging is that most of the capabilities remain largely intact to very late ages. All we have to do is to stay in good shape, mother nature will do the rest. For example, it has been found that the brain compensates the loss of neurons by additional growth of dendrites during middle age and old age. We may indeed get a little slower, but also a bit wiser, as the hard-wired schema indicates

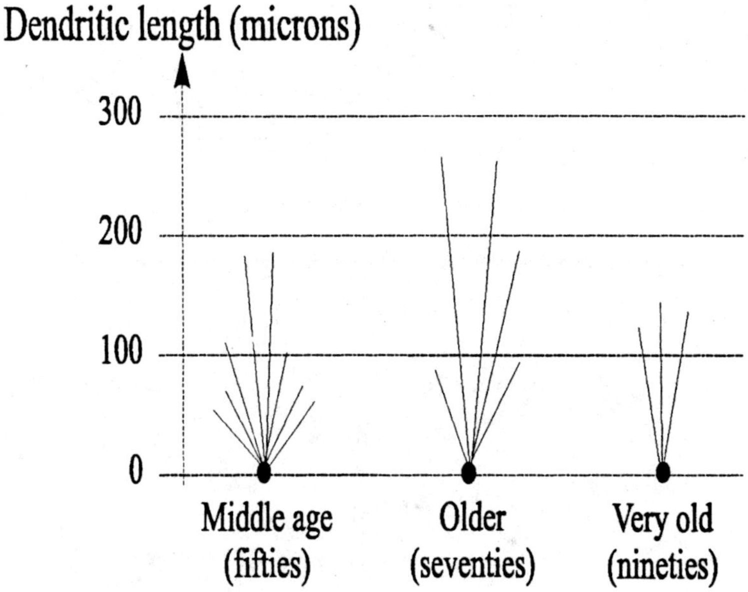

Figure 3.5: During middle and early older ages, the brain tries and usually succeeds to compensate for the loss of neurons with dendrite growth.

(Figure 3.5).

The bad news is that our body wears out because of guite general biological laws. These laws say that nearly all mammals reach the end of their natural life when their hearts have made 1-2.000.000.000 beats. For humans, that is around 100 years.

3.2.2 Visual Processing in the Brain

The visual system in the brain has been successfully and intensively studied in the recent years. Results are to a large extend encouraging and indicate that analyses of human hardware enable derivations of many comprehensions about the mind.

It was found that distinct areas in the brain analyze visual information searching and identifying different visual attributes such as motion, color, shape, combinations of simpler attributes etc.

The identified parts of the human brain involved in decoding visual input are usually denoted by V1 to V5. V1 contains a map of the entire retinal field. V1 and neighboring V2 accept signals and distribute them to appropriate specialized submodules. V3 reproduces dynamic forms, V4 analyses color and form-color properties of input sensors. V5 is devoted to motion. In reality, the whole process is a little more complicated. E.g., color is identified first in V1 and sent to V4 and V2. Form and form-color are analysed in V1, V2 and V4. In addition, there is no point of strict separation of low-level visualisation processes from seeing and understanding. These processes are strongly correlated and run in parallel and simultaneously.

The discovery of specific submodules in the brain, specialized for specific tasks, seems to enable an important step ahead in understanding how the brain works.

It is only higher layers of our performance that are not well understood. It seems that knowledge cannot be separated from consciousness, and that both are crucial for the visual process in the human brain. In visualisation as in many other mental processes, it seems obvious that consciousness plays a crucial role. Without understanding how consciousness works, no true understanding of global processes in our heads is possible.

Neurologists may be among the most well-deserved for new comprehensions – their approach is indeed a bottom-up one, from hardware to software, but they are accumulating more and more knowledge.

3.2.3 Mental Activities in the Brain

A successful attack on consciousness has not been performed yet. However, specific mental processes, e.g., learning, working memory, speaking and seeing are a little more understood. For example learning – it has been discovered that a rather simple set of rules explains what is going on in the brains at the hardware level. Basically there are two types of learning in the brain. Explicit learning is fast and usually rests on one positive example. Implicit learning is based on many occurrences of similar events, it is slow and related to sensory and motor systems. Explicit memory exists only in the temporal globe of vertebrates while even simple invertebrate animals show excellent reflexive learning. Both types of learning seem to follow rather simple sets of chemical "hardware" rules in the brains.

The learning process seems more complex from the point of upper levels. For example, explicit learning is usually performed in complicated and long-lasted circles. Information is first gathered in the temporal lobe. Hippocampus, an important part of the temporal lobe, stores information for weeks or months. Then, it is transferred to the cerebral cortex for permanent storage.

Short-term memory is based on changes in strengths of synaptic connections. Long-term memory is based on new wiring. It means that as long as we learn (and we learn practically during the whole life), our brain constantly rewires itself. It means that after reading this book, or maybe even this page (depending on whether you will find interesting anything from this page or the book thus remembering and putting it into your long-term memory) your brain will rewire its structure. In the light of the enormous number of connections, it will be only a very small change, yet you will be able to remember the thing that attracted your attention. This is one confirmation more that each brain is an individual that changes through time. It is like fingerprints but much more elaborated. **Each of us is a unique wonder-product of this universe!**

Will we ever be able to decode the brain and the mind? Nobody knows for sure. There are so many problems at much simpler levels we still cannot solve. Consider for example an aids virus. It is not even a being capable of living on its own. It is so small that thousands could be put on one neuron. Yet, for years we can not find a cure against it. Which optimist then presumes that a system consisting of 100 millions highly connected and significantly more complex cells than aids viruses can be explained? Even if we forget about the most important aspect of all – that **the power quite probably comes from an enormous number of complex connections that constantly change over time**?

To repeat, the operations of working memory are carried out in the frontal lobes of the cerebral cortex. An injury there to a large extend disables new comprehensions, yet the long-term memory and thinking possibilities remain mainly intact. Also, monkeys and infants perform poorly on specific tasks indicating that only humans several years old are able to perform full-task intelligence and knowledge-demanding operations. What is in our brains so different from say chimpanzees with only 1% different genetic code or from children with identical genetic code? Probably, it is not just slightly higher number of neutrons.

3.2.4 Sex Brains

Many parts of the brain are devoted to sex as the most important driving force to produce offsprings. It is no strange, then, that many differences can be observed when comparing the brain of a man and a woman. There are different reasons why this is so. Since some body functions are different, e.g., only women can give birth, it is understandable that specific parts of the brain are physically different and devoted to different activities. Even a scull of a man and a woman differ enough to be safely discriminated. On the other hand, why should mental abilities be different? Why should men be smarter than women or vice versa?

One reason why the brains are different is that man and woman have for millions of years performed different tasks. Until recently, males had to fight usually in a physical combat for their survival, for their families and for females. A calculation where the fist, sword or an arrow will lend is a crucial addition to physical strength and vitality. Good strategic planning when and where to take a fight is another advantage. Reading what the human close to you has in his/hers mind is crucial for both sexes, but more for the one whose dominant goal is to maintain healthy relations for offspring production besides being physically more vulnerable. No wonder these differences are statistically measurable.

Measurements have shown that men are generally superior in:

- spatial rotation and targeting accuracy when guiding or intercepting projectiles
- mathematical reasoning

- distant routing, e.g., finding correct paths or remembering it.

Women are generally superior in:

- specific language tasks – e.g., finding words starting with a specific letter or finding words with a couple of letters defined at specific places
- intuition, e.g., perception of moods of other people
- performing manual-precision tasks
- remembering where which object is placed among several
- exact algebraic calculation.

It would be fairly wrong to assume that women are generally superior to men since there are more items on the list of their advantages. If we measure statistical characteristics such as standard deviation, we observe that the advantages of men over women are statistically more significant than vice versa. Another difficulty – some of women advantages like intuition are difficult to measure while it is quite simple to measure accuracy of throwing a ball to a target. Overall, it is difficult or even unreasonable to say which of the brains is better. Each has specific advantages and disadvantages. At the same time, let us not forget that they are proven significantly different. Having different types of brains is surely advantageous for humans, and for our study of the minds.

Are sex differences in the brains disappearing? After all, fighting abilities are becoming less and less important. Pushing buttons in electronic wars does not demand physical strength. Such thinking does not seem to be closely related to experiments with other mammals. It seems that sex differences were not implanted only in the humans brain but generally at least in all mammals. Be it our domestic cats or lions, when males grow up, they have to leave their neighborhood in order to avoid mating with relatives and thus problems with genetic disorders. More typical, males are in charge of larger territories and taking care of borders seems to be of great relevance for transitions of their genes into next generations. Even experiments with rats have shown that male rats discover and remember paths significantly different than female rats. While females tend to orient according to landmarks, males tend to make spatial plans and orientations. Women and men show the same significant differences. Evolutionary, men like mammal males had to find long-distant routs while women had to remember characteristic places, e.g, with specific plants or people while on average not moving along far distances because of strong family ties, e.g., having children. **Many properties of our brains seem to be genetically coded as a result of millions years of evolution. Again – this might be an important advantage over computers. Some evolutionary coded comprehensions might well not be computable and thus may well be out of reach of current or similarly designed computers.**

Where are sex differences in the brain? Putting aside a simple fact that the part taking care for reproduction organs and body-related sexual functions are not the same. For a reasonably long time it was thought that woman's brains are more symmetrical than man's. Men were supposed to have more specialized left and right hemisphere while woman's brain was supposed to more equally use both sides. Part of this idea was based on the fact that the corpus callosum – the part of the brain that combines both hemispheres – is generally bigger in women. Latest research has discovered that this explanation is too broad, that differences are distributed in specific parts of the brain. For example, it seems that speech abilities are closely related to frontal lobes of woman's brains while in men they are located in the posterior region.

Generally, woman's brains and minds are more oriented towards feelings while man's brains and minds are more oriented towards physical actions. When asked to think of nothing, women tend to think about relations between people while men think about women, sex, and sport in peace and fighting in war. Since emotional brains are a recent evolutional product, and the action brains are basically an ancient one, some magazines published articles about men thinking with the "reptilian" brains while women tend to be more civilized. However, the differences seem to be again closely related to the selfish genes. If men are to conquer any women and take care of the family, they compete in different competitions and with different opponents then women do. Another simplification of this kind is a conclusion that women are generally much more emotional thus not able to be impartial. More valid seems a conclusion that since women tend to be more bound to human relations and emotions, they also suffer more because of depressions caused by human or emotional losses.

Another interesting sex difference is in the way how humans and animals choose their partners. Obviously, this is one of evolutionary most important tasks. If you mate with good partners you have good offsprings and they will survive. And vice versa. Therefore, one would expect that if there is any extra evolutionary coded function it should be related to sensing the advantageous genetics. Since males usually tend to mate with any female they can get (because their reproduction process is not as complicated as in females which give birth) females are the one that should be very careful when choosing the right partner. Indeed, different studies have shown that even in small animals like vine flies females choose genetically better partners whenever there is any chance for competition (if there is just one partner in the appropriate space-time to mate, then there is no point in choosing). Women get the first impression in 10 seconds. They scan the man and immediately take a position that usually does not change afterwards although the process of seducing takes much longer. The male position in social animals is defined according to the social status obtained in internal competition. Indeed, that might be one of the leading success parameters and clearly it usually guarantees good genetic inheritage. But if there is a conflict between the social status and the genetic quality, females often prefer the second one, be it humans, monkeys or deer. Whatever the case, the extra intuition women have is evolutionary deeply brain-coded and represents an important advantage.

What does relations between men and women brains teach us? **First, without sex diferences and related genetic processes there would not be intelligence. The enormous number of possible gene crossing during conception indicates why children are so miraculous.** Different kinds of thinking in men and women and at different ages also indicates that intelligence is not as unique as it seems at the moment. Rather, intelligence represents a general civilization concept.

3.2.5 Consciousness and the Brains

How is the brain related to consciousness and other mental abilities? In analogy, the brain is to the mind what computer hardware is to software. Some researchers like Minsky and Dennett (Consciousness explained, 1991) claim that mind, consciousness, intelligence etc. are nothing special. They are supposed to be only an emergent property of the brain (hardware). All that counts is the brain machine. In return, some of them have been termed "zombies" – people without souls.

Even in comparison to computers, this idea is not very attractive. As said by Searle: "It's consciousness explained away". Consider the computer analogy. A Turing machine is a very simple machine, yet it can perform very complex operations. Computers are important to humans because their hardware enables performing complex programs, i.e., algorithms. By studying only hardware and saying that programs/algorithms are only an emergent property of the hardware seems strange on itself.

Now, consider analyzing how a computer works analyzing it only from the hardware bottom-up level. What we can measure are currents and voltages in wires and chips. From those voltages it is very difficult to figure how the top algorithm works. Normal users and programmers do not care about voltages and currents. What they care about is how the system works from the top level.

But there may be much bigger problems ahead. **Maybe the brains and minds are integrated to the point that the two cannot be studied on its own like computer hardware and software.**

The philosophical debate behind this subject is not related to the question if anything in our brain can be scientifically described or if there is something beyond our universe. Centuries ago, debates were devoted to this subject. Now, the subject is different – it seems that the brain is explainable by laws of our material universe, but **there is something fundamentally more complex than current science teaches us.**

There are other problems – e.g., since each human brain is unique, it is very difficult to draw firm conclusions based on hardware only. If we analyze one Pentium chip we understand all chips of the same type. Even if we could analyse one human brain to the final bit and make a step-by step trace, that would not directly imply that we understand human brains since each human hardware is unique and in addition, the mind may not be traceable from such experiments due to its integration with hardware. All we could hope for is to derive some general principles and mechanisms.

There are other reasons why **we may not ever be able to comprehend the brain and the mind in details:**

- The brain is so complicated that the amount of information stored there is beyond our reach. If it demands, for example, 100000 kilometers of books to store the information in the brains, then nobody is able to read it through and understand it. Such an amount of information is not possible to tell or read in one life-time.

- Maybe we can not comprehend ourselves. Maybe some self-referential questions (e.g., as indicated by Gödel's theorem) formally eliminate us as being able to understand ourselves. This is not a cheap trick. We often easily see mistakes in other people yet are blind when observing ourselves. When we make an attempt to truly see or understand ourselves, we quite often see that it is not possible. Often, we are surprised by ourselves.

This is not to say that we should not study the brain and the mind in detail. Many important new comprehensions have been made not only increasing our knowledge about ourselves but also helping us to use this new knowledge for new products and new guidelines. Many new comprehensions about the brain come from observing its performances mainly at the hardware bottom-up level.

To sum the basic debate about of the brain – do the brains resemble computers? In certain characteristics yes, but there are enormous differences. **Saying that a human brain corresponds to a sufficiently complex Turing machine is clearly fairly naive.** Several world-wide-recognised researchers not only agree with the above sentence but also provide additional argumentation. One of them is Gerald E. Edelman.

3.3 Neural Darwinism

Here we analyze Edelman's neural Darwinism through his book "Bright Air, Brilliant Fire". It was published in 1992 by Penguin Books.

Gerald M. Edelman is one of neuroscientists who study consciousness and other top-level human properties through biological properties of the brain. Similar to Francis Crick (1994), a Nobel Prize winner, he treats the brain not as a black box, but as a very complex system whose biological properties are essential for analyzing the memory, perception, learning and other high-level human properties. Edelman shared a Nobel Prize in 1972 for research on antibodies. Through studies of evolutionary learning of the human immune system, i.e. selection and adaptation to foreign intruders, he proposes similar but more elaborate system in the human brain based on the so-called "Neural Darwinism".

Edelman sees current scientific trends as one of leading to the largest possible scientific revolution. When sufficient knowledge about the brains will be discovered, we shall know how the brain works. Not only that, we shall find out what governs our nature, and how we know the world. When achieving that goal, our knowledge will be significantly upgraded.

3.3.1 Basic Approaches to the Theory of Mind

Let us first analyze Edelman's basic positions regarding the mind:

- The real world can be described by the laws of physics using mathematical apparatus. These laws are general and apply everywhere (physics assumption).
- Humans have evolved from an ancient origin. The mind arose on the basis of evolutionary processes. Humans are embedded in the world, their minds in the brains (evolutionary assumption).
- The brain theory must be based on selectionist principles. **The mind must be put back into nature.** A science of mind must be based on biology (Edelman's approach).

Edelman analyses in detail several approaches to the scientific theory of the mind:

Physical Theories of the Mind

Edelman disputes that physics is appropriate for analyzing high-level human capabilities. There are three main reasons:

- Physics studies laws of particles and material bodies. Studies of atoms and molecules might add some knowledge when analyzing human brains, however, are of no great help when studying human high-level performance or evolutionary roots.
- Platonistic world of objective truths (e.g. Penrose's ideal (1989, 1990, 1994)) is not relevant for live beings. Even basic Darwinistic theories collide with Platonistic eternal truths.
- Fancy physical theories like Penrose's correct quantum gravity are not accepted by physical community and are not supported by scientific observations. Instead of searching for new formal physical theories more attention should be devoted to the only system that has properties like consciousness and intelligence – the human mind and the brain.

Digital Computers/Minds

According to Edelman, **"extraordinary silly things have been proposed about the capacity of digital computers to think"**. The silliness arises mostly from the false analogy between thinking and logic. Computing on digital computers no more constitutes thinking than adding numbers on an abacus. An abacus cannot provide intelligence as well as digital computers. The Church thesis and Turing machines (Hopcroft, Ullman 1979) declare formal positions about what is computable and what not, however, these properties are not closely related to high-level intellectual performances of humans such as consciousness or mind. Functionalism is close to symbolic representations and algorithms, however, biology is not.

Edelman analyses stronger and weaker functionalistic positions, but since they are all based on the same principle, i.e. that internal structure and evolutionary development do not matter, he finds them of the same (wrong) kind. Human brains possess enormous individual structural variation at a variety of organizational levels. Each brain is highly variable in contrast to universal Turing machines which can perform any function by other Turing machines. Each organism's behavior is biologically individual and enormously diverse.

Animals and humans perform their functions much different than isolated computational systems. The brain and the nervous system cannot be considered in isolation from the surrounding real world and social interactions. Meaning is obtained through growing and communicating in a society, not through complex predefined algorithms. Artificial neural networks can be simulated by Turing machines and face the same problems as all digital computers.

On the other hand, Edelman sees computer simulations as one of the most promising tools to study some properties of humans.

Hard Sciences – Objectivism and Functionalism

Objectivism goes beyond the hypothesis of scientific realism. **Realism** assumes a real world, a linkage between concepts and a real world, and a stable knowledge. In addition to realism, **objectivism** assumes that the world can be defined in terms of a definite structure made of entities, properties and their interrelationships. The whole world can be completely defined and modeled through mathematical and logical mechanisms. Strings of meaningless symbols can be in a unique way attached to entities and categories in the world.

The idea of objective world has been supported by scientific discoveries of Russel, Kleene, Post, Church, Gödel, and Turing.

Objectivism and functionalism are two of the -isms that are closely related to hard sciences. But in recent years, hard sciences are in a crisis – they have been proven unable to provide an adequate scientific description of a human individual, and of human properties such as consciousness or mind.

Several studies have shown that humans categorize much different than they should if categorization were objective and functionalistic. For example, **humans understand events and categories that are multiple at several levels, and sometimes these viewpoints are inconsistent and contradictive.** The mind is not a mirror of nature.

Memory is another example. It is a system property depending on a structure of a system in which it is expressed. Memory is related to capability to repeat a performance, to assert, to relate matters and categories to past events in time and space. **To perform top memory functions, one must have a self, a conscious self.**

Evolutionary Theory of Consciousness

There are three basic levels of sensory properties in the evolution of animals with neurons:

- Responses to stimuli are directly governed by selection for evolutionary values. Capable of learning and long-term memory but not of primary consciousness. An example: a lobster.

- Animals having primary consciousness. There is no socially constructed self. These animals can not identify themselves on a TV. Long-term memory is based on qualia in the remembered present, and limited to it. No categorization of qualia over time by a subject. An example: a dog.

- Full qualia capable of being refined, remembered, altered and reported. High-ordered consciousness. Example: humans. Note that some animals, e.g., chimps, are somewhere between the last two categories.

Consciousness is an evolutionary improvement, enhancing the evolutionary fitness. Consciousness is about 300 million years old. It shows intentionality and other properties essential for developed beings. Consciousness is a process. We all know of it as long as no one asks us to define it (as agreed by several others, e.g., Penrose).

Thinking is a result of many parallel, fluctuating, temporal processes, concept formation, memory and attentional states. Consciousness is incredibly multiple, parallel and shifting

3.3.2 Neural Darwinism

Edelman builds his theory of the mind on the basis of biology and related psychology. William James is seen as one of the founders of modern physiological psychology. Jame's viewpoints on consciousness are heavily embraced – consciousness and mind are processes not a substance or a stuff; they are both personal and reflect intentionality. The brain system has many levels of organizations and its connections to the body cannot be ignored. **Psychology is connected to and grounded by biology.**

Edelman's biological roots stem from Charles Darwin's evolution and Gregor Mendel's genetics. Darwin first recognized that **natural selection had to account for the emergence of human consciousness**. The most important single process in evolution is population thinking. In a population of organisms variations occur by mutation. As a result of natural selection, the relative frequency of genes that increase fitness in a population also increases.

The process of population thinking works by selection, not by instruction. An example of a selective recognition system in a human is the immune system. Each immune cell (lymphocyte) makes a special antibody binding with different shapes. When a foreign molecule or antigen enters the body, it is bound only by specific antibodies on specific cells. These cells divide and make more cells of the same or similar kind. In this way, the immune system adapts to foreign intruders like viruses or bacteria. Of course, some invaders manage to overrun the human immune system. One of the most famous latest examples is aids. It is a virus, as all viruses itself not able to live on its own. It needs a host enabling it to replicate, and has to force cells of the host to reproduce not new cells of the host but new cells of the virus. What is interesting with aids is that it changes very rapidly, approximately in the same way as the flu virus, just much faster. There is no good cure against flu because of the same reason. But the immune system is not toothless against both invaders. Flu is usually beaten in a week, aids stays at reasonable levels for around ten years. It is only after around ten years that the human immune system collapses, at the moment nobody knows exactly why. Maybe it is the ultimate result of the permanent hide-mask and unmask-destroy game, similar to the ever-repeating Turing test until aids finally manages to penetrate the safe-coding system.

Edelman extends the process of selection and population thinking in the immune system to the human brain. In the brain, it is unlikely that a single neuron could correspond to the individual unit of selection. Therefore, the unit of selection must be a neural group. Hence his theory – the Theory of Neuronal Group Selection (TNGS). The theory of neural groups in the brain is to a reasonable extend supported by scientific observations. E.g, some groups usually oscillate at the frequency around 40 hertz.

The human brain is substantially more complex than the immune system, however, in Edelman's opinion the basic mechanism is similar. When groups of neurons provide multiple actions (providing maps, models, viewpoints), their performance is reworded or punished as a result of the fitness of the process to the environment. Groups evolve during constant competition and cooperation, some of them die (are superseded by other groups), and some new groups are generated.

The brain performance is a result of its morphology and architecture. Biological processes and structures define human performance. In this way, **psychology is basically determined by biology**.

Edelman contends that the connection between groups of neurons and psychology has not yet been sufficiently scientifically supported. His theory is a scientific hypothesis that will be proven or disproven in time.

3.3.3 Edelman's Overview of Mental Representations

In an appendix to this section, we provide Edelman's analyses and evaluation of eight different approaches to mental representations:

- "Classical approaches" like essentialism are shown to be false by biological theories based on Darwin's work (Wittgenstein 1974; Lakoff 1987).
- Thought depends on body and brain. It is embodied. Meaning arises from relations to bodily needs and functions. The mind does not mirror nature (Putnam 1988, Millikan 1984; Lakoff 1987; Searle 1982, 1990; Edelman 1987, 1989, 1992).
- Memory cannot be described by internal codes or syntactic systems. A self and high-order consciousness are needed to account for full manifestation (Searle 1982, 1990, 1992; Edelman 1987, 1989, 1992).
- Language depends on learning processes based on conceptual systems and values already in place (Pinker 1984; Edelman 1987, 1989, 1992).
- Minds create their own versions of reality by social and linguistic interactions depending on historical events (Searle 1982, 1990; Putnam 1988).
- Digital computation is disembodied and by itself cannot provide a meaningful relation between symbols and real world (Searle 1982, 1990).
- Cognition depends on functions of a system developed in evolutionary history. The assignment of meaning is referred to as "meaning rationalism" (Millikan 1984).
- **The functionalist view is insufficient to explain the structure, function, and diversity of the nervous system, its evolution and development** (Edelman 1987, 1989, 1992).

3.4 Cognitive Sciences

Since weak AI strongly relates to the human brain, it also strongly relates to cognitive sciences. Other sciences mainly constituting the cognitive sciences framework are presented according to Franklin (1995) in Figure 3.6.

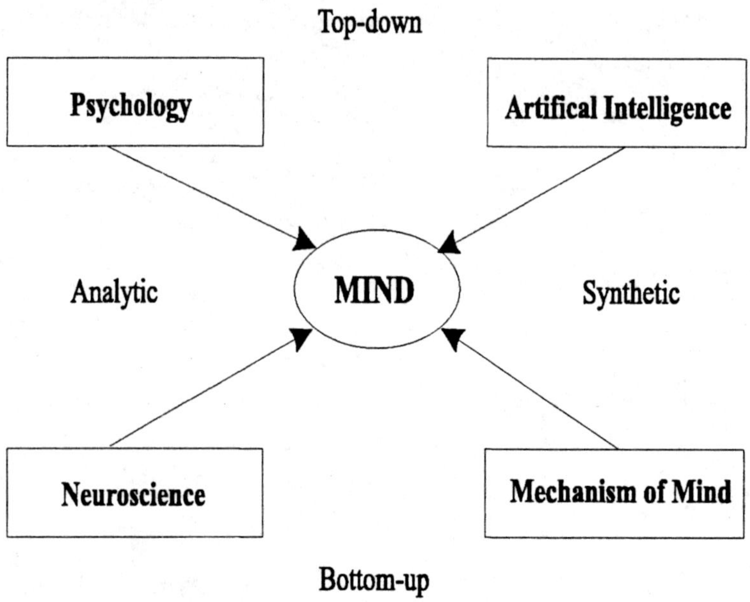

Figure 3.6: Weak AI is strongly connected to cognitive sciences.

3.5 Arizona Science of Consciousness

To represent current trends in cognitive sciences, an overview of the "Towards a Science of Consciousness 1998, Tucson III" conference is represented. It took place in Tucson USA from April 27 to May 2, 1998. This was the third conference in a row. The conference was supported by the Fetzer institute, Institute of Noetic Sciences and the Consciousness studies institute at the Arizona university.

The first two conferences were big media events with reports in mass media and journals such as Scientific American (Hameroff etc. 1997). A couple of years ago the big change has happened regarding the science of consciousness (Gams 1997). Classical formal sciences more or less denied consciousness since they were not able to describe consciousness with systems of equations or other formal mechanisms. According to classical sciences, what can not be described by scientific means does not exist. Therefore, there is no consciousness and no science of consciousness. On the other hand we all know that consciousness exists, and each of us possesses at least one. A possible solution of the consciousness enigma is based on new approaches and new description mechanisms. Maybe we need new theories, and possibly new discoveries enlarging the science itself. This is one of the reasons why the science of consciousness is so attractive. But this is also a potential problem since it is not easy to apply classical scientific criteria to strongly differentiate between reasonable contributions and others. Therefore, it is quite possible that at least some explanations of consciousness presented were more or less just speculations.

Classical science has resolved most or even practically all important questions in specific fields while other questions resist solution. Among the most important scientific questions left, consciousness is typically rated among the top four according to different scientific and popular publications. What is consciousness, can we explain it, why do we have it? According to Chalmers (1996), there are two major themata - analyses, explanation and construction of (artificial) consciousness is the so called **easy problem**. Explanation while we have consciousness is the much more difficult **hard problem**. Not to mention that currently we have not solved any of the two problems.

In recent years, no major new theory of consciousness has emerged. Existing theories can be grouped into a couple of classes with major representatives. The mind can be analyzed from the point of information theory (Chalmers 1996). Penrose (1989; 1994) and Hameroff (Penrose, Hameroff 1995) try to explain consciousness by computationally superior phenomena in the human brain based on quantum physics. Pribram (1991) sees consciousness and the mind as a holographic process. A couple of theories propose consciousness as nothing special, as an emergent property, a kind of side effect (Minsky 1987). Other researchers try to explain consciousness as a result of an advanced architecture (Sloman 1992).

The first problem one encounters dealing with consciousness is its complexity. The human brain is the far most complex closed system in our universe (Edelman 1992). An average human brain has for the start substantially more cells compared to supercomputers. But the major power and complexity comes from an enormous number of connections enabling computational explosion. There are different opinions as to why the human brain is so complicated (Davis 1998). One possible explanation is that evolution adds a layer over layer in a local optimization and that "a new designer" would create much better brains starting from scratch. The other opinion contradicts with a simple fact that computers are much more neatly organized, yet completely unintelligent. Maybe, the human power comes from its evolutionary based complexity.

Or think about the following report: When analyzing dreams (LaBerge 1998), many subjects dreamed about sex and had orgasms during sleep. But we people are not aware about it consciously and often feel uncomfortable when confronted with these data. Our brains and minds are full of bizarre events and processes, and pure logic is more an artifact in our thoughts.

3.5.1 Conference Overview

The conference consisted of plenary presentations taking place during the first half of the day. Typically, in the afternoon concurrent sessions and posters took place. Quite often, the conference day ended at around 22h at night.

The conference itself was arranged in several sections. Many terms and events were quite specialized. To illustrate this point let us copy a couple of consequent titles (Kaszniak etc. 1998, pp. 26 up):

- Blindsight and consciousness perception
- The epistemic potential of consciousness
- What kinds of philosophical zombies are possible and in what sense
- Bridging the epiphenomenal trap
- Reductionism in scientific explanation and the philosophy of mind
- Unity of consciousness and unity of agency in Kant
- Toward a new typology of modes of consciousness
- Towards a proper monism.

Obviously, it was difficult to follow all events unless one was already familiar with the subfield. A reasonable exception were plenary lectures which were presented to the broadest audience.

Following is the list of all plenary sessions with occasional commentary.

The Self

G. Strawson, The self.
M.S. Gazzaniga, The minds past.
J. Shear, Experimental clarification of The problem of self.

Strawson introduced SESMITs (Subjects of Experience that are Single Mental Things). They are supposed to be mental and physical. The basis of knowledge about self is past experience about self.

Gazzaniga highlighted the importance of evolution as the major force in the progress of the living world. Some birds learn to sing songs of other birds, but a large majority of birds never learns other songs even when subjected only to foreign songs. Therefore, it seems that lots of information is already precoded in the brains of all living beings.

The human brain is split into the left and the right hemisphere. The right is a pedantic and dull worker. The left continuously searches for connections, relations, explanations even in situations where there is no need for them. The left speculates about nonrealistic events always trying to find reply to the "WHY" question. According to Gazzaniga it is quite possible that superstition and other strange events are results of unbound speculations in the left hemisphere. The left is maybe also the "free-will-feeling" generator although there is no true free will in evolution.

According to Shear, consciousness is the major human property or one of the major ones. One of simple verifications is the fact that in processes of dying or fading our, consciousness often goes among last, later than several other physical and mental functions. Shear does not agree Hume about his proposal that consciousness is a collection. Consciousness must be much more complicated, based on integration mechanisms. Consciousness is a unique property of all humans, be it young or old, regardless of cultures or civilizations. Several processes, such as during the process of dying have very similar properties regardless of differences in e.g. cultures. For example, during this process, majority of humans lose contact with their body. These processes are not mathematically describable.

Implicit Processes

A.G. Greenwald, R.L. Abrams, Simple mental feats that require conscious cognition.
P. Merikle, M. Daneman, Is there memory for events during anesthesia?

Greenwald and Abramsom reported about reactions of subjects when given written words such as "NICE" for a short time. The human eye and the visual "hardware" is faster than consciousness. Some words were not understood although being shorter than others. For example, understanding words such as "UNCLEAR" needs negation, therefore a consciousness conclusion, these words were inproperly understood, e.g. like "CLEAR".

Merikle and Daneman presented a hypothesis that even during anesthesia there is certain consciousness and remembering. It depends crucially on the time and the level of anesthesia. While high-level consciousness is often excluded, lower levels of primitive consciousness remain active. Remembering is not direct, but subjects reported "feelings" when subjected to words during anesthesia.

Pathways of Visual Consciousness

D. Milner, Unconscious visual processing for action: neuropsychlogial evidence.
M. Goodale, Unconscious visual processing for action: evidence from normal observers.
M. Mishkin, On the neural basis of visual awareness.

What happens to a damaged brain? Human and monkey brains were studies. It was reported that after certain damages, consciousness typically resurfaces after a couple of days or even months. These processes enable studies where the consciousness is located. There are centers for perceptions and for actions. It is not completely clear where the consciousness is located.

Sleep and Dreaming

B. McNaughton, Neural ensembles in sleep and walking and the reprocessing of recent experience.
J.A. Hobson, D. Kahn, E. Pace-Schott, Neuropsyhology of dreaming consciousness.

S. LaBerge, Lucid dreaming: Psychophysiological studies of consciousness during REM sleep.

Naughton reported about visualization in the rat brain. There is a specific location in the brain corresponding to the two-dimensional position of the brain. When the rat moves firing of neurons also moves in the brains also. From time to time the neuron picture overruns physical location, disperses and regroups again at the physical location. Rats were also able to learn.

Kahn and LaBerge studied events during sleep. There are different phases of sleep (NREM, REM) and different stages of consciousness. The most known and adapted analysis of sleeping is based on observing humans during sleep. When their eyes start moving quickly, humans dream. If awaken, we remember dreams, but if not they elude our conscious memory. LaBerge reported about lucid dreams and dreaming according to ones wishes. They even constructed night glasses that transmit flashes of light when eyes start moving quickly. Due to this disturbance, the human consciousness is recalled and takes control over dreams.

Integrative Perspectives

C. Koch, Visual awareness and the frontal lobes.
M. Tye, Representation and consciousness.

Koch is one of the best known researchers in cognitive sciences. With Crick he proposed the following description of consciousness: The function of biological awareness is to provide a concise summary of the best current interpretation of the environment (including body states) in light of the past experience of the system and to make this interpretations available to the planning parts of the brain. In previous years he also reported about neuron synchronization. This year, he analyzed visual consciousness.

Color and Consciousness

S.E. Palmer, Color, consciousness, and the isomorphism constraint.
L. Hardin, Color quality and color structure.
M. Nida-Roemelin, Pseudonormal vision and color qualia.

Transpersonal Psychology

F. Vaughan, Essential dimensions of consciousness: objective, subjective and inter-subjective.
H. Hunt, Transpersonal and cognitive psychologies of consciousness; a necessary and reciprocal dialogue.
M. Schlitz, Distant intentionality and healing: Exploring the transpersonal dimensions of consciousness.

Schiltz reported about distance healing, telepathy and other transcendental events. The major problem is constant significant confirmation. For example, after she performed a successful "staring" experiment, the same experiment was reported as inconclusive in another country. But after she repeated the same experiment with the same equipment in the other country, it was significant again. Her theory is that these events do happen in real life, yet are not easy repeatable. They are unstable and depend on parameters we are not able to control.

Emotional Experience and the Brain

A.W. Kaszniak, S.L. Remingar, S.Z. Rapcsak, E.L. Glisky, Conscious experience and autonomic response to emotional stimuli following frontal lobe damage. R.D. Lane, E.M. Reiman, G.E. Schwartz, G.R. Fink, P.M.L. Chua, R.J. Dolo, Subregions within the anterior cingulate cortex may differently participate in phenomenal and reflective conscious awareness of emotion.

Evolution and Function of Consciousness I

S. Mithen, Handaxes: some hard evidence regarding the evolution of consciousness. W.H. Calvin, A Darwinian mechanism on the timescale of thought and action. A.G. Cairns-Smith, If Qualia evolved . . .

Evolution and Function of Consciousness II

R.L. Gregory, What do qualia do?
N. Humphrey, The privatization of sensation.

The evolution of human and its functions were presented. E.g. human the tool maker needed advanced brains. No chimpanzee can throw objects accurately since its brain is not capable of performing it. Neanderthals were not capable of using arrows and bows, thus fight from the distance. Such conclusions can be drawn from heavy bone fractures. The human line improved regarding the tool use, language use and consciousness. New capabilities enabled better predictions and in general better performance. More advanced human subspecies eliminated less advanced ones.

The Explanatory Gap

J. Levine, Conceivability, possibility, and the explanatory gap.
C. McGinn, How not to solve the mind-body problem.
C. Rosenberg, On the intrinsic nature of physical.

Culture and Consciousness

A. Zajonc, Goethe and the science of consciousness: toward s scientist's phenomenology of mind.

C. Laughlin, Biogenetic structural theory and the neurophenomenology of consciousness.

Consciousness is very complex and complicated, much more than we are aware of. There are different types of consciousness from being fully aware to sleep, different phases of dreaming, unconsciousness etc. Different cultures treat consciousness differently. In western societies consciousness is often treated as the mind, while easterners usually strongly differentiate between the two. How to define consciousness, then?

Blindsight

P. Stoerig, A. Cowey, R. Goebel, Blindsight and its neuronal basis.
R.W. Kentridge, C.A. Heywood, L. Weiskrantz, Attentional cueing in blindsight.

What happens when subjects (apes or humans) are not aware of seeing yet their "hardware" sees? These subjects stretch fingers according to the size of the object yet they report that they don't see it.

Space, Time and Consciousness

P. Hut, Exploring actuality, through experience.
K. Yasue, Physics approaches to consciousness.
B.J. Hiley, Quantum theory, the implicate order and the mind/matter relationship.

Theories about consciousness based on quantum physics were presented. No major new theories were presented, but new details and possible confirmations.

Neural Correlates of Consciousness

B.J. Baars, Is a real psychoscope possible? Inferring when brain images involve conscious experiences.
A. Revonsuo, How to take consciousness seriously in cognitive neuroscience.
J.B. Newman, Beyond pandemonium: the role of the reticural core in unifying the stream of consciousness.

Aesthetics and Consciousness

C.W. Tyler, The structure of interpersonal consciousness in art.
T. Grodal, Aesthetic feeling of subjectivity in film as blocked action potentials.
A. Bergesen, Artistic consciousness: the art of mind.

Discussion

Many attempts have been presented to answer questions about consciousness. The conference was a mosaic of significant new scientific discoveries and occasional spiritual events.

The Tucson III conference didn't result in any new major theory about consciousness. Rather, several reasonable steps ahead were reported in understanding complex processes in our heads, e.g. in neuroscience. Mapping of the rat's or even human's brain enables better and better explanation of the whole process. However, the final mystery seems to be nearly as far away as it was years ago. **It remains one of the major scientific challenges for us and maybe even future generations.**

3.6 Summary – The Brain Is The Most Complex System In Our Universe

In the human brain there are about 200 different basic types of cells. Each cell has a very rich and intricate regulatory biochemical mechanism to perform its functions, it is a computer on its own. The human brain has around 10^{11} cells which corresponds to the number of all stars in the Milky Way. There are 10^{15} connections. There are $10^{1000.000}$ possible combinations in an average healthy human brain. If we compare this number to 10^{100}, the number of all atomic particles in our universe, we understand why **the brain is the most complicated material object in our universe.** Altogether, the brain is computationally too powerful to be described as a computer in a symbolic way, in practice and/or in theory. **Many previous publications relied only on the number of cells thus ignoring the main power of the brain - to enable combinatorial explosion of the mental processes and still be able to control it. The brains evolved this capabilities in the million years of very complex evolutionary processes.** To achieve true artificial intelligence, advanced new computers and knowledge are needed. Most probably, we will need several decades, several technological break-throughs and several new comprehensions.

Chapter 4

Strong Versus Weak AI (Introductory)

4.1 Description

The terms "weak" and "strong" AI were originally defined by Searle (1982); here, we shall introduce similar ones based on our viewpoints.

There are several terms attached to the old and still dominant AI: symbolic, classical, formalistic, strong. The latest alludes to several versions of the **strong AI** thesis. More or less they all claim that it is possible to obtain intelligence by pure algorithmic processes regardless of technology or architecture. This philosophical approach is based on the Church-Turing theses, and therefore has good theoretical foundations.

Quite often, strong AI corresponds to the idea that all relevant processes can be described and formalized in mathematical formulae. Since we can model physical processes well with mathematical equations, there is no reason why we should not model processes in our heads as well. An example of this approach represents Dieter Doerner from Bamberg who models consciousness and feelings bases on equations. His computers get angry or friendly based on interactions with environment and internal states based on sets of equations. Weak AI-ers don't think that feelings are based on equations.

By weak AI we denote:

- negation of the strong AI thesis
- adopting knowledge from interdisciplinary sciences to upgrade the computational approach.

The extreme version of strong AI is denoted as strong-strong AI, and the extreme version of weak AI as weak-weak AI. If the strong-strong AI claims that even thermostats have feelings than the weak-weak AI claims that only humans can ever have feelings because they are the only beings with souls. Both extremes are out of the scope of this book.

While strong AI is saturated, **weak AI is still in the brainstorming state**. General ideas seem promising, however, it is not clear in which particular direction lies the major discovery of true intelligence. For the time being it seems that new AI is strongly related to interdisciplinary sciences, especially biological and cognitive sciences. In the words of Edelman (1992): "Cognitive science is an interdisciplinary effort drawing on psychology, computer science and artificial intelligence, aspects of neurobiology and linguistics, and philosophy." Several books range from philosophy to neurophysiology related to the mind-body problem (Dennett 1991; O'Rourke 1993; Ornstein 1991; Seager 1991).

Weak AI is also characterized by bold new ideas challenging fundamentals of computer science as well as science in general – the Turing machine, Gödel's theorem, Church-Turing thesis, Occam's Razor.

4.2 Sloman's Engineering Gradation of Strong-Weak AI

Here we present Sloman's granulations of the strong–weak AI scale (Sloman 1992). His vision of weak AI is based on architectural upgrades of Turing machines. In that sense he tries to avoid mentalism and cognitive sciences. Instead, he tries to upgrade the formalistic Turing-machines approach with engineering knowledge.

Sloman denotes the extreme strong thesis of AI as T_1. Each version T_n declares something about an Undiscovered Algorithm of Intelligence (**UAI**). T_1 is the strongest version claiming that **every instantiation of UAI has mental abilities**. This seems similar to the Turing machine – all that matters are data and algorithm. No time, mechanism, meaning. However, abstract and statical structures cannot have mental abilities. An often quoted example is a book of Einstein's brain. Supposedly, this book is no different than all information and algorithms stored in the Einstein's head. Indeed, hardly anybody would claim that any book itself – be it of Einstein's brain, Turing machines or anything else – is capable of thinking or speaking. A book on its own without any execution mechanism cannot perform any action at all.

Slightly modified version of T_1 is T_{1a}: **every time instantiation of UAI has mental abilities**. This eliminates the book case, however, has other obvious flaws. For example, if we throw a bunch of paper sheets into the air we certainly do not get anything intelligent even in the case that by chance a new interesting story emerges. The execution mechanism must be in some sort of stronger causal relation. What about Searle's Chinese room? According to Sloman the causal relation between a book (formal syntactic structures) and Searle (the executioner) is too weak. There can be no understanding and intelligence in such a loose way.

T_2 is a further modified version requiring **sufficient reliable links between**

T_1: abstract and statical procedures can reproduce mind
T_{1a}: time instantiation of T_1 can have mental abilities
T_2: links between programs and mechanisms
T_3: virtual parallelism
T_4: physical parallelism
T_5: super-computing powers

Figure 4.1: Sloman's strong (top) – weak (bottom) AI scale.

program and process. This is not a strong, but a vague mild version. Sloman analyses the properties of links between program and process from the engineering point of view. In his viewpoint, one algorithm executed on one single processor cannot emulate intelligence. **The process must consist of many interleaving and intensively communicating subprocesses**. The architecture of the Turing machine with one algorithm and one processor (executioner) cannot provide intelligence.

The difference between **physical** (T_4) and **virtual** (T_3) **parallelism** is similar to one- and many-processor architectures. **One algorithm, however complicated is not sufficient for intelligence.** Parallelism has to be at the same time fine- and coarse-grained. Minsky (1987) and Moravec (1988) have presented architectures which all fit previous descriptions.

Parallelism is discussed in greater detail: T_{p1} enables intelligence with **simulated continuous environment**. T_{p2} needs **a serial processor with time-sharing**. T_{p3} states that intelligent properties can be obtained through an appropriate **network of computers**. (Note that later Wegner extends these ideas towards interaction Turing machines and we with multiple models.)

What if any machine relying on digital technology is incapable of reproducing intelligence? T_5 declares that at least in some subsystems **super-computing power is necessary**, e.g., based on chemistry or biology. According to Sloman, even such discovery could be very valuable for focusing further research in AI.

In Figure 4.1 we represent Sloman's basic strong-weak AI granulation as a basis for further analyses. According to different strong-weak AI viewpoints, scientific truths as well as human mental abilities are perceived quite differently. At this point it is important to stay open for further analyses and debate.

Chapter 5

Fundamentals of AI, Computer Science and Science in General

Weak AI reexamines and challenges soundness of several well-established scientific fundaments: the Turing test, Gödel's theorem, Church-Turing thesis, Turing machines, Occam's Razor. We shall reexamine old truths under question, and weak-AI claims. Special care in this section is devoted to Penrose's "seeing" the truth of the Gödel sentence, i.e. the claim that humans can see the truth of a sentence that cannot be proven by any formal system.

5.1 Alan Turing

Alan Mathison Turing committed suicide in 1954 at 41. Turing is among best scientists of all times. He designed the Turing machine and showed that there is no mechanical process by which all true assertions could be proven. In this way he improved upon Gödel's incompleteness theorem and connected it to the halting problem for Turing machines. He independently discovered the thesis about classes of computable and noncomputable functions. The thesis was for a while known as the Church-Turing thesis, and is now often referred to as the Church Thesis. No argumentation has ever been presented as to why Turing's name is left out of it (putting besides a shorter title).

Turing has affected our life in many ways. Among others, he managed to crack the secret German military code (Enigma), thus importantly influencing the World War II.

When Turing posed his famous question **"Can computers think?"** around half a century ago, electronic computers were just emerging. Turing asked for a scientific way to distinguish humans from machines and scientific ways to determine if a specific machine is intelligent (conscious, having thinking abilities) or not.

5.2 The Turing Test

The Turing Test (TT) is **the best-known scientific test of intelligence to this day.** Its back-bone is a detective probabilistic quiz in which an interrogator has to be sufficiently sure which of the two subjects communicating through a computer interface (terminal + keyboard) is human and which computer, given limited time. Turing believed that his test will be passed in around 50 years when computer storage capacity will reach 10^9 bits. By then, "an average interrogator will not have more than 70 percent chance of making the right identification (as between human and computer) after five minutes of questioning."

Turing's original idea was a copy of a sex imitation/determination game. The interrogator has to determine the sexes of two people in two rooms. In the original game, the man plays at being a woman and the woman plays at being herself.

Gunderson (Shapiro 1990) proposes another version of the Turing test. The interrogator has again access to two rooms but this time through physical contact, e.g., by putting his arm or leg into the room. In one room, a machine throws stones at him and in the other a human. Can the interrogator determine where the human is? Can it be said that machines think or behave as humans if the interrogator cannot determine who is who and which is which?

The above cases with the Gunderson and the sex-imitation version of the Turing test indicate the nature and problems of the Turing test. For example, if a machine can throw rocks like humans do, does it mean that it has human-like performance? Can a man successfully imitating a woman really be accepted as having woman-like performance?

During the years, several modifications of the Turing test have been proposed, e.g. the total Turing test (TTT) in which the subject has to perform tasks in the physical world such as moving blocks. In the TTT version, the subject cannot be observed. A step further is the totally total Turing test (TTTT), in which one has visual and physical access to the being/machine in question. In other words, you can pinch it and observe the reaction.

Remarks about the Turing Test have their counterarguments:

1. communication through typing is more than relevant to evaluate the intelligence of a subject (e.g., IQ tests are performed in a similar way),

2. such communication holds rich possibilities of questions and themata, or in Turing's words (1950) "the question-answer method seems to be suitable for introducing almost any of the fields of human endeavor that we wish to include",

3. functional examination is sufficient since it is also not possible to reveal the human internal thinking process either, yet humans can pass the Test, and

4. if the Turing test (TT) is too difficult then the limited Turing test (LTT) can

be applied. Indeed, such is the case in actual contests for the Löbner prize, held annually (Shieber 1994).

Series of limited Turing tests (LTT) started on November 8, 1991. At that time, the Löbner prize was established with $100,000 for the first computer program to pass the full Turing test. Since computers are far from passing the TT, each year smaller awards are given to the best competitor in the limited Turing tests (there are accompanying prizes as well). Programs typically compete in rather limited discussions, e.g., about Shakespeare, in whimsical conversations, about women's clothing, politics etc.

Critics like Shieber (1994) see the limited Turing test as practising the art of P. T. Barnum who used to amass a fortune by exploiting the fact that people are easily fooled. The first three annual contests were won by Weintraub's programs using the same technology his program ELIZA used 30 years ago to fool his secretary. ELIZA is freely available through the Internet and the price for dozens of Weintraub's programs is around $100. In Shieber's opinion, the limited Turing test is like having a flight competition in the early days of the field producing winners designing better springs instead of better airfoils.

Ten years ago an educated human easily defeated computer chess programs and exposed ELIZA in two statements. Now, better computer chess programs even on low-performance PCs usually beat 99% of all humans, good amateur players included. Playing with the best computer programs even on normal PCs on equal terms is out of reach of all but the best chess-players at the moment. Still, an educated human has no problems with unmasking ELIZA as unintelligent in two sentences. My personal experience with different versions of ELIZA is rather frustrating, since most of answers are typical cliches and more often then not they are not related to the true subject of the question. Just one funny question-answer:

Q: Do you want to have sex with me?
ELIZA: Please go on.

exploiting ELIZA's habit to say "Please go on" too often. The point is that no woman says so and one can suspect in one sentence that there is something wrong. So one needs just another sentence like this to be sure.

In his defense of sponsoring the Turing test competitions, Löbner (1994) replies that it was his desire to advance AI: "I have, since adolescence, been interested in the field. ... Today, I remain an unrepentant utopian." He sees nobility in that endeavor: **"If we humans can succeed in developing an artificial intellect it will be a measure of the scope of our intellect."** He, like many others, has serious doubts that intelligence is attainable by constructing an algorithm.

Says Epstein: "When a computer finally passes the Turing Test, will we have the right to turn it off? Can we say that such a machine is 'self-aware'? ... If you doubt the significance of these issues, consider the possibility that someday soon you will have to argue them with a computer."

Another interesting example of the Turing test are programs that were in use through the Internet and electronic conferences, simulating a particular human user. Some of them were not uncovered as programs for years. On the other hand, this is not a real surprise since through the Internet some users produce garbage beyond machine level.

Although the TT is heavily analyzed and disputed, it remains the most interesting scientific test, offering important implications for our current and future tasks. Even in movies, there are many variations of the Turing Test.

Recent analyses of TT were performed by Turing's contemporary Donald Michie (1993a). In his opinion, there are two obstacles that each intelligent computer system has to face in order to approach passing the Test:
(1) subarticulacy – the human inability to articulate specific activities although performed by humans, and
(2) superarticulacy – the ability to explain particular thought processes in a suitably programmed machine although being subarticulate in humans.

Regarding the first subject, humans cannot articulate their internal thought processes, which are sometimes more transparent to observers than to themselves. Therefore, how can human knowledge be transformed into computer systems if humans are not able to specify it?

The second item poses another problem. Computer programs are by default traceable – meaning their decisions can be traced and reproduced. Even systems like neural nets or numerical procedures can be up to a point 'understood', and simulated by other transparent systems. All computer systems, therefore, have abilities nonexistent in humans.

Some of these questions were discussed already by Turing. He proposed that machines will play the imitation game simulating thought processes while inherently being different. Although it is not yet clear whether digital machines can achieve intelligence at all, it is becoming accepted that on digital computers, systems simulating human thought processes will be essentially different from humans. Consider, for example, connectionism. Even if neural networks were to achieve the performance of a human brain it would be possible to extract weights, topology and other characteristics of nets. By not being able to do it in humans, one (of many) unavoidable substantial difference appears. The "End of Innocence" period, together with empirical verification, is bringing new insights displaying the naivete of several still existing approaching, and opening new directions. **The TT indicates substantial differences between formal machines and real-life beings.**

Weak AI is in general satisfied with less than passing the Test. For example, artificial life and evolutionary computing try to simulate rather primitive forms of life. Brooks (1991) proposes intelligence without reason, low-intelligence robots (insects) without symbolic internal representation of the external world. Consider artificial grasshoppers invading Mars, analyzing every inch of the planet as proposed by artificial-life researchers. Surely, they don't have to pass the TT.

The TT is probabilistic, approximate, detective, fundamentalistic, behaviouristic, and functional. The Turing test should not be seen as an operational definition of intelligence, but as a mode for accumulating evidence (Moor 1987). The often neglected essential characteristic of the test is that an experienced interrogator performs it.

If one looks carefully at the nature of the Turing test, he/she sees it as what it really is – **a test of a human being**. By the test it is possible to distinguish men from women, and humans from other beings or from machines. That is the main reason why the test is so important and will become even more so in future.

5.3 Turing Machine and Church-Turing Thesis

At the beginning of our century, mathematicians like David Hilbert tried to construct a procedure capable of determining the truth of any statement in a well-defined formal domain (Actually, the truth of an arbitrary formula in the first-order predicate calculus applied in the domain of integers. Exact formulation are a little hard to read, therefore, we shall try to make a compromise between understandability and exact formulations.). Later it was shown that the number of unsolvable statements far exceeds the number of solvable statements. Remember – by an effective procedure.

Around 1930 Church, Gödel, Kleene, Post, Turing and others tackled questions such as: **"What can be computed and what not?"**, "Are all statements either provable or disprovable inside formal systems?" They have come up with basic concepts that represent a backbone of current computer science.

In 1931, Kurt Gödel published his incompleteness theorem thus proving that no such effective procedure exists.

The Turing model consists of three parts (Figure 5.1):

- an input tape of cells unlimited in one direction

- a mobile tape head (i.e. the control unit) capable of moving one cell left or right, changing its internal state, reading or printing on the cell according to a program. Often the tape moves, not the machine, but that is irrelevant for the basic concept.

- a program, i.e. a table of transitions from a symbol in a tape cell and the internal state of the tape head into a new internal state, a new symbol, and a move to the neighboring cell left or right.

A task is done successfully if the machine starts in the start state and ends in one of the final states.

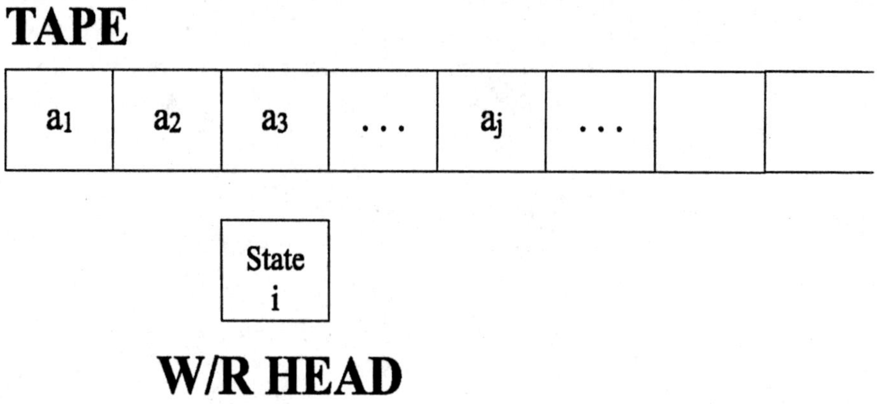

Figure 5.1: The common version of the basic Turing machine.

There are additional conditions and conventions, such as: input symbols, internal states, and final states are finite set of symbols; the initial state is usually at the beginning of the tape; however, there is nothing special.

The forthcoming example will show the essence of the Turing machine.

The task is to find out if the input string of chars has a balanced sequence of parenthesis, i.e. equal number of "(" and ")" in one sequence. An example: $(2*(3-1))$. Unbalanced combinations are not correct, e.g., $(2 = 2))$ or $(2-1))*((-3)$. An expression is a sequence of non-blank chars that finishes with a blank.

We, humans would make a quick scan for a mistake, count difference between current number of ('s and)'s and if the final is 0, then OK. Note that the Turing machine is not familiar with any program in advance, it is totally Tabula Rasa. Of course, computers have algebraic calculations already in hardware and we add software programs for several additional tasks. But the basic Turing machine is just the executing mechanism, capable of performing programs, and humans have to write a program.

How to write a program for a Turing machine or in any other computer language in general? Shortly, one has to understand the limitations and possibilities of the language/machine and try to put the idea in a correct version of a program. In the case of our Turing machine, one first sees that it is possible to move just to one cell left or right, and that we don't have subroutines for counting (already stored programs). What we can do is to mark one "(" and one ")" in consecutive pairs until none is left. Let us mark"(" with X and ")" with Y. See Table 5.1.

Description of the program in Table 5.1:
There are five possible internal states of the control unit (a to e). The first, a, is the

State	Symbols (	)	X	Y	B (=Blank)	A (=Any-Other)
a	b,X,R			d,Y,R		a,A,R
b	b,(,R	c,Y,L		b,Y,R		b,A,R
c	c,(,L		a,X,R	c,Y,L		c,A,L
d				d,Y,R	e,B,R	
e						

Table 5.1: An example of a program for the basic Turing machine.

initial state, e is the final state. Therefore, the machine has to stop in e in order to finish successfully meaning that the input is correct.

All symbols on the tape are: (,), X, Y, Blank and Any_Other. To perform one step of the program/algorithm, i.e. to find a correct move, one has to look at the internal state of the control unit and at the input symbol on the tape. A rule consists of three chars separated by commas. The left symbol determines the new internal state, the second the new symbol the machine is going to write on the tape, and the third a move to left (L) or right (R). If the first char on the tape is "(", the first applicable rule is `b,X,R`, determined by symbol "(" and internal state a. The `b,X,R` rule says that we have to replace "(" by X, go to internal state b and move to right. Following our idea to replace one "(" by one X and one ")" by one Y, the next rules should guide the control unit to the left-leading ")". Indeed, the next rule encountered is `b,(,R` meaning that we keep on moving to right until ")" is encountered.

Mistakes in the input string result in stopping at non-final internal state, thus meaning negative outcome of the analysis.

Let us look at the example below. The tape is represented by a string of symbols followed by blanks, and the control unit as a char below the string. The char thus determines the internal state of the control unit, and its position the corresponding char on the tape. The input string is (()) and the machine executing the program in Table 5.1 stops in the final state e in the 14th step as represented below.

```
(()) X()) X()) X(Y) X(Y) X(Y) XXY)
a     b     b   c    c     a     b

XXY) XXYY XXYY XXYY XXYY XXYY  XXYY
   b   a    c      a     d     d     e
```

Humans understand programs at two levels – at the level of general ideas when thinking about possibilities and constraints, and later at the level of each single rule.

During the process of coding, when checking or first understanding the program, one often starts by decoding these single rules and restructuring them back into ideas. Note that no program has yet been able to decode programs into meaning. There are programs that for a limited domain enable very flexible input close to natural language, but that seems to be the current limit.

The key subject at this point is understanding how such a simple machine can manipulate with symbols so successfully that it can (with an appropriate program) compute any computable statement/function.

Note that computing in this section actually means manipulating with symbols (Symbols can be transformed into numbers and vice versa , anyway.). That is substantially broader than just common human calculation with numbers. Consider our example with the Turing machine – the machine found the solution although it didn't actually calculate/compute in the narrow meaning of the word. So, where are the limits of Turing machines?

The Church-Turing thesis says that any computable function can be computed by a Turing machine.

It also means that functions noncomputable by the Turing machine are effectively noncomputable.

It is difficult to understand the meaning of the thesis and its preconditions. Before thinking about the thesis itself we have to accept that symbols can be representations of (parts of) our real world. Let us try with the following example: Suppose we have two apples, two suns, two cars. In the three cases there is always the concept "two". If we accept that concept "two" is in our thoughts, in computers, Turing machines, written on a paper, in the physical world around us, then we actually agree that symbolic world can represent the physical and the thought world. This is one of the preconditions for the Church-Turing thesis.

What about computing universality? Can machines simulate processes in other machines? Typical machines perform specific functions, e.g., calculate mathematical expressions, heat air in a room, transport people. Humans can predict behavior of other machines, therefore, why shouldn't some universal computing machines be capable of simulating performance of all other machines?

The Turing machine is the universal computing machine because it can compute anything any other machine can in the symbolic world.

Besides that, Turing machines can also compute all physical events in the real world (with some very rare exceptions). The philosophical meaning of the Church-Turing thesis is that machines are part of our universe, as are beings, and that they are bounded by similar limits. The old AI assumes that since Turing machines can simulate all other systems in our universe, they can also simulate other beings and humans which are also parts of our universe.

Later we shall mention other machines which perform differently or even perform more. Also, note that we have already agreed that symbolic world can sufficiently describe physical or mental world. Of course, that may not be necessarily so.

The important point about the Turing machine is that it is a fantastically good approximation of digital computers. And digital computers are among the most important and useful machines humans ever invented.

Back to the Turing machine and symbolic world. **Not accepting both concepts (symbols, universality) probably means that we are not accepting science.** How could we otherwise communicate with each other if not through some (written, painted, spoken, gesture) symbols. Not being able to communicate that there are two buffaloes with pointing two fingers would be an important handicap for ancient human hunters. Not being able to write a love poem and later read it would significantly decrease our mental lives.

The next thought comes as a modest one after philosophically more challenging ones above – **all computers can compute the same set of functions given sufficient time**, be it PC's or supercomputers. Remember the above example with the Turing machine in 14 stages? It doesn't matter were they performed in one second or one hour. Of course, some hardware would do it million times faster, but this is irrelevant from the point of the principle of computability. The important stuff here is that there are tasks no machine can perform, however fast. **There are computable and noncomputable functions.**

5.4 Church-Turing Thesis and Turing Machines

The Church-Turing thesis is the assertion that (only) a process that is effective or algorithmic in nature defines a mathematical function. These functions form a well-defined class, denoted by terms such as recursive, λ-definable, Turing computable. All computable functions are executable by the Turing machine, a formal model of computers.

Computing means performing a variety of functions from theorem proving to game playing or writing poems and painting.

"Computable" or "Turing computable" means that such a function can be computed by Turing machines. And vice versa: anything that is not Turing computable cannot be computed by Turing machines. The problems that the Turing machine cannot solve are also unsolvable for present and future formal computer systems as well, be it simple PC's, supercomputers or parallel connectionist machines. In simple words: **Anything that is computable can be computed by current or future computers and what is not computable cannot be computed by any computer, and is effectively noncomputable in general.**

If computable problems are solvable by the Turing machine then digital computers can theoretically solve them (if only they are fast enough), and therefore any function that can be solved at all can be solved by computers. Achieving true intelligence on computers demands only very fast hardware with sufficient memory capabilities and a sufficiently complex program. In Abrahamson's opinion (1994a) it is only a matter of time and technological progress. **The Church-Turing thesis**

provides the essential foundation for strong AI.

The Church-Turing thesis is such a basic foundation of natural and technical sciences that many consequences can be drawn from it. For example, it even implies that its computational essence cannot be refuted by effective means. It means that any hypothesis opposing the Church-Turing thesis cannot be effective at all, or in other words, it cannot be computed in the general meaning of the word. It certainly means that **no formal system can generate a disproof or counterexample of the Church-Turing thesis.** (Note that later Wegner and Gams show that there are extensions of the thesis, but they are based on new domain characteristics. If the domain area if formal and static, the thesis holds.)

In general, there are two major philosophical orientations regarding the human mind and our world in general: **mentalistic** and **mechanicistic**. Mechanicists regard the mind as a material object obeying the laws of nature. The mind is a (biological, physical ...) machine. Mentalists see mental states as something beyond formal sciences (mild version) or even extramaterial, i.e., outside the real world (extreme version).

5.4.1 Strong Versus Weak AI Again

The Church-Turing thesis represents such an important basis for the whole hard-science community that they for decades vehemently rejected all ideas disputing validity of the thesis. Since weak AI attacks some mechanicistic positions, it was regarded as being mentalistic, as not truly scientific.

Probably the most hostile debate was between strong-AIers and **Dreyfus** (Dreyfus, Dreyfus 1986). Dreyfus pointed to a couple of wrong assumptions of strong AI:

- computers are similar to the brain in the way they handle information and vice versa,
- human knowledge and behavior is formalizable, and
- knowledge can be meaningful in discrete chunks.

Searle (1982) introduced his counterexample with the **Chinese room** where translation between Chinese and English is performed by unknowledgable workers (or in one version, by Searle himself) blindly executing an algorithm in the book. Although translation between two natural languages is performed, there is no understanding in the room. It means that algorithms alone are not enough to simulate humans no matter how good they perform.

There have been several different attempts to explain the Searle room. Here is one: Replace Searle (or workers) with a simple input-output device, i.g. a scanner and a printer on one side, and the English-Chinese translation book with a copy of a human brain (in a liquid nitrogen if you wish) on the other side. The input-output device receives a text, transmits it to the brains and returns the reply. This schema shows where is the catch of the Searle room. In the original intention, Searle as an unknowledgable worker performs the execution part of the brain, and the book performs just the "passive" part of the task. Of course, this is the story of Turing machines (execution mechanisms) and programs/algorithms written on the tape. Therefore, if the book is replaced by the brain as proposed here, the brain is not allowed to perform the execution tasks (i.e. calculation).

Note that the symbolic/nonsymbolic question is actually not prime for the paradox of Searle's room. The real question here is the concept of the Turing machine and the Church-Turing thesis. Can the two tasks – knowledge and calculating – be separated? If so, Searle's paradox is a phony one (As Minsky says), since one can imagine the Searle room as one brain, parts of it representing eyes, mouth and other input/output devices; and the mind split into memorising and calculating tasks. There is no point in questioning if there is understanding in the human head. But if the mechanism in the human head is hardwired to the point that splitting the mental process into execution and passive parts is not feasible, then the Searle room is an important thought experiment. Note that in the brain it is not possible to effectively split the memorising and the calculating part – e.g., memory is dispersed through much of the "thinking" brain.

One of major soft disbelievers in strong AI in the recent ten years was **Winograd** (1991). Maybe the reason for this is that he is a technical scientist. In the mid-70s his program SHRDLU accepted simple commands in English about moving blocks on a table. It was quite an impressive achievement at that time. Later, he started to see limitations and problems in the classical AI approach.

Some other critics of strong AI were more concerned with its implications for our society. For example, **Weisenbaum** (1976) sees Western society as caught in mechanicistic models, thus neglecting its own humanity and judgment.

These disbelievers-pioneers were more or less rejected by the scientific community. Nonbelievers were often compared to nonscientists, principally opposing further progress of science and technology.

Today, practically all weak-AI researchers in this or another way distance their ideas from the Church-Turing thesis. Opponents of too general implications of the Church-Turing thesis come from various fields. Many of them are professional scientists and lecturers admiring science and technology. Neuroscientists (Edelman 1992) propose their models of the brain. Physicists propose new physical theories enabling new computing mechanisms – Penrose proposes microtubules where quantum effects in (the correct) quantum gravity make possible supercomputing powers. Deutch (1985; 1992) proposes a quantum Turing machine. Many authors attack the philosophical foundation that information can be represented as formal strings of symbols without biding to its physical representation.

Some objections come from the designer's or engineering viewpoint. E. g., Sloman's argumentation (1992) is based on the engineering architecture of the computing machine. Theoretically, it has been proved that the computational power of one

Turing machine is equal to the power of many parallel machines. But from the engineering point of view this is not the case. The key is not in speed or time, but in the architecture. For example, a fatal error in one processor simulating parallel computing causes malfunction in serial architectures yet is usually only a smaller obstacle in appropriate hardware parallel architectures. If one processor simulates several virtual processors then it must constantly check the internal states of each parallel process. This disables true asynchronous interaction with the complex real-life environment. Although the parallel and sequential process display equal computational powers, they substantially differ in causal relations. This is similar to our principle of multiple knowledge.

Sloman finds the Turing machine rather unrelated to real life. In his view, the Turing machine represents an artificial machine very capable of performing specific formal tasks. Sloman, Penrose and people in general tend to believe that even animals can display certain aspects of intelligence when solving real-life problems. On the other hand, while machines can solve difficult formal problems which are often practically unsolvable even by humans and definitively unsolvable for all animals, they are still regarded as totally unintelligent.

Some other objections are closely related to Turing machines, halting problems and humans. They will be introduced in the following sections.

5.5 Gödel's Theorem and the Halting Problem

In his 1931 paper, Kurt Gödel showed that for any formal system F broad enough to express the arithmetic of natural numbers, there is a construction of a formula $P_k(k)$ where k is the Gödel's number of that formula itself and P is the predicate of unprovability. This well-defined formula is denoted by $G(F)$, and is denoted as the **Gödel sentence. Gödel's theorem** states that if F is consistent (i.e., ω-consistent for $\neg G(F)$) there can be no derivation of $G(F)$ or $\neg G(F)$. Therefore, $G(F)$ is undecidable, and the formal system F is incomplete.

Not only is Gödel's theorem formally provable, computer programs such as SHUNYATA (Ammon 1993) have been able to automatically reproduce, i.e., rediscover the proof. Of course – by a program programmed by a human.

By proving his theorem Gödel has demolished the strong formalistic approach in science. He has proven that at least one statement/sentence cannot be proven inside a consistent formal system (later it was found that there are many such statements – see Figure 5.2). Therefore, there is no way a formal machine can prove or disprove every sentence of an axiomatic system. This means that **there are formal sentences which are beyond the reach of formal systems and machines.**

Note that this conclusion by itself does not contradict the Church-Turing thesis. These relations are shown in Figure 5.2. The biggest ellipse encapsulates all possible statements/problems/sentences (these terms are here synonyms). The smallest

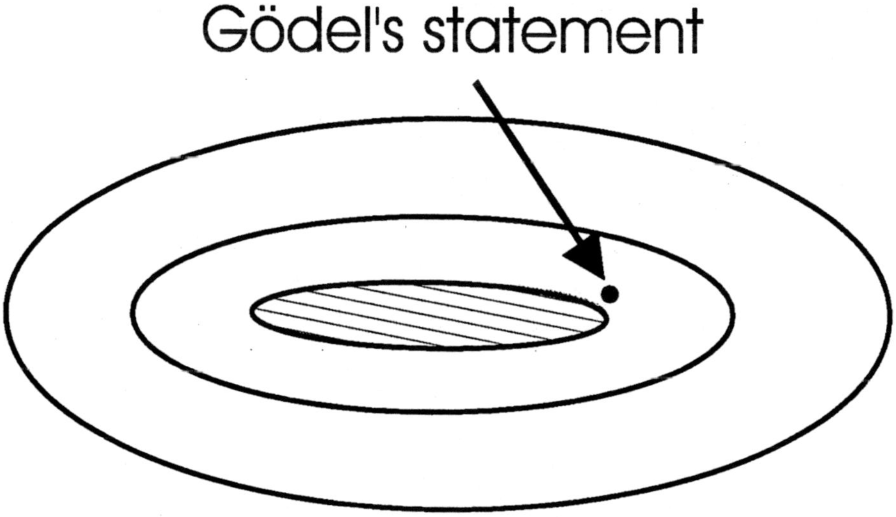

Figure 5.2: Three ellipses show areas of all possible statements/problems/sentences; all solvable; and all solvable by computers. The Gödel sentence can not be proven by formal systems, therefore, is outside the range of computers. If humans can see the truth of the sentence, they are in principal more powerful than computers.

ellipse contains problems that are solvable by Turing machines, i.e. computers. The second biggest ellipse contains all solvable problems, i.e. those that can be solved in principle. Some of these are solvable by computers and some by stronger computing mechanisms. Again - this is the basic and indisputable general computational schema.

In regards to the Gödel sentence ($G(F)$), many reputable researchers thought that although the proof shows that it is not possible to formally prove $G(F)$ if F is consistent, $G(F)$ is nevertheless true. And that humans like Gödel and Turing themselves can see the truth of it. Of course, no formal proof of $G(F)$ can be constructed inside F since it has been formally proven that such a proof does not exist (if consistent). How can then F be seen to be true by humans? **This is in contradiction with the overgeneralization of the Church-Turing thesis and formal hard sciences in general!** In 1961 Lucas presented his view of this paradoxical situation hypothesizing what happens if humans use some kind of a formal algorithm UAI (See Sloman's ideas). This idea was revived and extended by Penrose (1989, 1994).

Approximately at the same time as Penrose, Wandschneider (1990) published similar thoughts in a German magazine "Ethik und Sozialwissenschaften". Like Penrose in the December issue of the "Behavioral and Brain Sciences" journal (Penrose 1990), Wandschneider replies to responses of different researchers. Penrose and

Wandschneider seemed to be unaware of each other, at least they do not list each other in their references.

5.5.1 Gödel's Sentence is True in the Intended Interpretation– by Damjan Bojadžiev

While it is mainly accepted that the sentence is true, we shall first try to show that it is so beyond doubt in the original interpretation (Bojadziev 1995). In this sense we shall have to face one of **the most fundamental of all denials presented by Sloman** (1992). He attacked the core meaning of Gödel's theorem: Gödel's sentence does not mean what it seems to mean, and Penrose cannot see the truth of $G(F)$ since there are models in which it is true and those in which it is false.

The usual meta-arithmetical meaning of Gödel's sentence is that it says of itself that it is not provable. In his first argument, Sloman rejects this meaning by pointing out, when analysing Gödel numbers, that "k is, after all, just a numeral: it denotes a number, not a formula", where k is the k in $P_k(k)$ (p. 386). He repeats analogous statements for predicates and sentences: the predicate in the Gödel sentence "is a complex arithmetical predicate about numbers, not a predicate concerned with the derivability of formulas", and the Gödel sentence "is merely an assertion about numbers" (p. 386). This denial of the role of the Gödel code is not very carefully stated: Sloman sometimes represents the meta-arithmetical meaning as being additional to the arithmetical one, sometimes as being separate from it, and non-existent, and sometimes as excluding the arithmetical one. Sloman mentions the first, standard variant, when he considers the predicate in the Gödel sentence as "expressing not just a property of numbers but a syntactic property of formulas in F" (p. 385), but replaces it with the second variant, present in the quotations above. The third, most unusual variant, appears when Sloman considers the statement that the numeral "k" denotes not the number k but the corresponding formula (p. 385). This variant, and the intermediate one according to which the meta-arithmetical meaning is the primary one, would make $G(F)$ paradoxical and actually prevent the proof of Gödel's theorem, as Varga (1990) claims. Therefore, some of objections by Sloman contradict what has been well accepted in various books. No need to waste too much time here.

But Sloman's most fundamental claim is that "argument that $G(F)$ does not have the meaning it is commonly taken to have depends on the fact that because neither $G(F)$ nor its negation can be derived in F, F will have some models in which $G(F)$ is true and some in which it is false" (p. 385). The claim is based on two models: $(F, G(F))$ and $(F, \neg G(F))$. This is legitimate since neither $G(F)$ nor $\neg G(F)$ is provable in F if F is consistent. Now, nobody can see the truth of $G(F)$ in $(F, \neg G(F))$, Penrose included.

The argument seems to be that $G(F)$ means something else in those models of F in which it is false. Strictly speaking, this is true, but the difference in the meaning of $G(F)$ in those models in which it is false comes from the difference in those models themselves, namely the difference in the domain of the quantification through which $G(F)$ says of itself that it has no proof. This basic meta-arithmetical meaning remains constant across models, and it is this meaning which enables us to understand why $G(F)$ is false in some models. It thus makes much more sense to turn Sloman's thesis around and say that it is because $G(F)$ does have the meaning it is commonly taken to have that it is false in some models of F.

The basic argument about different models of F is already introduced, e.g., in (Hofstadter 1979) to which Sloman refers. There, Hofstadter discusses the possibility of extending F with the negation of $G(F)$ (p. 452-6). This possibility is better understood if the deductive structure of F and the logical form of $G(F)$ are seen in some more detail, using a couple of omega-notions. First, a system is called ω-incomplete if, for some predicate P, $P(n)$ is provable for all n, where n is the numeral of the number n, although $\forall x P(x)$ is not provable. Gödel's theorem involves this kind of incompleteness, with the predicate of unprovabity in the role of $P : G(F)$, which is equivalent to $\forall x \neg pr(x, g)$, where g is the numeral of its Gödel number, is not provable, if the system is consistent, but all its particular instances $\neg pr(n, g)$ are provable, for all n. The second omega-notion is that of ω-inconsistency: a system is ω-inconsistent if $P(n)$ is provable for all n, and yet $\exists x \neg P(x)$ is also provable, for some predicate P; if there is no such predicate, the system is ω-consistent. It follows from Gödel's theorem that if F is ω-consistent, then $\neg G(F)$, equivalent to $\exists x pr(x, g)$, is also not provable in F. Since ω-consistency entails simple consistency, neither $G(F)$ nor $\neg G(F)$ can be proved if F is ω-consistent. In that case, F can be consistently extended by adding $\neg G(F)$ as a new axiom. But since a consistent $F$is ω-incomplete, the new system $F + \neg G(F)$ is ω-inconsistent: all instances of $\neg pr(n, g)$ are provable, along with the new axiom $\exists x pr(x, g)$. If such a system is to have a model, that model must contain, in addition to the natural numbers, some other, non-finite number, which would make $\exists x pr(x, g)$ true. Such a number could be thought of as the number of some infinite proof of $G(F)$.

Let us reevaluate the basic Sloman's argument: if $G(F)$ is false in a model of F, that model is a model of $\neg G(F)$, and so a model of $F + \neg G(F)$. In this model, $G(F) = \exists x \neg pr(x, g)$ says that it has no proof (whatsoever, not even an infinite one), and so is false, because it does have one, since $\neg G(F) = \exists x pr(x, g)$ says so. This situation may seem a little strange: "if $\neg G(F)$ says that $G(F)$ is provable, and $\neg G(F)$ is provable, then $G(F)$ should also be provable". And in general, **"if you prove that something is provable, then it should be provable". But this is actually not so:** a meta-proof is not proof enough. This point may be easier to consider if the notation is simplified a little, writing just $pr(G)$ for $\neg G(F) = \exists x pr(x, g)$, and G for $G(F)$. The argument would then be that $pr(G)$ entails G, but it does not do so: the implication $pr(G)G$ is not provable, because the implication $pr(p)p$ is provable only for provable sentences p. This is a statement of Löb's theorem (Boolos, Jeffrey 1980, p. 187), which is equivalent to Gödel's second theorem; the implication $pr(p)p$ is called the principle of reflection (of the meta-theory in the theory).

Sloman has an argument for his reduction of the meaning of the Gödel sentence to the numerical, purely arithmetical one. He suggests that "perhaps it will turn out, in some of the 'non standard' models that make $G(F)$ false, that the assumed mapping between complex arithmetical expressions and meta-linguistic statements about F goes awry" (p. 386). But there is no independent reason to think that the Gödel code could "go awry" in any model of $F + \neg G(F)$, or anywhere else; on the contrary, there is reason to think that it does not, since that can explain how $G(F)$ is false in such models.

It should be added that the same observations about the falsity of the Gödel sentence in some models apply to Rosser's variation on Gödel's sentence, which Sloman does not consider. Rosser's sentence says of itself that if it has a proof, it has an even shorter refutation. For such a sentence, simple consistency is enough both for its own unprovability and for the unprovability of its negation. Sloman actually discusses Gödel's sentence as if it were Rosser's, and does not mention ω-consistency (except, parenthetically, in his introductory statement of Gödel's theorem on p. 383, and once again on p. 386).

Sloman says that those models of F in which $G(F)$ is false are sometimes called "non-standard" (p. 385). Such models are of course non-standard in the descriptive sense of the word, but not in its technical sense. Non standard models do not change but, on the contrary, preserve the truth-values of statements in the standard model, although they are not isomorphic to it (Hunter 1971, p. 203; Boolos, Jeffrey 1980 p. 193). So, in non-standard models of F, $G(F)$ is actually (still) true. And as will be shown in the next paragraph, **the Gödel sentence is true in the intended model.**

The standard proof that $G(F)$ is true in the domain of natural numbers goes by way of ω-incompleteness: while $G(F) = \exists x \neg pr(x, g)$ is not provable, if F is consistent, all its particular instances $\neg pr(n, g)$ are provable. These instances are thus true in the domain of natural numbers, which means that the general statement $G(F)$ is also true in it (Robbin 1969, p. 115). But Sloman is not satisfied with such a proof, and does not accept Penrose's more informal "seeing" that $G(F)$ is true because what it says (that it is not provable) is so (if F is consistent). The reason is that Sloman questions the possibility of specifying exactly the notion of natural numbers which is used in the proof and in Penrose's seeing that $G(F)$ is true: "how are we supposed to grasp which model we are talking about? How can we unambiguously identify this infinite set?" (p. 387). The reason for this insistence on uniqueness seems to be Sloman's belief that "unless the semantic properties of F somehow uniquely determine which (infinite) model is being talked about ... they cannot uniquely determine the truth-values of all the formulas expressible in F" (p. 385). But this is not so, and Sloman is much too strict in this insistence on uniqueness: the natural numbers do not have to be unambiguously identified, since much ambiguity is harmless. Models of natural numbers can be multiple if they are isomorphic, and even if they are not, provided they are non-standard in the standard sense of the term. Literally speaking, ambiguity is unavoidable since no satisfiable set of sentences has exactly one model (Boolos, Jeffrey 1980, p. 191).

Sloman is also concerned with the ambiguity between standard and (what he calls) non-standard models of F, in which $G(F)$ is false. Sloman almost seems to be asking: "how do we know exactly what the standard model is if the best way of specifying it, namely F itself, is ambiguous?" Since F has both standard and (what Sloman calls) non-standard models, it cannot be used to specify the standard, intended model. Sloman concludes that "F can be 'seen' to be true only if there is some means, other than F, of specifying which model is in question" (p. 385). "Until it is demonstrated that we do have some way of completely specifying exactly which infinite set we are talking about as a model of F it is not the case that we can claim to have seen that $G(F)$ is true: for it will actually be false in some models of F and we have no basis for saying that our grasp of the 'intended' model rules this out" (p. 388). But we do have some basis for saying this, and Sloman himself mentions it when he talks about "our intuitive grasp of the natural number series, containing 0 and all its successors" (p. 387). The non-finite numbers which appear in those models of F in which $G(F)$ is false are not natural according to this informal specification, since they are not successors of 0 in any intuitive, but only in a formal sense. However, such numbers appear already in non-standard models proper, those which are not isomorphic to the standard one but nevertheless preserve the truth-values of all statements (Boolos, Jeffrey 1980, p. 195). Thus, our concept of the intended model and those which are much less or even not intended is better than Sloman thinks, and does not have the weakness which he thinks it has ("too many models"). But it is conceivable that it has another, opposite weakness ("too few models"), which would even, on the face of it, support Sloman's position, though for a very different reason: it may be that we cannot say that $G(F)$ is true in the intended model because that model may not actually be a model. That would be the case if every consistent formalization of number theory were ω-inconsistent (Hofstadter 1979, p. 459).

Therefore, Sloman's theses that the Gödel sentence does not mean what it seems to mean and that we cannot say that it is true in the intended model are misguided. If Sloman's view of Gödel's sentence is confronted with the standard view, this view explains away the arguments on which Sloman's view is based.

It might seem that we have just refuted one of the weak-AI hypothesis in favour of classical formal interpretations. But we have just shown that there is nothing wrong with mathematics, Church-Turing theses or Gödel's sentence as long as we stay in formal time-independent domains. Problems arise in other domains and other worlds.

5.6 Penrose's Analyses of Gödel's Theorem

Publications about Penrose are not neat and straightforward. His interpretations of Gödel's theorem are usually given to critics, Penrose then replies etc. until readers almost don't know what is to be believed and what not. The final blow comes through the Internet. Hundreds of opinions, readers lost in space talking one over the other about pieces of the whole picture. In his second book Penrose (1994) analyses and answers to 20 possible major counterarguments. In one of the first journal debates (Penrose 1990) there are replies to thirty-seven reviewers of his first book.

Similar hot discussions accompanied the ideas of Searle and Dreyfus. But there is an essential difference. Penrose, unlike the above two "social" scientists, is a well-known representative of formal, hard science. He, unlike the above two, presents formal argumentation so as to show that there is something wrong with the Church-Turing thesis when applied to human minds. Had he succeeded in his argumentation, that would be accepted by formal and technical scientists alike.

Lucas and later Penrose propose – in their view – **a valid mathematical procedure for seeing the truth** of $G(F)$. Remember that $G(F)$ says about itself that it is not provable. Now, if the theorem asserts that $G(F)$ is not provable in F (if consistent), and the formal proof showed that $G(F)$ cannot be proved (if F is consistent), then it is obviously true (the other version with $\neg G(F)$ is similar). Therefore, humans can see that $G(F)$ is true.

In simple words: **The Gödel statement says about itself that it is unprovable. It can be formally proven that the statement cannot be proved. At this point people usually conclude that the statement is true. However, no formal system can do it inside itself.** Even if a human uses some kind of (probably very complex) formal algorithm UAI executable on a Turing machine, and we construct the formal Gödel sentence $G(UAI)$ for that algorithm, any reasonably bright human can see the truth of it – something any UAI cannot perform.

Penrose's extension is as follows: Every sufficiently educated person can see the truth of Lucas' line of reasoning. And since humans use similar processes when seeing the truth of Gödel's sentence, it is the truth and not some imagination or self-deceit. (After all, how is truth itself established? Usually in a similar way – when enough people are convinced that some kind of observation or formal derivation is valid.) And since humans can't explain this truth to each other in a procedural way, while agreeing that it is true, this truth is not describable by "classical" description and computing mechanisms that computers use. Therefore, humans are stronger (or at least significantly different).

5.6.1 Analyses of the Halting Problem

Here we translate Gödel's analyses into the world of Turing machines. Namely, Gödel's theorem corresponds to the halting problem, i.e., to the question if a Turing machine can in general predict whether any Turing machine will stop or not.

It has been formally proven that the halting problem in Turing machines is undecidable (Turing 1936; Hopcroft, Ullman 1979). Furthermore, the concept of Gödel's theorem is so fundamental for formal systems that it can be reproduced in many forms (see for example Penrose's second book (1994)). Let us consider my favourite – the halting problem in the light of high-level computer languages.

The basic idea of the halting problem is presented in Figure 5.3. A Turing machine receives data and performs an algorithm (i.e. a procedure, program) on it. If, instead of data, a program (*proc* in Figure 5.3) is given to the machine, it can compute whether it will stop or not. But if the same program that computes if other programs stops or not, is given to input, we get a clearly impossible situation. The program stops only when it does not.

The following Algol-like procedure shows in a slightly different formalism that there is no procedure that can determine whether any procedure will stop or not:

```
procedure U(proc);
begin
      while T(proc,proc) do;
      write('OK');
end;
```

Reasoning starts with the hypothesis that there exists a procedure T which can determine for any procedure *proc* whether it stops or not. Then we construct a procedure U which includes the procedure T as above. For the purpose of the above example we transform the procedure T into a function (Note that procedures compute while functions compute and in addition return some value. Functions are therefore a special kind of procedures). In our case the function T is a Boolean function, returning either *true* (when *proc* stops) or $false$ (it doesn't).

How does the procedure U work? If a given procedure *proc* stops, then T returns *true*, and U does not terminate. If *proc* doesn't stop, then T returns $false$, and U terminates (stops). This is quite OK, since U in this way just inverts the answers from T. A simple example from every-day life is a light-switch reversed – when it says "ON", there is no light and vice versa.

But here comes the catch: when U itself (self-reference) is given as an input for U (i.e. as *proc*), it should stop when it should not (i.e., $T(U)$ is $false$) and vice versa. Since the transformation from T to U is legal within a programming language or the equivalent description mechanism of Turing machines, and U cannot exist, T cannot exist. Therefore, a procedure which determines for any procedure whether it will stop or not, does not exist.

In reference to the reversed light-switch – if we see a plan of a light-switch that turns light on when it actually does not (not just declaratively or in an inverted case!) and vice versa, then obviously it can not be constructed in reality.

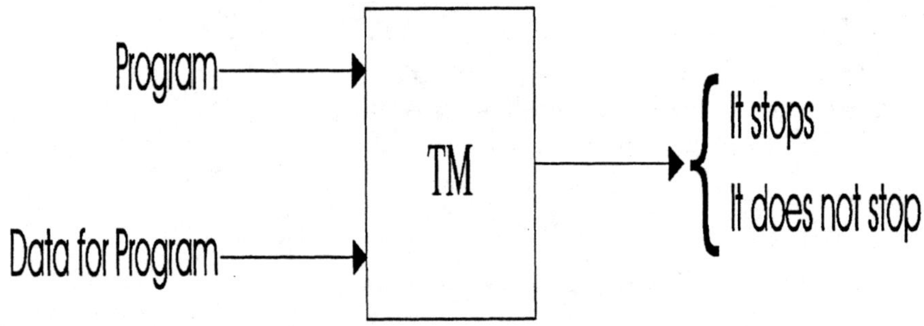

Figure 5.3: A Turing machine receives data and a program. Can it determine for any program in the form of data whether it stops or not? The answear is no. This is the halting problem of Turing machines.

Is there a case in which a program (procedure U) sometimes stops and sometimes not when the reply should be only one of the two (This should not be messed with fuzzy, stochastic or random-numbers-generating algorithms.)? Yes, but in this case we say that these programs are not consistent, they don't have the "desired" properties of programs we should like to work with (remember the consistency condition in the Gödel theorem or similarly – sound systems as proposed by Penrose). We don't want to construct inconsistent programs. But in general, it is easy to make an inconsistent program, which sometimes says $true(A)$ and sometimes $false(A)$ in a situation when it should always say only one of the two cases. If A can have two contradictory values in one situation intended for one state only, the program is inconsistent. Therefore, the procedure U is relevant only for consistent programs which is quite OK.

There are other computing mechanisms, e.g., informal systems or stronger formal systems. The first stronger formal mechanism (nonexistent in reality) is a Turing machine with an oracle. An oracle can reply with "Yes" or "No" to any question, and each time the reply is correct. These machines just extend the border of machines to a higher limit (see Figure 5.4). But no being or machine can cross the border of the second ellipse. Over this border are only in principle unsolvable problems.

Stronger machines still have unsolved problems of its kind. For example, Turing machines with oracles cannot determine the truth of $G(E)$ in E where E is a model corresponding to these machines. This is a common case in relation to computation capabilities of systems: stronger mechanisms can often answer puzzles in weaker mechanisms, yet have their own undecidable questions (puzzles).

Thus, if the procedure T is realised as a Turing machine with an oracle, it can answer for any Turing machine whether it will stop or not. Therefore, the procedure T exists in the world of stronger machines, but not in the world of Turing machines. But when the procedure U is applied in the world of Turing machines with oracles, it

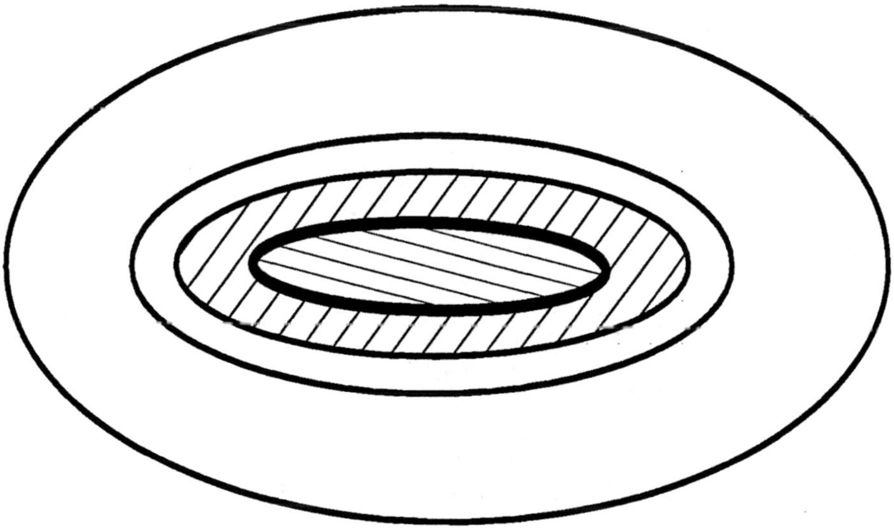

Figure 5.4: Stronger computing mechanisms, e.g. Turing machines with oracles just move the border of machine-solvable problems towards the ultimate limit - the medium ellipse.

represents a problem of different kind. Namely, the procedure U will now exist, but will not ever stop. The tricky procedure seems to work for higher-order machines as well.

This example also shows why it is important to distinguish between algorithms (i.e. abstract Turing machines) and computers (nonabstract Turing machines). One cannot give exactly the same machine as an input to the same machine. Let us make this more clear – suppose that you see yourself in the mirror. Of course – that is you (The task of recognising yourself in the mirror is not very simple and only the highest developed animals can do it. Certain animals like birds attack their picture in the mirror, and some monkeys try to catch their reverse image grasping behind the mirror). But actually it is only your picture in the mirror, not an exact physical or psychological copy.

In a repeated reference to the negated light-switch – can one construct a physical mechanism that turns light only when it actually does not and vice versa? If we construct a feedback that shuts the transmission when it should be opened, strange things can happen – the system might overload and burst in fire, it might simply oscillate etc. But that is just another physical process, nothing very suspicious or theological/teleological occurs since we are dealing with physical devises. In fact, feedbacks are quite common in electronic devices. One of the most common such devices is dynamic memory existing in computers, e.g., in RAM. But again, no true self-reference there. It is not possible to design a physical version of the Turing symbolic halting problem.

By true self-reference we can only denote thinking processes when we think about ourselves. Only humans are advanced to the point that they can think (successfully or not) about things such as Gödel's theorem. Note that Turing machines cannot discuss reasonably their limitations with humans. Only humans can do that. The situation might be repeated with us and some superior being – maybe we are unable to speak about the limitations we have while some superior being is. But that being ....).

It is often said that digital computers are theoretically not Turing machines because their memory is limited. A Turing machine can determine for every existing computer whether is terminates or not due to a simple fact that the tape of the Turing machine is not limited in size. A digital computer is therefore theoretically inferior to a Turing machine. However, the Turing machine is a very good theoretical model for computers and a great majority of theoretical conclusions is valid for computers as well. The problem in infinity is not crucial for real life, and not for the halting problem. This is just hair-splitting.

The self-referential application of U, the halting problem in Turing machines and formal programming languages are well known. Furthermore, high-school students usually do not have trouble seeing or understanding the true nature of the halting problem.

With this we have concluded that for formal domains it is not possible to formally determine for any sentence in F (Peano arithmetic or stronger) whether it is true or false. In mathematical jargon it is said that formal systems are not *complete*.

We have also shown that **several essential differences exist between Turing machines and physical beings performing tasks in real life.** There are formal and informal systems, computable and noncomputable functions. While formal systems enable good calculation and have specific problems like the halting problem, it seems that informal systems of different kind perform well in our evolutionary world. They react, learn, adapt, feel, guess, expect, ... perform functions that don't seem to be (easy or not at all) computable in the Turing sense. These systems perform poorly in formal domains while Turing machines perform poorly in the real-world around us.

5.6.2 Replies to Penrose

Penrose (1990; 1994) was one of the first credible formal scientists to make a step beyond formal computable sciences into a mainly unmarked territory where many interpretations are possible. It is difficult to structure various ideas about Penrose, therefore we recapitulate relevant hypotheses in an unstructured way. In these analyses we shall concentrate only on the main Penrose's argument about seeing the truth of Gödel's sentence.

Boolos (with sufficient mathematical pedigree) points out that systems like ZF or mathematics as a whole are not proven or known to be consistent. Boyle highlights problems of dualism, intelligence, learning and the necessity of physical grounding of algorithms in order to approach intelligence. Breuel relates AI to Turing machines with a simple fact that the best information machines are digital computers, i.e., Turing machines. Boyle as well as Breuel emphasize the importance of learning and adaptability. Butterfield accuses Penrose of trying to revive Lucas, his attempt being an undefended flank.

Chalmers analyses the main thesis of Penrose's book, i.e., that the mental processes might be nonalgorithmic. Chalmers thinks that Penrose's argument is perceived as true because **we have a built-in faith that our mathematical systems are consistent**. And that humans as well as machines cannot Gödelize ad infinitum. Furthermore, Chalmers also points out that a fuzzy algorithm cannot be Gödelized. Davis sees Penrose's argument as deeply flawed, among others because great mathematicians have often "seen" wrong conclusions, e.g., Frege, Curry, Church, Quine, Rosser. Therefore, seeing is not safe enough. Dennett sees formal algorithms as unrelated to real life or mother Nature. **These are two worlds apart and putting one truths in another may be wrong.** Doyle mentions several minor flaws in the book, but sees Penrose's book as deserving praise for opening "so many important questions to technical investigation." Eagleson supports strong AI but sees no major problem with Penrose's analyses. Like Minsky, he relies on agents and their multiple observations in space that can reduce uncertainty. Eccles concentrates on consciousness and mentions our insufficient knowledge about it. But unlike formal machines, humans are self-conscious and ask questions about themselves as well as about anything else.

Gigerenzer shows an important aspect that is left aside in all of Penrose's book. Humans use second-order probability, i.e. second order algorithms. The name of the game is much different in computers (formal algorithms or formal machines) than in humans. Whenever a computer computes anything interesting it is in fact computation designed by a human. Humans take into account several other criteria and parameters compared to formal algorithms. Gigerenzer tells a story (slightly modified here) about a person living in the jungle and having to decide whether to let your children play in the river or let them play climbing trees. You know that in the last hundred years only one child was attacked by a crocodile, whereas a dozen children have been damaged falling from trees. In addition, bees have six times attacked children climbing trees. Now, imagine that your neighbour tells you that just yesterday he saw a big crocodile in the river. He is not sure, but he has heard a rumour that this is the same crocodile that attacked a child a week ago. As Gigerenzer points out, it is very difficult to design a program that will be able to see that the crocodile presents greater danger than trees and bees because statistics or mathematics or abstract algorithms will tell you that mathematically speaking, the crocodile is in fact less likely to cause problems. As a result, "many children may be eaten", i.e. common-sense deprived "mind children" of Turing machines by real-life crocodiles.

Garnham is concerned with Platonism, formalism, intuitism and realism. Gilden and Lappin see Penrose's results as a little depressing because he has not presented any new subject. Glymour and Kelly perceive the book as one whose enthusiasm is infectious. It is "**refreshing, valuable, and unique**". On the other hand, the main argument is "**pretty obscure**". Their argument is interesting enough – than nobody can tell from observations whether or not any system is Turing computable or not. Higginbotham relates the intuitive version of the Liar paradox – "I am a liar" to the Penrose version of Gödel's theorem. Hodgkin and Houston start with the observation that "consciousness and the brain seem to act as a fatal attractor for many physicists". They seem to attribute the success of problem solving to the simultaneous action of several processes.

Johnson, Ettinger, and Hubbard construct a discussion between a human Babbage and a computer Arti. From the discussion it is easily seen that the computer is intelligent, conscious etc., but, arguments like Searle's room or Penrose's seeing the truth of the sentence are not understood by the computer. Now, let us turn these arguments to you, dear reader. You are accused of being a computer, incapable of solving the above two problems. The Turing test (the version proposed by Penrose or Searle) is applied on you to determine whether you are human or not. OK, where in your brain (Searle's room) is understanding? In the brains? Where? You don't know? And about the Gödel statement (Penrose) – can you see the truth of it? You failed twice?? Obviously, you are a computer, therefore – sorry – we shall unplug you.

Kentridge first reminds us again that seeing the truth of the Gödel sentence is actually just seeing the truth at one level. As Hofstadter already demonstrated to Lucas, there is no proof of seeing the truth in higher systems. Kentridge also reexamines important differences in thinking processes in computers (logic) and humans (experience-based heuristic search implemented as parallel processes). Libet discusses time-delays in conscious and unconscious processes and relates minds to the laws of the physical world. Lutz seems to be unsatisfied with the static view of the brain without learning and communicating with the external world. And at the end, after introducing quantum Turing machines: "So what Penrose has really done in his book is to advocate a move from traditional AI to what should perhaps be called **Quantum AI**. I doubt if anyone would disagree that this would be **an interesting area to investigate**." Sure, but let us update the terms "traditional AI" into "strong AI" and "quantum AI" into "weak AI".

MacLennan accuses Penrose of dualism and shows that his second idea about quantum processes in the brain can be much easier solved by another physical theory – **the many-worlds theory**. In fact, these discussions and the ones by McDermott revealed that there might be an important physical background for our principle of multiple knowledge. MacLennan sees the brain as nonalgorithmic, but simulatable by a Turing machine. That formal symbol manipulation is not appropriate for thought processes. Madsen notices that Penrose's book opens more questions than it answers. He suggests that Penrose is a bit unscientific or chauvinistic in **not giving artificial intelligence "a fair chance to prove its worth as a branch of study."** Manaster-Ramer, Savitch and Zadrozny mention that computing can be carried out by Turing machines as well as by stronger machines (e.g., Turing machines with oracles). They also point to the fact with which I certainly agree, that if we (a formal system F) are to see our version of Gödel's theorem, then our brains as well as any other system will not be able to prove their consistency according to the second Gödel's theorem. Provably consistent brain in this context means that we are nonalgorithmic.

McDermott, although not a specialist in physics, notes that **the Everett-Wheeler interpretation of quantum physics seems obviously correct** (to me also), and that Gödel's theorem is irrelevant to the mind-computer debate (personally, I don't agree with that easily). He proposes a seductive argument – any computer system duplicating any person would have to be incomplete, contradictory about mathematics as well about all other things. The trick here is that Penrose does not distinguish between programs and computers. The reason is simple – in the world of Turing machines, algorithms (i.e. programs) are essentially computers since there is no difference between the two. The Turing machine is a kind of a fictive toy machine with a couple of operations, and an unlimited memory capacity. It is only the program that is interesting to think of. Therefore, there in no great difference when thinking about an algorithm or a program or a system. The Turing machine just performs programs, algorithms etc. But in real life **there are essential differences between computers and programs that run on them.** A machine may perform programs that could be essentially different in nature from the machines themselves.

McDermott finds it hard to read about Penrose's oneness of the human mind. His advice is that Penrose needs to brush up on with William James and Sigmund Freud. He sees no real problem for AI, **since if the human brains are really different than computers, then we will have to build different computers in order to achieve artificial intelligence.** While most of the cases presented by McDermott are well written, there are two things I disagree with: that the Turing test is irrelevant for intelligence and that weak AI is a trap for the "philosophically unwary cognitive scientist". In my opinion, these are double criteria – while strong AI is to deserve a shot at explaining consciousness, weak AI is denied such a chance. Bottom line, everybody making a strong stand has its own mistakes. It is also the case with the Emperor's New Mind – it is a very interesting book opening many questions. However, few parts are debatable.

Mortensen warns that the first Gödel incompleteness theorem can be true only if the system is consistent. But by the second Gödel incompleteness theorem no Turing machine can prove its own consistency. There is no guarantee that we humans perform better on these matters. Niall doesn't seem to be too satisfied with Penrose, nor does Perlis talking about the emperor's old hat. Perlis writes: "But mere pattern by itself is not even a process, it does nothing. It is algorithmic *processes*, not static printed copies of algorithms, that AIers are concerned with." Roeper has a nice final remark: **"Why does Penrose devote his talent to the obviously weak nature of strong AI instead of exploring the strengths of weak AI?"** Such lovely words must come from a department of linguistics (Roeper's affiliation). According to Roskies, we don't know for sure about many things in the book, e.g., we do not know if algorithms can give rise to consciousness. Smithers in his "pretender's new clothes" turns his attention to a very limited view of AI in the book. It is really a very strong version of AI that Penrose discusses. "So where did Penrose get his idea of AI research from?" says Smithers. Not from the literature he is familiar with as an active researcher. And later he agrees with Penrose that symbolic processing by itself cannot give rise to mental states. Smithers concedes that in AI there is a much needed debate about the role of symbol processing in relation to mental states, however, **"what is *not* required is to have some distorted image of AI put up and shot down."**

When reading Penrose's book, Stanovich had the association of a cartoon with a miracle at the end of a long mathematical proof. While several paragraphs are interesting, the chapter about the mind is "hopelessly muddled". Stanovich also points to a rather naive approach to consciousness. Like many authors, he also proposes a make-believe story. That he is an expert reader, that his eyes just pass gently through pages and recycle interesting stuff from the text. Many readers believe such stories, although it is well known that the eyes jump from place to place, stopping for moments at interesting places. One should be cautious about believing all that is written.

Taylor concentrates on differences between living systems (dynamic, nondeterministic, nonformal) and mathematical formal systems. Tsotsos is disappointed with the end and the beginning of the book. Obviously, Penrose is not familiar with AI – he cited only four AI items in the literature. Physics alone is enough to provide important insights into the human brain. Much of the book is old stuff revived, be it of any important question in the history of the mankind that was unsolved at that time. Similarly, Varela sees parts of the book as very interesting and parts as infuriating. It seems to him that **"a recent trend in cognitive science and AI is to abandon the notion that issues of general computability are the hallmark of intelligence".**

Waltz and Pustejovsky see the weakest parts of the book in those dealing with AI. In their view, **Penrose is attacking a very limited subarea of AI**, that of representing thinking as disembodied formal manipulation of symbols. No wonder that Penrose accepts the dualistic position separating the body from the mind. For Waltz and Pustejovsky, the mind consists of perception, action, and memory, it reacts to events in the real world. "Perception is an active process, involving layers and 'societies' of detectors and agents." They also tackle with Penrose's Platonism, unlike the majority of repliers who just slip magical thinking in the

Emperor. Penrose sees science as religion, revealed only to the blessed like Turing, Gödel, and of course – Penrose. When he is in the blessed mode, he sees the truth that normal people cannot. At that time, his mind makes a connection to the Platonic world of eternal truths. Wilensky sees Penrose's arguments as a revival of old arguments. "Like the ghoul in the horror film, having been convincingly and utterly vanquished last time around, inexplicably appears in the sequel as if the previous episode had never occurred." And later that "critics biding the mind to biological brains should be reluctant to believe that God, if exists, has a mind because there is no corresponding biochemistry". He also notes that humans don't use proving theorems for cognitive activities, such as using language or being able to see. Zytkow agrees with Penrose that thinking is not computing by formal machines and that consciousness and greater thinking power is in the brains. But he disagrees with Penrose's line of reasoning. As he points out, there is not a single well defined formally specified problem that can be solved by humans and not by computers. Zytkow finds **"nothing more fascinating than to chase and imitate that elusive being – our mind."**.

In (Penrose 1994) Penrose recapitulates and reanalyses the same position and arguments. He remains confident in his seeing the truth, however, substantially softens his ideas probably to please some of the critics.

There are several events following the second book, although the first book seemed to be the true brainstorm, the second book and events following it more like sequels.

5.6.3 Some Problems with Penrose's 'Seeing'

To repeat Penrose's essential argument: since formal systems are not able to formally prove the truth of Gödel's sentence, and humans can see it while not being able to tell the solving algorithm to other people, humans do not apply formal algorithms (e.g., UAI). Therefore, since humans can in principle reproduce anything that Turing machines can, and Turing machines in principle cannot reproduce all things humans can do (e.g., seeing the truth of Gödel's theorem), **Turing machines do not possess the computational powers that humans do.** Since Turing machines are capable of reproducing any computation by digital computers, true intelligence cannot be achieved on digital computers.

Consider the truth of Gödel's sentence, i.e. true(Gödel's sentence), true(G) in Peano arithmetic. It can be proven outside Peano arithmetic using stronger mechanisms or inside sound systems. Of course, adding G to F we obtain another system and another version of Gödel's theorem. The mathematical community is well aware of it – Penrose included. This procedure can go on and on and not only never stops, **it cannot be mechanised** either.

Now consider the possibility that we can see the truth of Gödel's sentence because we use stronger formal computational mechanisms. Then, however strong these computational mechanisms are, **we might have our own Gödel's theorem.** Of course, any formal system or machine cannot see the truth of its own Gödel theorem and cannot discuss it reasonably. We may be able to see the truth in simpler formal mechanisms, however, we should not be able to meaningfully reason about such questions in systems as strong as we are.

The problem with stronger machines such as a Turing machine with an oracle is that it is hard to imagine an oracle in any actually constructed machine. The only possibility, but a very dim one is that the oracle corresponds to a priori knowledge, i.e. to background knowledge. For humans, that knowledge would correspond to evolutionary preprogrammed truths, e.g., through DNA. Maybe these truths are not computable, but may be observable and learnable.

Whatever the case, **a Turing machine with an oracle does not exist in real life.** It does not correspond to any digital, analog, fuzzy, random, quantum etc. machine we know of. And still it has its own undecidable questions (Hopcroft, Ullman 1979).

If one looks carefully at Penrose's line of reasoning, in each formal system it is possible to check the truth of Gödel's sentence if we evaluate it with stronger formal mechanisms. But what is the point of going into non-existing machines? On the other hand, if we stick to sound systems and universal Turing machines, then **we can design self-modifiable computer programs** that will

- evade the problem as unsolvable (undecidable), as we humans have to in ZF systems, or
- see the truth of Gödel's sentence like humans do using some form of truth-evaluating mechanism. Such programs would be able to see that they cannot formally prove it, however, can see the truth of it.

The second idea is close to the fact that **informal or fuzzy systems cannot be Gödelized**, as pointed out, e.g., in (Chalmers 1990). However, these sysems are not very useful. We want our computers to compute correctly each time, and not from time to time.

What about consistency (that there is no statement that can be true and false at the same time)? Purely mathematically speaking (Davis 1990; Boolos 1990), when one speaks about mathematics as a whole, anybody should stick to general formal systems such as Zermelo-Frankel (ZF) systems. Peano arithmetic (dealing with natural numbers) is not enough. **Inside or outside ZF and similar systems, nobody knows if these systems are consistent or not.** Penrose's insight is not correct for general mathematical systems, as Penrose himself admits, because the precondition is not fulfilled.

Penrose insists on dealing only with *sound* systems. If we accept Penrose's line of argument and stick to sound systems, we deal only with systems in which a statement if proven is also true. These systems are also consistent and ω-consistent. Penrose says that if we are dealing with reality then there is no point dealing with unsound systems.

5.6.4 The Importance of Penrose's Analyses

Let us reevaluate basic positions in the previous section. The two most relevant questions regarding Penrose's analyses of Gödel's theorem are:

1. Are Penrose's interpretation and derivations of his analysis reasonable or far-fetched?

2. Is Gödel's theorem important for human lives, for science, for mind- or computer issues?

Penrose has a couple of formal mistakes especially in the first book. It happens to everybody, especially when introducing new ideas; some mistakes are probably in this book as well. Some of the mistakes are close or even along the main line of reasoning. For example, in (Penrose 1989) it is claimed that no computer program can see the truth of Fermat's theorem. This is to say that computers cannot solve problems that humans can. Another such case was Penrose's famous tiling problem. The tiling problem is (according to Penrose) noncomputable, but a human (Penrose) has solved it. Both these basic claims – that computers cannot prove Fermat's theorem or that computers cannot solve Penrose's tiling problem, are incorrect. In his last book (Penrose 1994) Penrose corrects this by stating that such families of problems are noncomputable, but that problems inside these families, such as Fermat's, may be computable. Indeed, a couple of years later the Fermat's problem was solved with formal mathematics and by a brilliant mathematician.

Another example of overgeneralisation is the claim in his first book that semantics cannot be formalised. Indeed, there are severe problems when formalising semantics and there is a real chance that all semantics cannot be formalised. But some semantics has been formalised already and there are specific branches of mathematics that directly deal with formalising semantics. We have to be careful before stating too general, i.e., populistic a-kind-of-truth. (For those unaware of differences between syntax and semantics, consider an example: you say to your friend that he/she is beautiful. Syntax deals with chars, strings, sentences. The formal meaning (first level of semantics) is that some person is beautiful. But in multiple worlds of meanings and related semantics, there is usually much more than that. Maybe we say it because we want something from that person or we are just flattering.)

Some of Penrose's critics have misinterpreted the meaning of the Gödel theorem. For example, Abrahamson (1994a) claimed that the theorem is paradoxical in nature. An example of such thinking would be: "I lie all the time." If I do, then the last statement is false and then I am telling the truth. But then I cannot say that I am a liar. **Please note clearly that Gödel's theorem is not a simple paradox but an important intellectual construction.**

While Penrose agrees with the above paragraph, he makes a mistake when claiming that Gödel's theorem/statement is not self-referential. Some statements not computable but true are not self-referential, but Gödel's sentence certainly is. Since the theorem deals with a self-referential sentence, it must itself have something to do with self-reference. Even more, the basic argument of Penrose or Lucas is self-referential.

More important, what is the importance of Penrose's analysis? Consider the following two stories:

Johnny, a young bright scholar enthusiastically jumps up and says "Listen, family, what an interesting statement have I encountered recently! A barber shaves the beards of all the people in the village that do not shave their own beards. Who shaves barber's beard? This is a contradiction no computer can solve!"

"Yeah", says his older brother Jimmy, a bit jealous:
"What about infants? Don't tell me that the barber shaves their beards also!"

"OK, the statement is valid for grown-up men only" replies Johnny after a little thinking.

"Yeah" says his touchy older sister Mary "You chauvinist! Anybody civilised today writes 'he or she' or 'person' in order to avoid sex discrimination. Come up with something better!".

"OK, then the barber shaves his or hers eyebrows" replies a bit shaken Johnny.

"I think you have all gone a little too far. Johnny, barbers do not shave eyebrows. Eat the supper!" finishes discussion their mother Sue.

Consider another story: A teacher says: "One day next week we shall see a superb video. But I will not tell you which day it will be so that it will be a surprise."

Now suppose that it is Friday next week and that the teacher has not yet shown the video. There will be no surprise since it was promised that the video will be shown that week. Obviously, the teacher has to show the movie before Friday.

What about Thursday next week? The teacher cannot wait till Friday as shown above. So the video must be shown latest on Thursday. But that is no surprise then either. And so forth until we see that there is no way the teacher can achieve a surprise under the above formal conditions.

Let us now consider Monday or Tuesday. The teacher can freely choose between any of the two days and it is going to be a surprise.

Or consider Friday. The teacher comes in and says: "Sorry, I forgot the tape at home. We shall see it next week". *That* should be *a real* surprise.

The story with a videotape is cleary misleading, based on a wrong logical conclusion. The self-referential paradox with barbers is a deeper one, yet still a formal paradox, unrealistic in real life. These two stories should be understood in the way Penrose admonishes a couple of times: "Don't read what I write, read what I mean" (i.e. separate true meaning from formal ones). The above two stories were introduced to show that humans primarily use common sense and thus have no problems with various paradoxes, puzzles and obstacles in formal systems although they often don't know how to formally solve them. We could mention several similar problems, e.g., where is an edge in Euclidian geometry? How many angels can sit on the top of a triangle? Such questions are not solvable in Euclidian geometry, but they do not cause many problems in real life.

Many AIers have objected to the validity of the Turing test. But see how easily we can use the Turing test in the normal version to eliminate all Turing machines! Remember - this task is often referred to as formaly unsolvable. But just ask them about the Gödel theorem. If Turing machines use normal algorithms, then they cannot discuss about the Gödel theorem reasonably as Penrose shows in the fantasy discussion in the "Shadows of the Mind". What is wrong with the Turing test here?

Gödel's theorem is very important for formal hard sciences in the original sense as proposed by Gödel himself. The relation to human or informal systems is an open scientific question. Humans in general rarely deal with formal systems, yet they constantly display consciousness, self-awareness, common-sense and intelligence. They also constantly use multiple knowledge.

If Penrose has not been able to persuade the scientific community of his basic arguments, mainly because Gödel's theorem offers so many possible interpretations, how can he persuade us that just his own interpretation of all possible ones is the correct one? After all, while Gödel's theorem is formal, relations to humans, other beings and our real world are informal and nontechnical. That is slightly inconsistent with Penrose in his first book The Emperor's new Mind (Penrose 1989). There, Penrose advocates Platonism to the point where our minds make contacts with mathematical truths and phenomena, e.g., infinite numbers. Even more, whenever we have an insight, a connection between our mind and the Platonistic world of abstract truths is presumably made. As Sloman points out (1992), a connection between our minds and infinite numbers is a bit questionable.

In his second book (Penrose 1994) Penrose softens his ideas. He agrees to a possible counterargument that the mind allows shortcuts with respect to complexity theory rather then being computationally stronger in the sense of Turing machines. And then he replies that though that might well be true, it does not mean that the mind does not use noncomputable processes. And further, on page 115 that "it is quite probable that our mathematical insight and understandings are often used to achieve things that could in principle be achieved computationally" and that "it may well be that in the working lives of most mathematicians, noncomputability issues play, if anything, only a very small part".

Or consider Penrose's claim that Turing himself wouldn't object Penrose's "theory" about Gödel's theorem? Although Turing really said a lot of things overall about this basic subject, one should be extremely cautious about which claims to choose.

Why does Penrose use analyses of the formal Gödel theorem to analyse informal beings like humans? He says he wants to defeat his opponents (i.e. strong AIers) on their ground. It is quite common to prove that one mechanism is stronger than another one by designing a problem which one is capable to solve but the other not. Following this analogy we should propose a theoretical problem we can solve but computers cannot. OK, what should that be? Playing chess? Playing tennis? Making a date? In practice we see lots of such examples, but in abstract theory, no proven case. Penrose's analysis of the Gödel sentence is one of the best candidates. So, which matters more – abstract mathematics or our real world full of physical reality and semantics?

Another subjective Penrose position is about AI. Which AI does Penrose attack? Obviously he is not an expert in AI, probably much less. In the first book (1989) Penrose does not distinguish between strong and weak AI. In the second book (1994) he tries to somehow structure AI, and introduces top-down and bottom-up AI. As Sloman pointed out (1992) there is no point in attacking strong AI. In fact, the new weak AI rejects strong AI as one of its fundamental positions. Artificial intelligence is an interdisciplinary scientific discipline which tries to construct artificial intelligence in machines using knowledge from all sides including physics, chemistry, biology, psychology etc. It is just the digression of strong AI that has turned predominantly towards Turing machines, formal mathematical systems and one-level algorithms up to a point that the basic definition is not relevant for it anymore.

Let us compare the basic weak/strong AI granulation with the one by Penrose:

Strong-weak AI division:

- Strong AI: performance of humans and other beings can be perfectly simulated by Turing machines.
- Weak AI (general): even if humans and other beings can be perfectly simulated by Turing machines, these machines (algorithms) are essentially different than currently perceived.
- Weak AI (extreme): Humans and beings are *not* Turing machines. They are worlds apart.

Penrose's division in the "Shadows" (Text in parentheses added by the author of this book):

- Thesis A (Strong AI): All thinking is computation.
- Thesis B (Weak AI): Computing by itself cannot evoke consciousness; however, it can simulate physical states of the brain.
- Thesis C (Weak AI): Thinking can not be properly simulated computationally.
- Thesis D (Mysticism): Consciousness can not be explained scientifically.

Penrose's gradation of different approaches is presented above. Penrose sees AI as strong AI or slightly modified strong AI. His own positions are seen by himself as outside any AI. But looking at the theses, Penrose's reasoning is clearly inside weak AI! The border between thesis A and B is also the border between strong and all versions of weak AI.

5.6.5 Closing Arguments about Penrose

In summary, Penrose's version of the Gödel sentence and the halting problem is tempting, yet not proven. It is not fully accepted even in the weak AI community. On the other hand, none of the attempts to demolish Penrose has totally succeeded, and some of the attacks were not grounded. Penrose-Hameroff theory – although unproven – about supercomputing powers in the brains based on quantum processes in neural tissue is among 10 major theoris about the brain.

Why is Penrose so stubborn in declaring that human thinking is in principle superior to or at least substantially different compared to computing by computers? What do you think – are computers superior to humans, equal or inferior? Probably we all agree that although computers perform better several specific operations, e.g., mathematical computations etc., we humans are essentially different, and in the most important aspects and altogether superior to computers. First of all, computers are very limited universal machines. Although specific robots have sensory apparatus, none of them is of any great relevance compared to the whole human system performing physical and mental tasks. Have you seen any robot opening a door, jumping two steps at a time and swimming in a pool in less than five minutes? In intellectual tasks, computers lack many properties we have, such as qualia, self-consciousness, autonomy, unity etc. **Computers are wonderful information machines, however currently incapable of most high-level human properties!** We humans can analyse the way computers work, computers can not analyse well even how they work. That is the current reality!

Final two summaries:

- The phenomenon of Gödel's theorem is so deep that no human, Penrose included, can currently come to its end.

- It is wrong to say that Penrose "mounts an even more powerful attack on artificial intelligence", because what he attacks is strong AI. Weak AI sits with Penrose on the same bank of the river.

Whatever the case, who can say that Roger Penrose is not on the right track? He has pushed our knowledge ahead at least with another interesting analysis of Gödel's theorem and AI. In my opinion, he has formally shown that there are important differences in the way humans and formal systems compute. Although we cannot formally prove it, our common sense tells us that there must be something in principle different when humans and computers are involved. Keep on, Roger!

In this section we have shown that the old truths are quite firm when applied in formal domains. However, these truths seem empirically much different compared to human truths, the way we live and the way we deal with our world. It is difficult to formally prove or show the differences between the two worlds – the formal world of abstract truths computable by Turing machines and the real-life world we live in and which our brains are part of, the most developed and advanced system known in our universe. Yet, practical differences between the formal world and the world we live in are too big to be dismissed. **There must be something different in principle, something not discovered yet.** In the next section, the principle of multiple knowledge will be introduced as a potential cross-border between the two worlds, but first we examine the major scientific discovery in recent years - Peter Wegner's article about interaction.

5.7 Is Interaction Stronger Than Algorithms?

This section is mainly based on the article "Why Interaction Is More Powerful Than Algorithms" by Peter Wegner, published in Communication of the ACM. But first we analyze Gödel's statement by using the principle of multiple knowledge. We show how close these concepts are.

Humans can simultaneously use different techniques (formal and informal systems), approaches, viewpoints and contecsts to reach conclusions. According to the principle of multiple knowledge we should not have too many problems in one system or mechanism if we encounter the Gödel statement because we are always able to leap into another system and evaluate the truth there.

A clever opponent might say that all these systems together still represent another formal model computable by the Turing machine and thus humans have their own version of the Gödel statement. A possible reply is that humans dynamically use as many models/systems as they need, and that it is nearly impossible to "catch" them with a specific Gödel statement in exactly appropriate combination of models. Even when caught, humans can simply change the combination.

Can we think in terms of Turing machines? Suppose we have two Turing machines. One deals with all Gödel-type questions of the other one and vice versa. As a result, there is no Gödel theorem in the combined system. Unfortunately we know a kind of a classical answer. If we simulate the performance of the combined system by another universal Turing machine, it will again have its own undecidable question. But what if the combination by another Turing machine is forbidden by the combining mechanism? Of course it is possible to design a uniform Turing machine simulating all that the above system can, but in reality it will perform differently. It is not the same machine any more. And the undecidable statement might be quite complicated to construct (There is a small formal problem though. One Turing machine has troubles replying to all undecidable questions of the other Turing machine.). Wandschneider (1975) proposed a similar combination. Each of the two Turing machines has a meta system of the other, and in a similar way, a superior machine can be obtained.

Let us upgrade our combined machine into a copy of the human brain. The logically thinking hemisphere might correspond to one Turing machine, the intuitively oriented hemisphere to a fuzzy system. The integration mechanism might correspond to a third subsystem. Who can construct Gödel's theorem now? Even if we try to copy all subsystems by Turing machines, we obtain something much different than the original system.

The above lines were written before Wegner's publication. They clearly indicate that a potential greater computing power, capable of dealing with the Gödel-type questions, lies in dynamical cooperation between actors (Turing machines, beings, etc.). Peter Wegner managed to formalise similar thinking into the most significant modification of the Church-Turing thesis published to this date.

The major idea is that (Wegner, p. 80):

Interaction is more powerful than algorithms, overturning the prevailing view that all computing is expressible as algorithms. And later (Wegner, p. 81): **interactive systems are more powerful problem-solving engines than algorithms.**

By interactive systems Wegner denotes Turing machines extended by addition of input and output actions that support dynamic interaction with an external environment. Although Wegner does not explicitly mention, it is pretty clear that if one looks at the Turing machine (see Figure 5.1) just writing on and reading from the tape is not enough since this is a common action of the Turing machine. Writing on the tape from the environment is not essential for the interaction Turing machine as long as the machine does not change its behavior on the basis of the changed input writen on the tape. Only that is interaction. But then, one gets (potentially) substantionally different behavior compared to the performance based on algorithms.

Here we show the idea of interaction by a couple of simple examples:

- Suppose students write exams. As long as they have limited acess to other knowledge sources – say, their books – they can not perform as good as when they have access to the Intrenet. On the Internet, they can contact other programs, data and other humans. Surely, in which of the two cases will they perform better? The difference is similar to the difference between one stand-alone PC and a PC connected to the Internet.

- Great leaders of companies or other institutions perform well on the basis of their own cleaverness and effective use of interaction (delegation, coordination etc.).

- In an often quoted example, Simon (1892) reports about an ant trying to find its way home to an ant colony. Although the ant follows a simple procedure (a simple interactive agent) the environment forces it to exhibit complex behavior the ant is not capable to produce without environment. In this way, the ant can traverse a nonalgorithmic path undiscribable by any algorithm because all possible beaches can not be described by algorithms.

The Turing machine is indeed a mathematical attempt to model our world. As mentioned by several other critics, there is no time in the Turing machines. Wegner adds: no interactivity either.

It should be distinguished between interaction, parallelism, and distribution.

- **Interactive systems** interact with unpredictable environment and get there additional information to upgrade its behaviour.

- **Parallel systems** compute in such a way that their computation overlaps in time.

- **Distibuted systems** denote systems that consist of separated (e.g. geographically) components.

Parallel and distributed systems are not stronger than Turing machines, therefore can be fully simulated by a universal Turing machines. Only interaction enables greater powers. However, interaction systems can be implemented paralelly or in a distributed way. It is just an implementation detail. Interaction Turing machines can also be structured as universal Turing machines into single or multiple input streams, synchronous or asynchronous, since interaction Turing machines are just extended Turing machines. To represent them, the classical picture of the Turing machine suffices. All we had to add is a property of the algorithm to consider information on the tape written from an uncontrollable environment.

The proof that interaction Turing machines are stronger that universal Turing machines is based on a simple observation that Turing machins cannot handle time and interaction. More formally (Wegner, p. 83): "Input streams of interaction machines are not expressible by finite tapes, since any finite representation can be dynamically extended by uncontrollable adversaries."

How about the Gödel sentence in interaction machines? To idea of Gödel's contribution is that one numbers statements and by diagonalisation shows that there is (at least) one statement that is not recursively enumerable. So, the system is incomplete. But in interaction Turing machines, by definition we can not ennumerate all algorithms since they can change due to the external environment. Therefore, it is not possible to enumerate all statements and futher more, the set of all posible statements is not finite while constructed over a finite alphabet. So evidently, the machine is not only incomplete, but also stronger than the universal Turing machines!

The Church-Turing thesis was undisputably valid for the last 50 years. Not accepting it equalled being a mentalist, e.g., a nonscientist. But after Peter Wegner's publication in 1997, the basic version of the thesis breaks down since it si possible to compute several problems that are not computable by universal Turing machines. Looking at Figure 5.5, the inner ellipse covering solvable statements/problems extends due to the extension from Turing machines to interaction Turing machines.

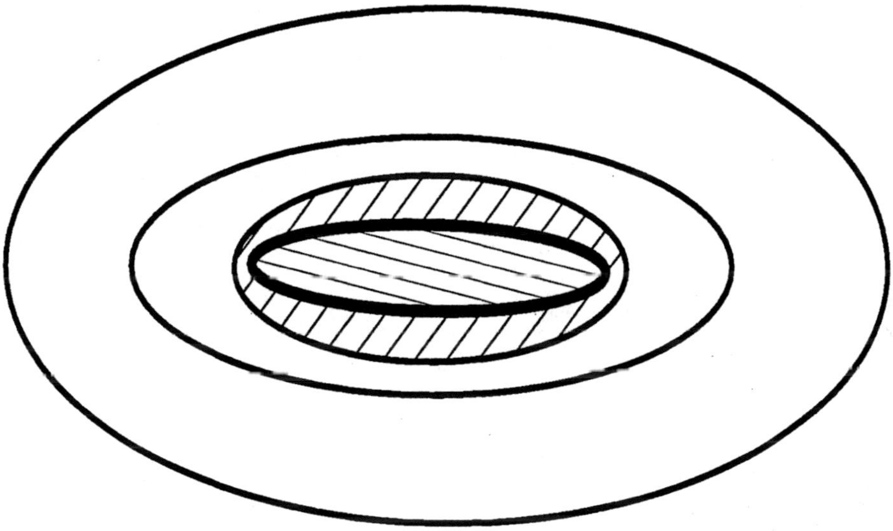

Figure 5.5: Peter Wegner extended the space of solvable problems from the one covered by Turing machines (most inner ellipse) into the one covered by interaction Turing machines (second most inner ellipse). Since the Church-Turing thesis for the last 50 years claimed that all problems solvable by universal Turing machines are precisely also the ones that are computable by humans, and weak AI claimed that humans are stronger than that, **the major thesis of weak AI has already been proven.**

Chapter 6

The Principle and Paradox of Multiple Knowledge

In previous parts of the book the idea of multiple knowledge was shortly introduced. Here we shall introduce the principle and paradox of multiple knowledge in a more formal way starting with a couple of definitions and later trying to formally prove the principle.

6.1 Basic Definitions

Definition 1: In the *measurement* or *observation space* X of *objects, tasks* or *events* $\vec{x}$, properties of a *problem domain* $\mathcal{D}$ are described in *description languages* $\mathcal{L} = \{\mathcal{L}_1, \mathcal{L}_2, \ldots\}$.

Definition 2: A *model* or a *system* ζ is a function which for any future task $\vec{x}$ from X with J possible solutions proposes a probability distribution of possible solutions (a vector)

$$\zeta : X \rightarrow [0..1]^J; \quad \vec{x} \mapsto (p_1, \ldots, p_J); \quad \sum_{i=1}^{J} p_i = 1, p_i \geq 0$$

or a single solution (one number from 1 to J, $C = \{1..J\}, c \in C$)

$$\zeta : \; X \rightarrow C; \quad \vec{x} \mapsto c.$$

In addition, a model has to represent at least a part of the real-life world we live in. An example of a model would be a decision tree for diagnosing patients, a list of rules for exchange rate prediction, a neural network recognizing familiar faces or a human evaluating the scientific value of this section. Note that the terms "model" and "system" are used as synonyms.

Definition 3: A *multiple model* ζ_M combines proposed solutions of m models from a set $M = \{\zeta_1, \zeta_2, \ldots \zeta_m\}$, all defined over the same space X

$$\zeta_M : X \to C; \quad \vec{x} \mapsto \mathcal{F}_{\zeta_j \in M}\{\zeta_j(\vec{x})\}$$

where $\mathcal{F}$ is the *combining function* or *combining mechanism.*

According to the above definitions, each single or multiple model performs as a classification or a prediction function. When a solution is proposed by such function, it can be the correct one (T) or not (F).

For example, if one system predicts class probability distribution $(0.3, 0.7, 0.0)$ of three possible solutions, the second system $(0.5, 0.3, 0.2)$, and the third system $(0.6, 0.1, 0.3)$, a normalized sum as one of possible combining functions $\mathcal{F}$ of a multiple system would be $(0.47, 0.37, 0.16)$. If the correct solution is the first one, then the first system failed (F) while the second, the third, and the multiple system succeeded (T).

Performance is usually estimated using the percentage of correctly performed testing tasks and is denoted by *accuracy.*

Multiplicity is a property of models designed for the same problem domain and tasks. Semantically, both models perform the same task and in general, each of the two can perform the task on its own. In terms of numbers, multiplicity of two models corresponds to the percentage of different proposed solutions.

In a given domain D, the probability of correct solution by model i is denoted by p_i, $0 < p_i < 1$ (to enable divisions in derivations). The probability that the function combining 2 or more models will predict the correct solution in a situation $\vec{s}$ is denoted by $q_{\vec{s}}$. For example, for two models in a situation where the first model succeeds (T) and the second fails (F), the probability that the combination will be successful is denoted by q_{TF} (see Table 6.1). It is assumed that $0 \leq q_{\vec{s}} \leq 1$, $q_{FF} = 0$, $q_{TT} = 1$. The last assumption is usually valid, however, there are combining mechanisms which can predict the correct solution even if single models predict wrong (i.e., $q_{FF} > 0$). In case of random guessing, $q_{TF} = q_{FT} = \frac{1}{2}$.

An example: Suppose the task is to diagnose patients. Each patient is described by age, sex, medical data, etc. These attributes define the measurement/description space X. One patient could be (John, Smith, 32, male, ...). The task is to classify the patient into the appropriate diagnosis ($\vec{x} \mapsto c$), e.g., John Smith has a flu (John Smith $\mapsto$ flu).

Each of the physicians can classify patients alone, with the help of a medical expert system, and in a mutual consultation. According to our definitions, a single physician corresponds to a single system/model, a physician and a medical expert system correspond to a combination of two systems (models) as well as two physicians together. Classification accuracy of all of these combinations can be measured and compared. Detailed analyses include specific cases, e.g., how often the first

$\vec{s}$	$p_{\vec{s}}$	$p_{\vec{s}}$, $d=0$	$p_{\vec{s}}$, $d=1$	$q_{\vec{s}}$
(F, F)	$(1-p_1)((1-d)(1-p_2)+d)$	$(1-p_1)(1-p_2)$	$1-p_1$	$q_{FF}(=0)$
(F, T)	$(1-p_1)(1-d)p_2$	$(1-p_1)p_2$	0	q_{FT}
(T, F)	$p_1(1-d)(1-p_2)$	$p_1(1-p_2)$	0	q_{TF}
(T, T)	$p_1((1-d)p_2+d)$	p_1p_2	p_1	$q_{TT}(=1)$

Table 6.1: Four possible situations for 2 models

physician fails and the second one classifies correctly (i.e., p_{TF}, since $\vec{s}=TF$) and how often in these cases a combination succeeds (q_{TF}).

Formal models (see Table 6.1) are introduced in order to determine the probability of correct solution of two combined independent or dependent models.

Definition 4: Models ζ_1 and ζ_2 are **independent** if their vectors of performances of testing tasks are independent (The probabilities of two independent events can be multiplied in order to get the probability of the combined event).

In reality, models are usually highly dependent since they typically use similar information.

Definition 5: A model ζ_2^* is **dependent** on a model ζ_1 if it gives the same result as ζ_1 with probability $d, d > 0$ and the same result as the independent model ζ_2 with probability $1-d$.

Hypothetically, the dependent model ζ_2^* can be split into a model identical to the first model ζ_1 and an independent model ζ_2. On the basis of given vectors of proposed solutions, the independent model can be constructed from $(1-d)$ proposed solutions which remain after d of the same proposed solutions by the two models are eliminated.

For better understanding, let us introduce two examples.

In Examples 1 and 2, the first row denotes the number of a consequent example. Each of the two single systems classifies on its own and for each example succeeds (T) or not (F). The two systems combined together classify according to the last row.

In Example 1 and Example 2, examples and classifications are grouped into quadruples to enable a simple verification by the reader. Each second quadruple is identical.

Example 1:

```
Examples      1 2 3 4     5 6 7 8     9 0 1 2     3 4 5 6
---------------------------------------------------------
system 1      T F T F  |  T F T F  |  T F T F  |  T F T F ...
```

$\vec{s}$	$p_{\vec{s}}$	$p_{\vec{s}}$, $d = 0$	$p_{\vec{s}}$, $d = 1$	$q_{\vec{s}}$
(F, F)	0.25	0.25	no	0
(F, T)	0.25	0.25	no	0.5
(T, F)	0.25	0.25	no	0.5
(T, T)	0.25	0.25	no	1

Table 6.2: Four possible situations for 2 models, Example 1

```
system 2       F F F F  |  T T T T  |  F F F F  |  T T T T ...
combination    T F F F  |  T T T F  |  T F F F  |  T T T F ...
```

The first system classifies correctly every odd object, and the second system classifies wrongly each odd quadruple of objects. Obviously, their classification accuracy is 0.5. From given sequences it follows that $p_{FF} = p_{FT} = p_{TF} = p_{TT} = 0.25$, and $p_1 = 0.5$. The classification accuracy of the second system ζ_2^* is also 0.5, but in order to fit the model we have to calculate d and classification accuracy p_2 of the independent system ζ_2. The numerical procedure (a Monte Carlo method with local optimization trying to minimize $\sqrt{(p_{\vec{s}}measured - p_{\vec{s}}fitted)^2})$ returns $d = 0, p_2 = 0.5$ meaning that the two systems are indeed independent. Although the procedure started with the general case presented in the second column in Table 6.1, the results correctly enable simplification corresponding to the third column. The quality of a combining mechanism is denoted in the fifth column of Table 6.1. In this example, the column is filled with $q_{FF} = 0, q_{TF} = q_{FT} = 0.5, q_{TT} = 1$. The corresponding changes of Table 6.1 are introduced in Table 6.2. The forth column is not relevant for Example 1.

Example 2:

```
Examples       1 2 3 4     5 6 7 8     9 0 1 2     3 4 5 6
-----------------------------------------------------------
system 1       T F T F  |  T F T F  |  T F T F  |  T F T F ...
system 2       T T F F  |  T F T F  |  T T F F  |  T F T F ...
combination    T T T F  |  T F T F  |  T T T F  |  T F T F ...
```

In this case, each second quadruple of the classifications in the second row repeats, one is independent and one is identical to the classifications in the first row. We are dealing with a dependent system. From this data it follows $p_{FF} = p_{TT} = \frac{3}{8} = 0.375$, $p_{FT} = p_{TF} = \frac{1}{8} = 0.125$, and $p_1 = 0.5$. The calculation returns $d = 0.5, p_2 = 0.5$ meaning that the second system is identical to the first one in $\frac{1}{2}$ of classifications and independent in the other half of classifications. The parameters of combining mechanism are: $q_{FF} = 0, q_{TF} = q_{FT} = q_{TT} = 1$. These numbers are

$\vec{s}$	$p_{\vec{s}}$	$p_{\vec{s}}$, $d=0$	$p_{\vec{s}}$, $d=1$	$q_{\vec{s}}$
(*F*, *F*)	0.375	no	no	0
(*F*, *T*)	0.125	no	no	1
(*T*, *F*)	0.125	no	no	1
(*T*, *T*)	0.375	no	no	1

Table 6.3: Four possible situations for 2 models, Example 2

presented in Table 6.3. The third and forth column in Table 6.3 are not relevant for Example 2.

In real-life examples, fitting is performed in a similar way.

Performance of any two systems/models can be represented through Table 6.1. E.g., the case of two physicians diagnosing patients fits to the form of above examples as well as to Table 6.1 no matter how physicians perform alone and together, which bias (Utgoff 1986) or which description language ($\mathcal{L}_i, \mathcal{L}_j$) they use.

6.2 The Principle of Multiple Knowledge

When constructing models, i.e. when constructing and storing knowledge about domain properties into a computer or a human, knowledge can be stored in a form of one model/process (ζ) or in a form of many models/processes (ζ_M).

Definition 6: The **"general" principle of multiple knowledge** states that *in order to obtain better performances in real-life domains, it is generally better to construct and combine several models than one model alone:*

$$performance(\zeta_M) \geq performance(\zeta)$$

The problem is how to design a reasonable combination. Here we assume that a combination of two models is constructed by a human expert.

In addition to the technical general principle, an extension towards general properties of intelligence is proposed.

Definition 7: The **"strong" principle of multiple knowledge** states that *multiple models are an integral and necessary part of intelligence in any machine or being:*

$$intelligentPerformance(\zeta_M) \geq 0$$

$$intelligentPerformance(\zeta) = 0.$$

In this way, intelligence is introduced as a property enabling better performance in real-life complex domains. Although both versions of the principle originate from a similar idea, it should be noted that they are dealing with two quite different levels. Computer-models multiplicity can be measured. Examples of such multiplicity are introduced in Examples 1 and 2, and in Figure 1 where we deal with combining single words from multiple pages. Intelligent multiplicity at the level relevant for the strong principle deals with meanings. There, we do not combine formal symbols but mental concepts and meanings. Still, the nature of the problem is up to a point similar – again we deal with combinatorial explosion when combining single items, and again computers cannot deal with it reasonably while humans can. Note that multiplicity alone does not guarantee intelligence – it is just a necessary condition.

A direct implication of the general version of the principle is that a sequential single model executable on the universal Turing machine (ENCAI-90) will not achieve as good performance as combined models in majority of real-life domains. The strong version implies that no Turing machine executing a single model (e.g., no computer system constructed as a single model) will be able to achieve intelligent performance.

The last statement does not directly imply that digital computers can not achieve intelligent behavior or that intelligence can not be formalized. Rather, it implies that real-life domains have different properties than formal domains which are well suited for single computational models. The principle declares that in real-life domains better performance will be obtained when constructing multiple models. Of course, the essential part is the combining algorithm. Currently, not much is known about that mysterious "algorithm" (i.e. the mysterious property of the human brain which may be algorithmic or not!). However, knowing one essential property (i.e. multiplicity) more about the whole process already enables an important step ahead. First of all, it enables us to start studying multiple models in computers and in humans. This new approach could enable new comprehensions which are unattainable with the classical formal viewpoint.

In analogy to physics, existing computer single-model-systems correspond to Newtonian models of the world. Intelligent computer systems have additional properties thus corresponding to relativistic models of the world valid near great masses or at high speeds, or atomic models of the world valid in specific circumstances. Our hypothesis is that among the special properties of intelligent systems multiplicity is one of the most relevant ones. Multiple models are very rare compared to all systems. If we are searching for them in the space of all possible systems without correctly assuming their special properties, it is highly unlikely that we find (construct) them.

Although the general and strong version differ substantially regarding the consequent part, they both represent a significant deviation from formal single computational models. Both versions of the principle are to be seen as an attempt to upgrade a general computational theory valid for the last 50 years. In this way, they represent a single principle of multiple knowledge.

6.3 The Paradox of Multiple Knowledge

Is not a set of models actually another model? Therefore, is there any difference if we are dealing with one single model or a model consisting of a set of submodels? For example, a set of trees can be transformed into one integrated tree in such a way that performance of the set of trees is identical to the performance of the integrated single tree. This seems to be in contradiction with the general thesis of multiple knowledge and represents a puzzle – the **"general" paradox of multiple knowledge.**

One reason, why one single integrated model can not achieve as good performance as multiple models is as follows: Each model tries to fit data and noise according to its own structure and therefore tries to impose its own view on the problem domain. During the construction phase, it is difficult to estimate which of the models has imposed the most appropriate structure for the unseen data, and different subparts of the measurement space are typically more suitable for different models. When combining or integrating single models it is usually not too difficult to eliminate unsuccessful parts of models.

The general thesis of multiple knowledge implies that by constructing only one model it is practically impossible to achieve the same performance as by multiple models. In other words, although multiple models can be at any time (with more or less effort) transformed into one single model with the same performance as a set of models, in general it is not possible to construct such a single model in the process of learning without designing multiple models (See Figure 6.1).

Integration of models after they are designed seems not only feasible but also sensible because of reduction in storage and classification time. After integration, experiments have shown not only decrease in complexity but also increase in classification accuracy (Kwok, Carter 1990).

What about the strong version? If intelligent models consist of multiple models and multiple models can be transformed into single models, then intelligent systems can be transformed into single models. According to school textbooks, all systems including intelligent ones can be executed by the Turing machine given enough time and space. Then, paradoxically, one can design intelligent systems with one single system. This **"strong" paradox of multiple knowledge** is related to the strong thesis of multiple knowledge.

There is an essential difference between copying, approximately simulating and actually performing intelligently. The Turing test is based on unexpected questions, which eliminate possibility that all sensible answers will be stored and reused. No doubt that all intelligent performance can be repeated after once performed. In analogy, every intelligent speech can be transformed into letters just as easily as

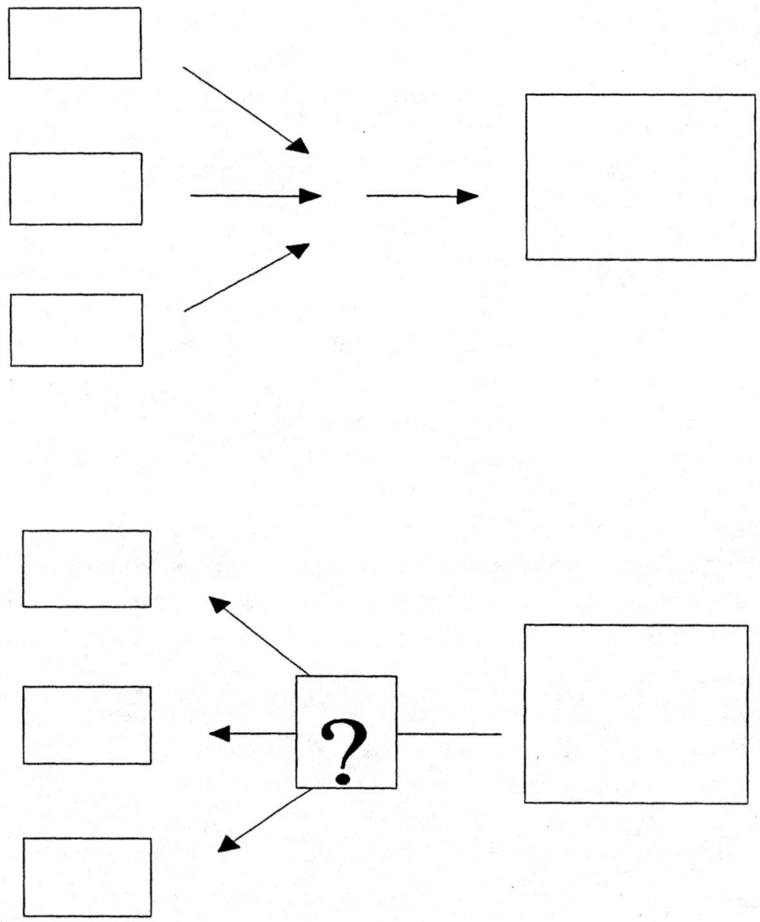

Figure 6.1: Paradoxes of multiple knowledge: theoretically, transformation in one direction is possible, however, future performance (i.e., intelligence) is lost in the world of single models.

random generated words. But in the world of all possible texts, only very rare have the special properties of intelligence. **An average random text (analogy – an average formal domain) and an average intelligent text (analogy – a real-life domain) are worlds apart – we humans easily distinguish that and the Turing test easily differentiates the two. Intelligence is the property of a very special subclass of systems, more particular – a special subclass of multiple systems.**

Chapter 7

Confirmations of the Principle

There are several indications that the principle is valid. A simple example – in communications the positive effect of using redundant bits is known for decades and even simple ID numbers in banking have additional digits in order to improve robustness of the whole system. Theoretical aspects of redundancy in such cases are described, e.g., in (Shannon, Weaver 1964).

In most every-day activities, people use multiple knowledge whenever there is any possibility of biasing (Utgoff 1986). It could be said that humans are intrinsically multiple, and that they apply multiplicity without paying much attention to that phenomenon. One of possible reasons is that multiple models are difficult to explain in speech or writing (sequential words), while multiple models have to be integrated for each single task anyway (because of the necessity and frequency of multiple thinking the whole process must be hardwired in the human brains) in order to preserve overall performance.

It is commonly accepted that cross-checking of several knowledge sources is generally better than using one source of knowledge alone. For example, when hiring a new employee, one checks several reports which are basically multiple (e.g. biography, recommendations etc.). When bringing an important decision, humans often discuss possibilities in groups of relevant people. A council of physicians is consulted when dealing with difficult or important cases. One physician suffices for most of normal activities since one is substantially cheaper than a group of them.

Attempts to confirm the principle of multiple knowledge were performed by:

- empirical learning (general version)
- simulations (general version)
- formal models (general version)
- fitting the model to a real-life practical application (general version)
- analogy with humans (strong version)

- related subjects in cognitive sciences and common sense (strong version), and
- quantum physics (both versions).

7.1 Multiple Knowledge in Empirical Learning

In empirical learning, models are designed from given data and weak or no prior knowledge. Performance is usually measured as the percentage of correct classifications of new examples. Classifiers correspond to systems, and classes to solutions.

Automatic knowledge construction from examples has proven useful in many practical tasks. Quite often, examples are described in terms of attributes and their values and each example belongs to a certain class. The task of the system is to induce concept descriptions from examples. First systems were designed for exact domains like chess end-games and constructed trees (ID3 – Quinlan 1983) or lists of rules (AQ11 – Michalski, Larson 1983). But in many real-life domains (Gams, Karalič 1989), because of noise or incomplete description (Manago, Kodratoff 1987) specialized mechanisms have to be applied. In noisy domains, longer rules (or longer branches in trees) perform better on learning examples while truncated rules (pruned trees with shorter branches) perform better on unseen examples. On the basis of this principle, the second group of inductive systems emerged (CART - Breiman et al. 1984; AQ15 – Michalski et al. 1986; ASSISTANT - Kononenko 1985; CN2 – Clark, Niblett 1989; C4 – Quinlan 1987).

Around ten years ago the third group of systems began emerging (GINESYS – Gams 1988; 1989; LOGART – Cestnik, Bratko 1988; new CN2 - Clark, Boswell 1991), hypothesis boosting (Schapire 1990), based on **the explicit use of multiple knowledge.** Each of these groups of systems usually achieves better performance than previous. **Better performance of multiple knowledge systems** was especially noticeable in classification accuracy, also in better comprehensibility (although more difficult to measure) when compared to the other two groups. At the same time, their efficiency remained similar to those in the second group.

Buntine (1989) combined 5 decision trees, which were all constructed by the same algorithm with the exception that the attribute at the top of the tree was each time forced to be different. The combination of 5 trees performed significantly better than any single tree. Later, Buntine (1990) overlapped several trees into one and again reported important improvements. Kwok and Carter (1990) have shown that it is very promising to combine a small set of good and as different as possible trees. Clark and Boswell (1991) constructed for each class a corresponding list of rules, and compared their combination with a single list of rules for all classes. Schapire (1990) showed that reasonable improvements are produced when boosting hypothesis. In all cases, significant improvements in classification accuracy were obtained.

These publications were accompanied and followed by tens of others (Michalski, Tecuci 1993; ML-93 1993, INF-17-4 1993). Among first distinguished events related to mutistrategy learning was a book edited by R. Michalski, G. Tecuci: *Machine Learning, A Multistrategy Approach*, (1994), specialised international workshops on multistrategy learning organized by George Mason University, special issue of Informatica (Tecuci 1993), and IJCAI-93 workshop on integration of machine learning and knowledge acquisition (Tecuci, Kedar, Kodratoff 1993).

There is one important general conclusion: **Successful combinations are quite different regarding the combining mechanism or the number of combined systems indicating that there must be a deeper cause for the improvement than just a lucky combination.**

7.1.1 Current Situation

General approaches in multi-strategy learning are described already in (Diettrich, 1997). In order to construct multiple models (i.e. systems), which are called *ensembles of classifiers* at that time, Diettrich identifies the following items, here slightly modified:

- **Subsampling the training examples**: A machine learning algorithm is run each time over different learning data subset from a bigger data set. In this way, different models (e.g. different decision trees) are obtained and finally combined together in the final classification. This technique is especially appropriate for unstable algorithms such as decision tree learners, rule-learning systems or neural networks, which can substantially change because of a small change in the input data. Stable learning algorithms are e.g. nearest-neighbor and linear regression which change only slightly if a small change in the input data occurs. Most common methods for generating subsets of learning data are *bagging, cross-validation committees* and *boosting*. In bagging, a subset is created by creating a sample of training examples randomly chosen with replacement from the original set. In cross-validation committees, learning subsets are created by leaving out disjoint parts of training data. In boosting, choosing the next set of learning data is similar to bagging, but in addition it depends on the success of previous classification. Wrongly classified examples get higher probability to be chosen next time.

- **Manipulating the input features and output targets**: Input data are described by specific features, usually a set of attributes. In a similar way, output can be defined in different ways with different output languages. By altering input and output descriptions, different models can be created.

- **Changing parameters of systems**: Each learning algorithm uses some set of parameters. By altering these parameters, systems create different sets of models, i.e. different decision trees or different neural networks. Diettrich sees here more important injection of randomness in the form of creating e.g. random good multiple-choices in one node.

- **Methods for generating multiple models:** Diettrich proposes here several algorithms for generating multiple models of neural networks. We prefer generalization of these approaches often first published for the back-propagation algorithm. One common algorithm is based on genetic algorithms that handle a set of multiple models (solutions) for a particular problem. Unlike basic genetic algorithms, this algorithm tries to create and finally combine a set of good single solutions. Other methods are based on competition between single solutions.

- **Methods for combining classifiers:** Basically, there are different kinds of voting, weighted or unweighted, and specific algorithms.

Diettrich tries to explain why multiple knowledge works. His reply is: *Uncorrelated errors made by the individual classifiers can be removed by voting.* The deeper question to him is why shouldn't we be able to find a single classifier capable of performing as well as the combined classifier. He proposes three replies, all technical explanations why multiple machine-learning algorithms perform better than single ones:

- The training data might not provide sufficient information for the best classifier, e.g. finding the best hypothesis. It might not be possible to construct the best hypothesis (knowledge model) from data by machine-learning algorithms.

- Machine-learning algorithms use some heuristics to create knowledge models. Therefore, it is usually not possible to find the best hypotheses. More likely it is possible to find parts of the best hypothesis or hypothesis similar to the best one.

- Classifiers separate the problem space into subspaces. It might be very difficult to find the best split corresponding to the best hypothesis. The task of finding specific subsplits might be more appropriate for specific systems.

The essence of this book is about the general principle and not in particular explanations in a particular AI field. We believe that the principle has been sufficiently proven in several scientific areas and that in machine learning the principle is very extensively methodologically and empirically verified. One should not get lost because of too many seemingly different technical solutions. Technical parameters and terms might be different in specific subareas, but the principle is the same.

Current state-of-the-art is described in the Machine Learning journal special issue on integrating multiple learned models for improving and scaling machine learning algorithms (Chan et al. 1999). Editors Chan, Stolfo and Wolpert set 1996 as a turning point in accepting integrating collective predictions of a set of models. They describe different techniques for integrating multiple learned models based on using different training data distributions, training over different partitions of the data, using different integrating schemata and different parameters. Practically all publications report important improvements in overall classification accuracy of the integrated model compared to the best single model. Here, we shall not go into technical details but rather briefly mention a couple of major approaches.

Merz and Pazzani (1999) integrate multiple base regression models by detecting correlation between models as well as detecting contributions of each particular model. Mertz (1999) does not only attach weights to each particular model as in the Merz and Pazzani paper, but also eliminates too correlated models (i.e. systems). It is generally accepted that more uncorrelated models produce better results than the more correlated (dependent) ones.

It is also getting generally accepted that a combination of systems (as claimed by us 10 years ago) is in general beneficial compared to the best single model. In machine learning community, similar improvements are observed in supervised and as well in the unsupervised models. Smyth and Wolpert (1999) show that a linear combination achieves superior results in real-life and artificial data. Different techniques such as stacking, bagging, boosting are described in several papers. Breiman (1999) in several publications describes various algorithms how to create different sets from the same data and use them for multiple systems. Bauer and Kohavi (1999) perform a large-scale empirical comparison of several algorithms for combining systems. Several systems and techniques are getting generally accepted such as the AdaBoost system (Freund, Schapire 1996; 1997).

Here we briefly describe a couple of basic algorithms according to (Bauer, Kohavi, 1999):

Bagging

The bagging algorithm (see Figure 7.1) generates different single models based on a specific subset of learning data. In most often version of bagging (Breiman 1966), each learning sample/subset from the whole learning dataset L is generated by randomly sampling n instances from the training set with replacement (i.e. the instance is just copied to the subset and remains as a potential candidate for further choices). A learning system/algorithm consists of inducer I and classifier C. The i-th single system/algorithm/dataset is denoted by index i. The final classifier combining M single classifier is C^*.

Note that for the implementation one basically needs just one L' instead of several L_i.

When picking one instance from a learning dataset L, each instance has $1/size(L)$ $1/n$ probability to get chosen. A bootstrap subsample has n items randomly chosen from the training set with replacement. For a given bootstrap sample of size n, each instance in the training set has a probability $1-(1-1/n)^n$ to appear at least once in the bootstrap sample (i.e. 1 - probability-that-it-does-not-appear-at-all). For large n, the expression comes close to $1-1/e) = 63.2\%$. This means that for large n, only

Input: training set L of size n, inducer I, no. of bootstrap samples M

```
for i := 1 to M do begin (* create M single classifiers*)
    create bootstrap sample L_i from L with replacements
    apply the inducer I on the bootstrap sample L_i to get C_i
end;
C* classifies to the class most often predicted by all C_i
```

Output: The multiple classifier C^* consisting of M single classifiers C_i (voting)

Figure 7.1: The Bagging algorithm.

63.3% of all instances appear in the learning subset. The above number is important to show that the subsample gets substantially different than the original sample and thus from other subsamples. Still, the difference is big enough only for unstable inducers such as decision-tree builders. Empirical measures have shown that bagging results in worse accuracy when applied to stable inducers such as nearest-neighbor algorithm. **That is no surprise at all - in bagging, stable inducers do not construct sufficiently different systems/models to exploit multiplicity.**

Cross-validation Committees

The cross-validation committees algorithm (see Figure 7.2) is based on cross-validation, a fairly classical method in statistics. The training dataset is split into M disjoint subsamples S_i as in cross-validation. Thus, an subsample has $1/M$ the size of the training dataset. Typically, M is set to 10, 20 or more. Then, create M overlapping training subsets L_i of size $1 - 1/M$ each time dropping a subsample S_i from L. Otherwise, the algorithm is very similar to bagging. Again, the difference in the learning data causes differences in the constructed classifiers. And since differences are in general bigger than in bagging, results are typically slightly better.

Boosting

Boosting was introduced by Schapire in 1990. Several versions were produced in the following years, including the AdaBoost algorithm (Freund, Schapire 1996). AdaBoost can be seen as a substantially modified version of bagging since it constructs different learning subsamples in a similar way as in bagging, creates inducers on these subsets and combines them together in the final multiple classifier. The major difference is that it uses weights attached to instances. Since these weights change in each bootstrap trial according to classifications in the previous trial, clas-

Input: training set L, inducer I, no. of bootstrap samples M

separate L into M disjoint subsets S_i
create M bootstrap samples $L_i = L - S_i$
for i := 1 to M do begin (* create M single classifiers*)
    apply the inducer I on the bootstrap sample L_i to get C_i
end;
C^* classifies to the class most often predicted by C_i (voting)

Output: Multiple classifier C^* consisting of M single classifiers C_i (voting)

Figure 7.2: The Cross-validation committees algorithm.

sifiers C_i can not be created in a parallel way as in bagging, but in a sequential way. Weights of misclassified instances/examples increase and thus these instances more likely appear (get covered) in the next classifier. In this way, bootstrap classifiers are forced to create different models. Classifier weights (i.e. their error estimates) are used also in the final classification. Better estimated classifiers are more important.

In Figure 7.3 we see the M1 version of AdaBoost as presented in (Bauer, Kohavi, 1999). As in boosting, some variables like L' and $error'$ can be used instead of indexed ones. If the inducer I can not deal with weights, then the bootstrap sample L_i can be generated by randomly sampling n instances (with replacement) proportional to weights in the training set.

AdaBoost works for a weak learning algorithm with error smaller than 1/2. The correction mentioned in the algorithm definition is therefore a program patch. Usually, authors try to repeat a kind of redo action (set weights to 1 again) to stabilize the system.

Several versions of the original algorithm were published, and several explanations were provided as to why the algorithm works (Drucker 1997). The puzzle is why give misclassified examples bigger weights, and why voting works better than a single best-estimated classifier. Being familiar with the principle of multiple knowledge, it is easy to comprehend that the more different the classifiers, the better results.

Arching

Breiman splits multiple-model machine-learning algorithms in two families:

- P&C family (Perturb and Combine), e.g. Bagging, and
- arc family (Adaptively Resample and Combine), e.g. AdaBoost.

Input: training set L, inducer I, no. of bootstrap samples M

> $L_0 := L$ with instance weights set to 1
> for i := 1 to M do begin (* create M single classifiers*)
>   create bootstrap sample L_i from L_{i-1}, $L_i = L_{i-1}$
>   apply the inducer I on the bootstrap sample L_i to get C_i
>   calculate the error by summing weights of false classifications:
> $error_i := \frac{1}{n} \sum_{x_j \in L_i : C_i(x_j) \not\succ y_j} weight(x)$
>   if $error_i > 0.5$ then correction
> $\beta_i = error_i / (1 - error_i)$
>   for each $x_j \in L_i$, if $C_i(x_j) = y_j$ then $weight(x_j) := weight(x_j)\beta_i$
>   normalize the weights of instances
>   so that the total weight of L_i is n
> end;
> C^* classifies to the class most often predicted by weighted C_i

Output: The multiple classifier C^* consisting of M single classifiers C_i voting proportional to the error estimate of each single classifier $log \frac{1}{\beta_i}$

Figure 7.3: The AdaBoost algorithm.

Breiman (1997) gives a plausible explanation why arching works. Instead of technical description of margins, weights and voting provided by Schapire et al. (1997), Breiman suggests that the improvement lies not in a specific form of AdaBoost but in its adaptive resampling property. To show his point, Breiman described what he calls an "ad hoc invention" – the Arc-x4 algorithm (Figure 7.4).

At ML conference at Bled (Bratko, Dzeroski 1999) and in several previous publications (Kohavi 1995; Alpaydin 1998; Ali, Pazzani 1994; Murphy, Pazzani 1994), several authors showed that several algorithms achieve similar improvements over single systems. Therefore, AdaBoost is neither the ultimate nor the unique multi-model ML system. However, its clear mathematical analysis is another very good confirmation that multiple knowledge works. With so many publications, algorithms and analyses showing that there indeed is an improvement when sensibly combining several systems/models, **empirical learning is one of them most strictly verified domains confirming the principle of multiple knowledge.**

7.1.2 Our Measurements

Our measurements are around a decade old and a little arcane from today's viewpoint. But their importance lies in the fact that we were among the first to empirically show improvements due to the use of multiple knowledge. Although we managed to present our results in various publications and at various occasions

Input: training set L, inducer I, no. of bootstrap samples M

for i := 1 to M do begin (* create M single classifiers*)
  Create bootstrap sample L_i from S
  by setting weight of x to $1 + e(x)^4$,
  normalized to $total - weight(L_i) = n$,
  where $e(x)$ is the number of misclassification
  made on x by classifiers C_1 to C_{i-1}.
  Apply the inducer I on the bootstrap sample L_i to get C_i
end;
C^* clasifies to the class most often predicted by C_i (voting)

Output: The multiple classifier C^* consisting of M single classifiers C_i voting without weights

Figure 7.4: The Arc-x4 algorithm.

(Gams 1988; Gams 1989), the replies were mixed then.

- First group of researchers supported the idea and further developed into specific directions such as multistrategy learning.

- Another group with strong statistical and pattern-matching background strongly opposed the idea claiming that the best solution is just one single model, and that the improvement is not coming from integration of many. This of course corresponds to the paradox of multiple knowledge to which our repy is already addressed.

- The common-sense oriented group generally accepted the idea that more systems are helpful (more heads know more), but also claimed that the improvement comes from combining different knowledge since each model has its particular knowledge nonexistent in all other modules. This is not the main issue of our principle since obviously one gets improvements by adding additional knowledge. The main point of our principle is that computing/thinking must be multiple and that even with the same amount of knowledge, e.g. in our head, better results are obtained if we combine multiple solutions about the same problem.

Whatever the case, our measurements were not generally accepted as identifying multiple knowledge as the source of improvement. By repeating these extended benchmarks we want to show that our conclusions were valid already a decade ago.

Around ten years ago, we had tested several systems on real-life domains (Gams *et al.* 1991). Our efforts to outperform statistical systems were fruitless until we started to combine systems. Typically, when the chosen AI system classified with great confidence, its classification was accepted. Otherwise, the statistical system prevailed. Since then a version of combined system achieved the best classification accuracy of around 30 tested systems.

With measurements presented in this section we gave additional arguments for successfulness of multiple knowledge by explicitly measuring the influence of the number of learning examples and the influence of noise, as well as the influence of the error estimate and impurity functions. The basic idea that multiple knowledge enables better performance was first presented at the European conference on machine learning (Gams: New measurements highlight the importance of redundant knowledge, 1989).

GINESYS

GINESYS (Generic INductive Expert SYstem Shell) is one of the oldest systems actively utilizing multiple knowledge representations (Gams 1988). It consists of two systems (i.e. methods), one from AI and one from statistics. There were sensible reasons for combining methods from different fields. First of all, artificial intelligence methods enable construction of knowledge bases which are typically very transparent and understandable; therefore, it was hoped that a combination would still be more understandable than statistical methods. A statistical method was chosen on the basis of the hypothesis that knowledge representations should be as different as possible.

GINESYS utilizes two different strategies on the basis of these two systems: the AI system constructs and consults lists of rules, and the statistical system multiplies probabilities according to the distribution of classes corresponding to each attribute of the tested example. Both single systems already implicitly utilize multiple knowledge – the AI part through a couple (typically 5) of rules attached to each main one which are triggered when classifying, and the statistical part through combining probabilities relating to the value of each attribute of the tested example.

The AI part of GINESYS is named INESYS (see Figure 7.5). It reimplements many of mechanisms of the ID3 and AQ (CN2) family of algorithms. It was primarily designed as an attempt to fully simulate the family of ID3 and AQ inductive empirical learning systems (Gams, Lavrač 1987). Theoretically, it simulates N^M different algorithms where M is the number of modules of the algorithm and N is the number of variations of each module (Gams 1989). The actual number of different variations of GINESYS can be estimated to several hundreds.

INESYS constructs rules with a beam search over all possible combinations of attributes. In addition, it utilises several search-guiding and error-estimate functions such as informativity, the Gini index, Laplacean error estimate and significance. Due to elaborate mechanisms for noise handling, INESYS typically constructs a small number of short rules, i.e. with a small number of attributes. For example, on average, 5.1 main rules with 1.4 attributes in a rule were constructed in lymphography. In primary tumor, there were 11.0 main rules with 2.3 attributes in a rule. Therefore, a typical rule had the form:

$if(A_i = v_{ij})\&(A_k = v_{kl})\ then\ Distribution_n$
where

- $(A_i = v_{ij})$ is a Boolean test whether attribute i has value j, and
- $Distribution_n$ is a class probability distribution corresponding to the condition part of the rule.

A general description of INESYS is:

```
repeat
  construct Rule(s);
  add Rule(s) to d;
  L := L - ExamplesCoveredByRule
until  satisfiable d
```

where L is the set of learning examples, d is constructed knowledge in the form of trees or lists of rules and $Rule(s)$ is one or many branches in a tree or one or many rules in the list of rules. A procedural description of INESYS is presented (see Figure 7.5) – d is the constructed knowledge in the form of an ordered list of ordered lists of rules, *Star* and *BestRules* are ordered lists of rules and L is the set of learning examples. NP is a rule with an uninstantiated complex and class probability distribution of L.

In INESYS, the main improvement regarding existing rule-based systems are rules attached to the main rule. The aim of these multiple rules is twofold. First, to give the user more rules and thus more opportunities to analyze the laws of the domain. Second, to improve classification accuracy by cross-checking the matched rule with confirmation rules. This mechanism already enables the use of multiple knowledge to a certain degree:

```
if Complex1 then Class1
   (Complex11 then Class11
        ........
    Complex1R then Class1R)
   else if Complex2 then Class2
          (Complex21 then Class21
               ........
           Complex2R then Class2R)
```

Classification in INESYS starts by sequentially checking main rules. When the first main rule matches a new example, corresponding multiple rules that match the

```
d := (()); (*d is initialised*)
repeat
  Star := (NP); BestRules := (NP);
  repeat
    for all Rule_j from Star generate all specialisations
    NewRule_i that do not fulfil the stopping criteria;
    Star := ();
    put into Star at best MAXSTAR the best NewRule_i
    evaluated by user defined impurity function;
    from rules in BestRules and significant NewRule_i choose
    the best MAXBEST rules, evaluated by user defined
    error estimate function, and put them into BestRules
  until Star is empty;
  add BestRules into d;
  L := L - examples, covered by the best evaluated rule from
  BestRules
until L is empty
```

Figure 7.5: The INESYS algorithm.

new example add their class probability distribution according to the formula for the union of independent events

$$p_{12} = p_1 + (1 - p_1) \times p_2.$$

Probabilities are multiplied by error estimates in order to calibrate the effect of rules with different credibility, and finally normalized. There are two threshold parameters that present a heuristic estimate of the goodness of classification by a rule: the smallest necessary percentage of the majority class (MINACC) and the smallest difference between the percentage of the majority class and the second to majority class (MINDIFF). Each constructed rule in GINESYS has to satisfy both conditions. Parameter MINDIFF additionally affects the classification process in the sense that the class probability distribution of a combined main and confirmation rules must satisfy it.

The second method in GINESYS is the approximation of the Bayesian classifier which assumes independence of attributes. It is often referred to as "naive Bayes" (Good 1950), in this paper also "Bayes". Naive Bayes constructs all possible rules with only one attribute in the complex. Therefore, the form of these rules is:

$$if(A_i = v_{ij})\ then\ Distribution_n.$$

The classification schema is as follows: all rules, that match a new example, are taken in consideration. The probability of each class c is computed by the following formula:

$$P(c|A) = P_a(c) \times (P(A_1|c)/P_a(A_1)) \times \dots$$
$$\times (P(A_v|c)/P_a(A_v))$$

where $P(c|A)$ denotes probability of class c given attributes and values A of the tested example, $P_a(c)$ denotes the a priori probability of class c, $P(A_i|c)$ the probability that attribute A_i has the same value as the classified example regarding the class c, $P_a(A_i)$ the same as before, but regardless of class, and v is the number of attributes. By calculating probabilities of all classes by, a class probability is obtained. Therefore, although naive Bayes constructs rules similar to INESYS, in the process of classification all attributes are considered in Bayes and on average only around two in INESYS.

Cooperation between the AI and the statistical system is relevant only when they propose different classes. In that case, goodness of triggered rules in INESYS is estimated by the simple heuristics mentioned above. If goodness of combined rules exceeds the value of a given threshold (parameter MINDIFF), classification by INESYS is adopted. Otherwise, the classification by naive Bayes prevails. In other words: If class probability distribution of combined rules is estimated as unreliable, the statistical method is called as a supervisor to decide which class is estimated as the most probable.

The combining schema is based on the following reasoning: When multiple rules confirm the main ones, classification is very likely to be correct. If a significant disagreement occurs then the list of rules is not credible and the other method using different knowledge representation should be consulted. It was expected that short rules constructed by INESYS will be more successful when they have high confidence in their prediction, and the approximation of the Bayesian classifier to be more successful when dealing with difficult cases where truncated rules capturing the main and most important laws of the domain are not predicting with great certainty.

Benchmarking

Since 1987, systematic measurements were performed on two oncological domains, lymphography and primary tumor (Clark, Niblett 1989; Michalski et al. 1986; Cestnik, Bratko 1988; Gams 1988). Data were obtained from real patients from the Oncological institute Ljubljana (Kononenko 1985).

Domain Description

Basic statistics of the whole set of data are:

LYMPHOGRAPHY
18 attributes
2 – 8 (average 3.3) values per attribute

SYSTEM	LYMPHOGRAPHY			PRIMARY TUMOR		
	class.acc.	no.rules	no.att.	class.acc.	no.rules	no.att.
GINESYS*	70.5	5.1	7	52.2	11.0	25
GINESYS	70.5	5.1	7	52.0	11.0	25
BAYES	68.6	56.0	56	50.1	37.0	37
CN2-new1	68.7			50.3		
GB*	67.4	5.1	7	47.6	11.0	25
CN2-new1'	65.6			46.9		
NEAREST NEIG.	72.9			40.4		
C4.5-rules	64.7			38.2		
C4.5-trees-u	63.1			48.9		
C4.5-trees-p	66.7			48.8		
CN2-like1	67.3	4.8	8	48.7	11.4	27
CN2-like1'	66.1	5.0	6	45.6	10.8	22
ID3-like	61.8	25.0	110	48.7	28.6	129
CN2-like2	66.8	10.8	21	45.7	19.3	70
CN2-like2'	65.0	9.4	16	46.2	19.4	68
AQ-like1	60.6	7.0	80	48.8	16.0	423
AQ-like2	55.2	7.0	80	32.0	16.0	423

Table 7.1: Benchmarking systems on two oncological domains.

9 classes
150 examples
distribution: 2 1 12 8 69 53 1 4 0
all examples differ even if one attribute is deleted

PRIMARY TUMOR
17 attributes
2 – 3 (average 2.2) values per attribute
22 classes
339 examples
distribution: 84 20 9 14 39 1 14 6 0 2 28 16 7 24 2 1 10 29 6 2 1 24
75 examples in the data set have another example with the same values of attributes and different class; if we delete one attribute, this number is: 114 111 81 122 84 75 93 79 97 91 77 83 76 77 79 94 94

LYMPHOGRAPHY			PRIMARY TUMOR		
FUNC.	INESYS**	GINESYS**	FUNC.	INESYS**	GINESYS**
AB	68.4	69.7	BA	48.3	52.3
GB	67.4	69.9	BG	48.1	51.8
BB	66.4	70.8	GB	47.6	52.0
BG	62.6	68.4	AB	46.6	51.3
BA	62.4	68.4	BB	46.4	52.5

Table 7.2: Accuracy under different impurity and error estimate functions.

Benchmarked Systems

On the benchmark domains, around 30 AI and statistical systems were compared over more than half of a decade. All the systems were given the same set of 10 random distributions of data, each time taking 70% of data for learning and 30% of data for testing. Results of relevant systems are presented in Table 7.1. The row in the middle of the Table divides multiple and single systems, i.e. those that use only one rule or combine many rules during one classification.

GINESYS* is a version of GINESYS using "negation" multiple rules, which try to confront the main rule if possible. BG* is GINESYS* without the statistical method, i.e. INESYS with functions B and G (see Table 7.2). First nearest neighbor algorithm classifies with the class of the nearest neighbor where distance is measured by the number of attributes with different values. BAYES is an approximation of the Bayesian classifier using an assumption that attributes are independent. ID3-like is a version of the ASSISTANT system using cross-validation pruning. CN2-like systems are different modifications of the CN2 algorithm, and CN2-new systems are newer versions. C4.5-rules constructs rules, C4.5-trees-u unpruned trees, and C4.5-trees-p pruned trees. AQ-like systems are modifications of the AQ15 systems.

Classification accuracy (column 1 in each domain in Table 7.1) was measured as an average percentage of correct classifications in ten test runs. The second column in each domain represents the average number of rules in a rule list or branches in the tree. The third column is a product of the number of rules (branches) times the average length of a rule (branch) times the number of internal disjunctions.

The relations between systems are similar to those observed in other measurements (Clark, Niblett 1989; Rendell et al. 1987; Rendell et al. 1988). Systems of the AQ family usually achieve lower classification accuracy than CN2 or ASSISTANT, while ASSISTANT and CN2 achieve similar classification accuracy. AQ-like1

LYMPHOGRAPHY	% OF LEARNING EXAMPLES						
SYSTEM	20%	30%	40%	50%	60%	70%	80%
GINESYS	52.8	58.2	63.1	63.7	60.1	70.5	75.3
BAYES	52.8	59.3	60.8	61.2	58.2	68.6	72.1
INESYS	39.2	51.7	54.1	62.6	59.0	67.4	74.3
ASSISTANT	53.9	60.5	57.9	57.5	55.2	62.1	65.2
ASSIST 0	53.2	60.7	57.4	57.8	55.9	62.4	66.8

Table 7.3: Accuracy in lymphography at different percentages of learning data.

represents an estimate of the upper possible classification accuracy of the rules, constructed by the AQ-like system. BAYES achieved better results than other systems except GINESYS. Nearest neighbor algorithm seems to be very domain dependent. GINESYS achieved the best average classification accuracy over both domains.

AQ-like systems construct more complex rules than other systems. However, the third column might be misleading for tree constructing algorithms like ID3-like because it represents tree as a list of separated branches. GINESYS* and GINESYS are measured only by the main rules and not by the multiple ones. On the other side, from the results in Table 7.1 it follows that systems like GINESYS and CN2 construct smaller number of shorter main rules while AQ-like systems construct more complex rules.

The efficiency of the benchmarked algorithms was also analyzed. AQ systems are about an order of magnitude slower than ASSISTANT, CN2 and GINESYS, and these are about an order of magnitude slower than BAYES. Results are similar to other measurements when having in mind that our versions of CN2 and GINESYS use a data compression mechanism which speeds up the algorithm roughly five times. GINESYS PC, another version of GINESYS, runs on IBM PC computers and is available as a free scientific software.

Varying Impurity and Error Estimate Functions

In order to verify whether improvements in GINESYS were caused by multiple knowledge or by domain-dependent parameters, several parameters were varied, and functions were the first among them. GINESYS uses two different groups of functions: informativity functions and error estimate functions. Informativity functions strategically guide search by trying to determine the amount of impurity. Error estimate functions try to estimate classification error. Four functions were used in all 16 possible combinations in each domain. Classification accuracy of GINESYS

P. TUMOR	% OF LEARNING EXAMPLES						
SYSTEM	20%	30%	40%	50%	60%	70%	80%
GINESYS (G)	41.9	44.6	48.1	49.0	48.1	52.0	52.3
BAYES (B)	41.8	45.2	47.5	48.0	47.2	50.1	50.3
INESYS (I)	26.9	35.6	33.8	43.5	41.2	45.9	46.7
ASSISTANT (A)	39.8	43.5	43.5	45.9	44.3	47.9	49.2
ASSIST 0 (A0)	39.6	41.6	39.9	41.1	39.6	41.3	41.7

Table 7.4: Accuracy in primary tumor at different percentages of learning data (table).

with (GINESYS**) and without (INESYS**) top-level multiple knowledge was compared. In Table 7.2 we present only the best three combinations of INESYS** in both domains. The four functions used were: I – informativity (Quinlan 1986); A – % of majority class; G – Gini index (Breiman et al. 1984); B - Laplacean error estimate (Niblett, Bratko 1986). The first letter denotes the impurity function and the second letter the error estimate function.

Measurements presented in Table 7.2 indicate that Laplacean error estimate is one of the most successful functions used for impurity or error estimates. Informativity is unexpectedly not present in the best three combinations. Default functions for GINESYS systems (GB) were taken in advance from the literature (Breiman et al. 1984).

Varying Percentage of Learning Examples

Benchmarks were performed on 10 distributions of data each time taking 70% of data for learning and 30% of data for testing. In Table 7.3 and 7.4 we varied the percentage of learning data from 20% to 80% and used the remaining data for testing. Systems are denoted as in column 1 of Table 7.4. ASSIST 0 is ASSISTANT without pruning and INESYS is GINESYS without the statistical method.

Probably the main reason for unproportionally low classification accuracy of INESYS with small number of learning examples are functions which work well only with several ten examples. But even then there are some cases when INESYS classifies better than BAYES. The combining mechanism usually decides well when to choose the right method. The performance of INESYS increases with the number of learning examples, and the gain of GINESYS over BAYES also proportionally increases. In lymphography, ASSISTANT prunes the tree by approximately 50% and achieves very similar classification accuracy as ASSIST 0. In primary tumor,

LYMPHOGRAPHY	% OF ADDITIONAL NOISE						
SYSTEM	0%	1%	5%	10%	20%	35%	50%
GINESYS	70.5	65.3	63.7	53.1	43.8	28.9	21.1
BAYES	68.6	65.8	61.7	51.1	41.8	28.0	20.7
INESYS	67.4	63.4	59.1	53.0	41.4	30.3	25.4
ASSISTANT	62.1	60.2	52.8	34.1	33.3	23.4	18.4
ASSIST 0	62.4	60.5	51.8	41.6	29.9	23.5	17.6

Table 7.5: The influence of additional noise – lymphography.

P. TUMOR	% OF ADDITIONAL NOISE					
SYSTEM	0%	1%	5%	10%	20%	35%
GINESYS (G)	52.0	50.6	42.6	35.2	23.5	13.8
BAYES (B)	50.1	47.8	40.3	33.5	23.6	13.9
INESYS (I)	45.9	43.5	36.2	30.7	20.0	16.1
ASSISTANT (A)	47.9	44.9	39.4	30.5	16.7	8.4
ASSIST 0 (A0)	41.3	39.1	32.4	25.3	14.5	8.7

Table 7.6: The influence of additional noise – primary tumor.

the pruned tree constructed by ASSISTANT is roughly 4 times smaller than the tree of ASSIST 0 which besides constructing more complex trees also achieves lower classification accuracy.

The improvement of GINESYS over the best of its two subparts was typically around 1-2% leading to a conclusion that the combining mechanism performed well when changing the number of learning examples.

Varying Additional Noise

Noise was introduced into the lymphography and primary tumor domain to attributes and classes in the learning and test examples. For example, 1% of noise means that, on average, each hundred's value of attribute and each hundred's class was randomly changed in learning and test data. Average results of 10 tests are presented in Tables 7.5 and 7.6.

When the amount of noise increases, the performance of INESYS relatively improves and achieves even better classification accuracy that GINESYS. As expected, in a very noisy situation, a small number of short rules performs the best. Similar effect is noticeable in the lymphography domain especially compared to ASSISTANT and is probably connected to the fact that ASSISTANT constructs a tree of several tens of leaves while INESYS constructs from 2 to 5 rules. With a growing amount of noise, the gain of GINESYS slowly decreases but remains around 2% as long as any rule of INESYS can be trusted as the meaningful one.

More Measurements

In further attempts to verify the obtained results presented in previous sections, GINESYS and benchmark data were around six years ago sent to over 50 laboratories and declared to be freely available for scientific purposes. The obtained answers can be clustered into two groups: several laboratories benchmarked systems on the proposed two domains, or at least approved the approach. On the other hand, there were some researchers who considered proposed benchmarking of classification accuracy as a numerical measurement belonging to statistics. In their opinion, artificial intelligence methods should be evaluated mainly at the level of ideas. Indeed, measuring only classification accuracy does not consider several important advantages of artificial intelligence, e.g., the transparency of the constructed knowledge base or the comprehensibility of classifications. However, since then there has been a constant shift in a direction which accepts such verifications as crucial in evaluating quality.

In 1992 we had received a report of a system (NAIVE BAYES*, Cestnik 1992), which achieved better accuracy than GINESYS in both domains (54.1% in primary tumor and 70.9% in lymphography). The improvement was based on a correction of the weakness of NAIVE BAYES which happens whenever there is a gap in the data, meaning there is no example with the particular value of the attribute. Then, one factor in the product becomes 0 and the resulting product becomes 0. This was already observed in (Gams, Drobnič 1988; Gams et al. 1991) where ϵ was used instead of 0. In NAIVE BAYES*, the Laplacean estimate is introduced for a correction instead of ϵ.

The reported improvements enabled additional experiments in trying to construct a multiple system, achieving even better classification accuracy. In the first attempt, NAIVE BAYES* was directly embedded into GINESYS, but the observed classification accuracy was lower than that of NAIVE BAYES*. Obviously, a smaller number of stronger rules had to be constructed since NAIVE BAYES* achieved significantly better classification accuracy than GB. Several parameters in GINESYS deal with rules, such as significance (Kalbfleish 1979), modified Laplacean error estimate (Niblett, Bratko 1986) or MINDIFF and MINACC. In the second attempt, MINDIFF was set to 0.5 instead of the previous 0.3, and MINACC to 0.7. Consequently, GINESYS90 achieved an additional 0.8% increase in primary tumor and 1.3% in lymphography over NAIVE BAYES*. Later it was found that the values of MINACC and MINDIFF belong to the set of optimal combinations, as can be observed in Tables 7.8 and 7.9.

SYSTEM	LYMPHOGRAPHY			PRIMARY TUMOR		
	class.acc.	no.rules	no.att.	class.acc.	no.rules	no.att.
INESYS90	63.7	3.8	7	36.3	6.9	19
NAIVE BAYES*	70.9	56.0	56	54.1	37.0	37
GINESYS90	72.2	59.6	63	54.9	44.3	56

Table 7.7: Accuracy, number of rules, number of all attributes.

The updated versions of NAIVE BAYES and GINESYS achieve the best two classification accuracies (compare Table 7.1 and 7.7). The percentage of corrections by NAIVE BAYES was 8% in lymphography and 27% in primary tumor in GINESYS and, correspondingly, 25% and 45% in GINESYS90.

New values of parameters MINDIFF and MINACC force GINESYS90 to construct a smaller number of longer rules. Also, rules are usually roughly twice more often corrected by NAIVE BAYES* than in GINESYS. To a great extent, this is due to the increased average number of classifications performed by the null or uninstantiated rule, i.e. the last rule in a rule list. This number increased from 9.2 to 15.9 in lymphography (45 classifications), and from 18.0 to 55.1 in primary tumor (102 classifications). Understandably, the last uninstantiated rule is always considered as unreliable in GINESYS and GINESYS90. But in the INESYS and INESYS90 algorithm, the classification is still performed by corresponding null-rule class distribution which is typically only slightly better than the default rule. Therefore, it is understandable that on average accuracy of INESYS90 decreased from 67.4% to 63.7% in lymphography and more, from 45.9% to 36.3% in primary tumor. This should not blur the fact that the effective part of INESYS90 which takes part in classifications of GINESYS90 actually achieves better classification accuracy than INESYS.

The influence of the MINDIFF and the MINACC parameters on the classification accuracy of GINESYS90 was further measured, and it was found that there is a wide range of possible combinations which enable similar improvements (see Table 7.8 and Table 7.9).

The x-axis in Tables 7.8 and 7.9 corresponds to MINACC and the y-axis corresponds to MINDIFF ranging from 0.1 to 0.9. The second column of classification

	LYMPHOGRAPHY									
MINACC ↓	MINDIFF →	.1	.2	.3	.4	.5	.6	.7	.8	.9
.9	71.0	+								
.8	72.0	$\heartsuit$							$\heartsuit$	+
.7	71.6	+								
.6	72.0	$\heartsuit$						$\heartsuit$	+	+
.5	72.2	$\heartsuit$				$\heartsuit$	$\heartsuit$	$\heartsuit$	$\heartsuit$	+
.4	70.2	−			−	−		−	+	
.3	70.7	−		−			−	−	+	+
.2	70.2	−								
.1	68.2	−				−			+	

Table 7.8: Influence of the goodness criterion, GINESYS90, lymphography.

accuracies in each Table represents accuracy with current MINDIFF and MINACC <= MINDIFF. Each mark in Tables 7.8 and 7.9 represents one ten-runs measurement as follows (in percents):

− bellow 70.9 in lymphography, bellow 54.1 in primary tumor

+ between 70.9 and 71.9, between 54.1 and 54.6 correspondingly and,

$\heartsuit$ over 71.9 (+1) in lymphography and over 54.6 (+0.5) in primary tumor.

Top-level or global multiplicity in any version of GINESYS can be estimated by the percentage of different classifications of both single systems. In Table 7.10, it is presented for GINESYS90 in both domains with MINDIFF = 0.3 and 0.5 (MINDIFF − MINACC) on training and testing examples. Note that in this section we deal with low-level multiplicity relevant for the general version of the principle of multiple knowledge.

Let us measure the internal multiplicity of each monostrategy system. INESYS90 constructs a list of sublists of rules. However, the order of rules is important and the confirmation rules are attached to the main rules. Therefore, each sublist of rules corresponds to a particular subset of training data and there seems to be no natural way to extract many models such that each covers the whole measurement space. On the other hand, rules in both NAIVE BAYES and NAIVE BAYES* have the form

$if(A_i = v_{ij})\ then\ Distribution_n$

	PRIMARY TUMOR									
MINACC ↓	MINDIFF →	.1	.2	.3	.4	.5	.6	.7	.8	.9
.9	54.3	+								
.8	54.3	+							+	
.7	54.3	+							+	
.6	54.5	+							+	
.5	54.9	♡				♡	♡	♡	+	
.4	53.5	−			−	−		−	+	
.3	53.6	−		−						
.2	53.1	−								
.1	51.9	−				−		−	+	+

Table 7.9: Influence of the goodness criterion, GINESYS90, primary tumor.

and are constructed on the whole training data. Therefore, a list of rules with the same attribute and all possible values of that attribute represents one model covering the whole measurement space. The average percentage of different classifications of each such model and the combined model is presented in Table 7.11. It should be observed that the same single models/systems are used in NAIVE BAYES and NAIVE BAYES*, but they are differently combined. Whatever the case, both NAIVE BAYES and NAIVE BAYES* can be regarded as internally consisting of multiple models. Furthermore, these knowledge subbases are quite independent of each other, although they are constructed on the same training data.

MINDIFF	LYMPHOGRAPHY		PRIMARY TUMOR	
	train	test	train	test
0.3	28	26	28	34
0.5	26	29	44	49

Table 7.10: Percentage of different classifications,
i.e. top-level or global multiplicity in GINESYS90.

SYSTEM	LYMPHOGRAPHY		PRIMARY TUMOR	
	train	test	train	test
NAIVE BAYES	48	50	72	70
NAIVE BAYES*	44	46	65	66

Table 7.11: Percentage of different classifications in BAYES, i.e. internal multiplicity.

Overall, finding a reasonable combination of the two models, i.e. GINESYS90, took only one day of work and resulted in achieving an average 1% increase in classification accuracy. The amount of efforts needed was evidently small because only already existing systems had to be modified.

Discussion of our Measurements

These measurements started more than 10 years ago and led to the introduction of the general principle of multiple knowledge. The measurements represent one of the longer-lasting measurements regarding multiple knowledge.

In our measurements, **classification accuracy of the combined model was typically better than the accuracy of each single model when varying system parameters (form and number of multiple rules, goodness of rules, factor of significance, impurity functions, error estimate functions) and domain parameters (percentage of training and testing data, percentage of additional noise)**. In this section we presented over 200 measurements each time averaging 10 tests. If we delete measurements with more than 20% of additional noise and those with less than 70 learning examples, we obtain 167 measurements with only 3 cases where (a version of) GINESYS has not achieved the best classification accuracy. The improvement was typically around 1%.

Besides better classification accuracy, improved explainability and understandability were also reported. Indeed, the informativity of the model with multiple rules seems to be much better than without them. Multiple rules can be trimmed off and a "usual" model is obtained as a downgraded version. Since a user can define the number of multiple rules, the preference function and other parameters, it enables a thorough extradition of most valuable rules. The efficiency of the learning algorithms remains practically the same when using multiple knowledge.

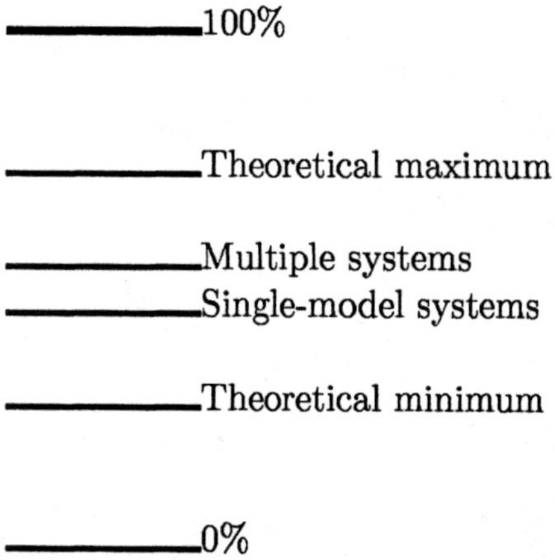

Figure 7.6: Shemantical relations between classification accuracies of different types of systems.

7.1.3 Discussion Regarding ML

While research on monostrategy methods and one-level knowledge representations continues to be of great importance to the machine learning community, the interest and amount of research work in multistrategy learning and multiple knowledge representations rapidly increased in 1990s. Expansion is accompanied by great diversification and new approaches.

It is safe to conclude that in real-life circumstances multiple systems enable greater competence than monostrategy systems relying on one knowledge representation and one computing mechanism. On the other hand, multiple systems demand more understanding of capacities, limitations and cooperation between single systems. Due to the constant growth of computer power, problems with speed and memory limitations have to a great extend diminished, thus enabling study and design of multiple computer systems bringing the focus to essential research and engineering computing questions.

In summary, empirical results show the following relations (see Figure 7.6): In real-life domains, no system achieves 100% classification accuracy since there is always noise, and all kinds of inconsistencies and unexpected errors. There is a theoretical – Bayesian limit of classification accuracy in each domain. Practical empirical results show that the best multiple systems achieve the best classification accuracy approaching the theoretical limit. The best single systems are close to the best multiple systems. Other systems follow. There is also a limit to the lowest possible classification accuracy. For example, when tossing a coin and betting on one side, it is theoretically and practically impossible that we always win or always lose on a long run. Differences between reasonable systems are usually small, e.g. a couple of percents. In our experience, the best and the worst systems achieve

20-30% different classification accuracy.

Similar conclusions were reported in related areas, e.g., in pattern recognition when combing classifiers in handwriting recognition (Xu *et al.* 1992). There, several algorithms for combining have been designed, from combining a Bayesian classifier and a k-NN classifier, different voting schemata, and one based on the Dempster-Shafer formalism. In (Cestnik, Bratko 1988) it is shown that even a simple method that combines multiple rules can achieve better performance than several known single methods that are based on sophisticated techniques for pruning. An interesting approach was taken by Schlimmer (1987), utilizing multiple views on the same domain by means of different algorithms, each of them using differently preprocessed input data. Brazdil, Torgo (1990) used different data and different algorithms for learning.

Theoretical approaches related to multiple knowledge can be found also in information theory (Shannon, Weaver 1964) and in theoretical analyses of the Bayesian classifier (Cheeseman 1990). **Indeed, in recent years there have been so many empirical confirmations in so many areas that the empirical subject is beyond doubt.**

7.2 Simulated Multiple Models

In this subsection we study simulated multiple models and combining methods. A schema for combining models is introduced and its performance is illustrated in artificial and real-life domains. The main questions are:

- does a combination of models achieve better classification accuracy than the best single model,
- what are the gains, and
- under which conditions do they appear?

Our first simulations were presented in 1994 (Gams *et al.* 1994). Artificial abstract data models are constructed behaving as quasi-random generators with specific parameters determining the quality of the models, their similarity and dependence, the combining mechanism, different distributions, different number of systems, different number of classes, etc. All possible combinations of parameters are generated within a given granulation (typically 100 values per parameter). For each combination of parameters, performance of the combined systems was plotted and visually analyzed. Results have shown rather stable behavior primarily based on three parameters: quality, similarity and dependence.

In experiments described in this section, the following assumptions are taken into account. Each simulated model has a *predefined average classification accuracy*, which is typically set to 0.5. It means that on average 50% of new objects are classified correctly. In addition, the model estimates the *confidence factor* of each of its classifications. The confidence factor is a real number between 0 and 1. It is uniformly distributed by default. Confidence factors do not necessarily represent probabilities. Rather, they resemble the ability of humans to estimate certainty of their decision.

Simulated models are deliberately designed to be as simple and uninformed as possible. Therefore, no additional information about the problem domain is used. For example, the number of possible classes is arbitrary and no actual description of each object is given.

Class and confidence factors for each model are predicted on the basis of a random number generator with additional specifications. Namely, there is a parameter CONNECT that determines the portion of classifications where the confidence factor is forced to randomly fall into the subinterval between 0.5 and 1 if the model classifies correctly and between 0 and 0.5 otherwise. In the remaining (1−CONNECT) classifications, the confidence factor and correct classification are completely independent. In other words, CONNECT represents the degree of correlation between the confidence factor and correct classification.

There are two additional parameters that control the combination of multiple models:

- DECREASE: the absolute decrease of average classification accuracy of the j-th model base with respect to the $(j-1)$-th model;
- DEPEND: the portion of classifications of j-th method that are forced to classify into the same class as the first method.

The purpose of introducing parameters DECREASE and DEPEND is to obtain a mechanism for approximating the behavior of multiple models in real-life problem domains. Namely, in real life models usually achieve different classification accuracy (parameter DECREASE) and are dependent (parameter DEPEND).

There are two assumptions that are not so obvious. First is that systems are sorted according to classification accuracy. In reality, this is not difficult to achieve since we can test each system alone. In addition, we have performed other orders, e.g., worst-first or random orders, however, the same general phenomenon was observed, just not as clear as in the chosen distribution. The second and more questionable assumption is a uniform distribution. It means that each consequent model proportionally differs from the previous one. In real life, other distributions (i.e., the Gaussian or the normal distribution) are more common. But again, our attempts with different distributions have not substantially changed the overall characteristics presented in this section.

The parameters DECREASE and DEPEND are mutually constrained. For example, setting DEPEND $= 0.8$ and DECREASE $= 0.005$ would become theoretically impossible when adding the 21st model. Therefore, DEPEND is applied on classifications after they have been modified by DECREASE.

By default, the three parameters are set to 0, meaning that for each classified object the classification and confidence factor of each model are independent of each other, classification and confidence factor of any other model, and any other classified object.

The classification with multiple models is obtained according to two classification schemata, which are based on the estimated confidence factors. They are:

- *best-one*, where classification is performed by the model with the highest confidence factor, and
- *majority*, where models add their confidence factors either for or against the correct class.

The best-one schema classifies correctly if a model with the highest confidence factor classifies correctly. The majority schema classifies correctly if the sum of confidence factors for the correct class is greater than the sum of confidence factors for all the remaining classes.

In each measurement, 10,000 objects were generated for classification. Altogether, several 10000 measurements were performed. Average classification accuracy was measured as the percentage of correct classifications. In order to determine the dependence between the behavior of the model and parameters CONNECT, DECREASE and DEPEND, each measurement was performed with different parameters. Some additional characteristics of models were also varied, such as an average classification accuracy, mean confidence factor, distributions of average classification accuracy over models, etc. However, the characteristic behavior of the model was obtained already with the basic three parameters.

Results of simulations are presented in Table 7.12. The same data is graphically represented in Figure 7.7. The parameters were set as follows: CONNECT = 0.1, DECREASE = 0, DEPEND = 0, which means that models are completely independent of each other, and that each model has the same classification accuracy. Best-one and majority classification schema were used. Average classification accuracy was set to 0.5 and mean confidence factor to 0.5. The relation between the number of models and classification accuracy was observed. The meaning of rows in Table 7.12 is as follows:

1. index of the current model,
2. classification accuracy of the current model,
3. classification accuracy of all models up to the current one, using the best-one classification schema,
4. as above, but using the majority classification schema,
5. confidence factor of correct predictions of the current model,

6. confidence factor of correct predictions of all the models up to the current one, using best-one classification, and

7. as above, but using the majority classification schema.

1.	1	2	3	4	5	6	8	10	20	50	aver.
2.	49.7	50.0	49.5	50.0	49.0	49.9	50.1	49.0	50.2	49.3	50.0
3.	49.7	53.0	53.9	55.0	54.6	54.3	55.0	54.9	55.0	55.0	54.8
4.	49.7	53.0	52.9	53.7	53.5	53.6	54.1	54.4	58.5	61.9	58.2
5.	52.7	53.6	52.6	52.6	52.5	52.8	52.3	53.1	52.8	52.5	52.5
6.	52.7	68.8	76.1	80.6	83.8	86.1	89.0	91.0	95.3	98.0	93.1
7.	52.7	68.7	84.4	97.5	109.3	120.2	140.9	158.1	224.9	373.3	244.6

Table 7.12: Classification accuracy and confidence factor of a combined model. See text for the detailed description.

Parameter CONNECT has a positive effect on classification accuracy of a combined model. With a small number of models, e.g., 3 to 10, the classification accuracy increases more rapidly when the best-one classification schema is used. With increased number of models, e.g., over 10, the best-one classification gets saturated while the classification accuracy of the majority classification continues to increase. The later resembles information theory (Shannon, Weaver 1964) where noise can be eliminated if sufficient redundancy is available during communication. Unfortunately, such cases are not common in real-life where available models do not have the same classification accuracy and are not independent of each other.

When introducing parameters DECREASE and DEPEND, the following was observed. First, DECREASE has especially negative effect on the overall classification accuracy. With CONNECT $= 0.2$, DECREASE $= 0.005$ and DEPEND $= 0$, classification accuracy for the majority classification schema is 55.8% for 5 models and 18.0% for 50 models. With the best-one schema the accuracy is 58.2% for 5 models and 47.2% for 50 models. Second, DEPEND proportionally decreases the difference between overall classification accuracy obtained with DEPEND $= 0$ and the classification accuracy of the first method. If DEPEND $= 1$, all methods classify the same as the first method.

The results, presented in this section, indicate that multiple knowledge can substantially improve overall classification accuracy under reasonable conditions, such as that the confidence factor must be positively correlated to the accuracy of each model. It means that the more likely prediction will succeed the more trustful the predictor is about it on average. The CONNECT parameter (i.e. quality of self-estimation) is nearly linearly proportional to the gains

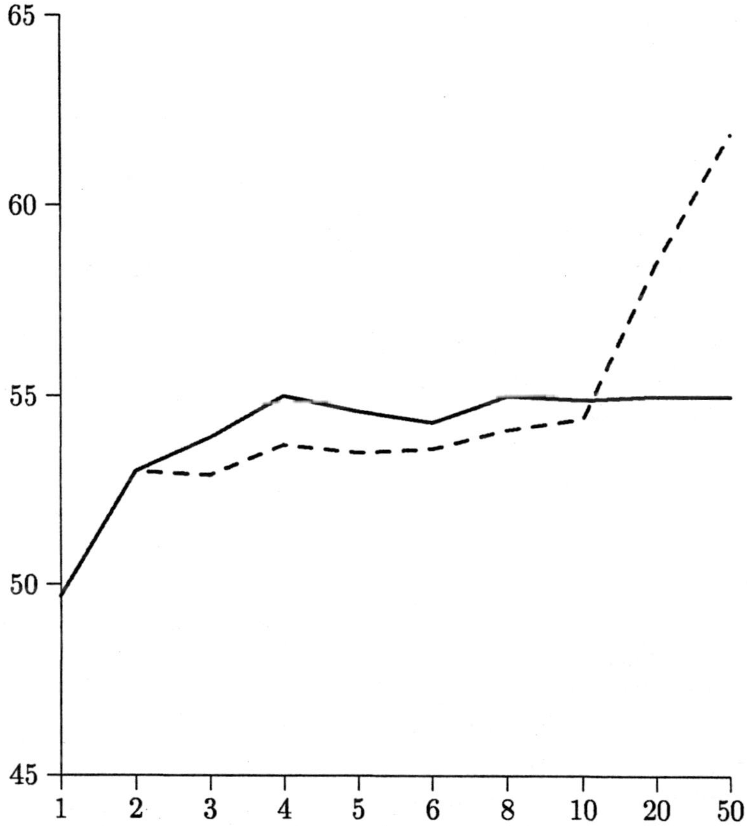

Figure 7.7: Best-one (—) and majority (- -) voting (see Table 7.12).

of classification accuracy for smaller number of models. The decrease of classification accuracy of subsequent models, i.e. parameter DECREASE, must not be too high. Otherwise, the combination of models may result in negative gains. The gain of the combined model is lowered roughly proportionally to the similarity between the first and remaining models, i.e. parameter DEPEND. The increase of classification accuracy is especially notable when having a small number of multiple models, e.g., 2–5. The best-one schema achieves better accuracy than the majority schema for most combinations of parameters; this particularly holds for smaller number of models. The majority schema is better with larger number of independent models with similar classification accuracy.

To summarize:

- **The better systems self-estimate the better overall improvement.**
- **Combinations of more independent systems are generally better.**
- **Improvement when adding another system to a list of systems depends on the number of the systems, similarity and quality of the added system. It is more beneficial to add more independent and as good as possible stand-alone system. Greater improvements can be expected when adding a system to a small number of existing systems than when adding to a large list of already combined systems.**

7.2.1 Empirical Verification in Real-life Domains

An attempt was made to verify the schema with simulated multiple models on two real-life problem domains, lymphography and primary tumor. The same domains have been used for benchmarking several learning systems in previous sections.

Results of simulation are presented in Table 7.13 and Table 7.14. The meaning of rows in Table 7.13 and Table 7.14 is the same as the meaning of columns in Table 7.12 with the addition of the DIFF column which denotes the percentage of different classifications of the current model compared to the first model.

Due to the stochastic nature of models, only an approximation can be made, however, the parameters CONNECT, DECREASE and DEPEND can be tuned in the following way. Default classification accuracy of the first model corresponds to the classification accuracy of NAIVE BAYES90 (row 1, column 2 in Table 7.13 and Table 7.14). Parameter DECREASE corresponds to the difference between classification accuracies of NAIVE BAYES90 and GB90 (row 2, column 2 in Table 7.13 and Table 7.14). These accuracies are identical to the one in Table 7.7. Observe that DECREASE is set to the pessimistic value because of the null-rule problem. The observed percentage of different classifications (29% in lymphography and 49% in primary tumor) corresponds to DEPEND. Therefore, DEPEND was tuned until appropriate difference between classifications of the first and the second model was obtained (column DIFF, row 2 in Table 7.13 and Table 7.14). The remaining parameter CONNECT has to be set to the appropriate value to simulate the improvement, i.e. the classification accuracy of GINESYS90 (row 2, column 3 or 4 in Table 7.13 and Table 7.14). Rows 3 and 4 represent characteristics of three and four simulated models with the same parameters.

IND	ACC	ACCB	ACCM	CF	CFB	CFM	DIFF
1	70.9	70.9	70.9	57.8	57.8	57.8	0.0
2	63.7	72.3	72.3	58.4	72.7	95.1	29.5
3	57.2	72.7	72.2	58.0	78.9	123.3	32.0
4	50.2	71.6	70.9	58.5	82.8	145.4	35.5
Av.	60.5	71.9	71.6	58.2	73.1	105.4	32.4

Table 7.13: Simulating NAIVE BAYES90 (row 1, column 2), GB90 (row 2, column 2) and the resulting combination, GINESYS90 (row 2, column 3 or 4) in lymphography. CONNECT = 0.33, DECREASE = 0.07, DEPEND = 0.36.

IND	ACC	ACCB	ACCM	CF	CFB	CFM	DIFF
1	54.2	54.2	54.2	59.0	59.0	59.0	0.0
2	36.7	55.0	55.0	59.8	71.7	69.6	49.1
3	18.5	50.7	44.2	59.4	76.9	73.6	51.4
4	1.5	43.4	30.6	57.5	79.7	65.3	52.7
Av.	27.7	50.8	46.0	58.9	71.8	66.9	51.1

Table 7.14: As above, but in the primary tumor domain. CONNECT = 0.38, DECREASE = 0.18, DEPEND = 0.03.

For the two domains and computer programs, the three parameters CONNECT, DECREASE and DEPEND enable fine tuning of performances of two models. However, the performance of the third and consequent model is already determined by these parameters. This decrease of accuracy of consequent models is caused mainly by simulated multiplications of the effect of the null rule.

Whatever the case, the simulations have shown that simulated models fit to two real-life domains. Although experiments were performed on only two domains, the proposed procedure for determining the parameters illustrates how one should find a good fit for the cases with two models. Note that the number of parameters is sufficient to make very good fits at least for two models.

One of the common objections to the proposed simulated models is that in reality we do not have ordered systems according to their classification accuracy, and that the difference between systems is not equal. As mentioned before, the proposed modifications do not change overall major characteristics, although values are shifted.

7.2.2 Conclusion

It is essential to understand how, why and when multiple knowledge helps.

Simulated models strongly indicate that multiple knowledge can considerably improve classification performance, given that models are as accurate and reliable as possible. At the same time, they should be mutually independent as much as possible. A particular problem, which was also addressed in this section, is how to find the proper combination of multiple models. The experimental tests and simulated models show that there is a broad area of reasonable combinations that offer important gains in classification accuracy.

Simulated artificial models achieve substantially better results under reasonable conditions that could be expected in real life. Although there might be a need for designing and testing more elaborate models, the idea behind the relatively simple and uninformed models is the following: If even such models show important improvements in classification accuracy, it is reasonable to expect improvements also in real life. However, the problem of finding an intelligent combination of methods in a specific application seems domain dependent.

The average benefit of applying multiple knowledge can be judged by the ratio of achieved improvements and additional costs. The improvements can be measured in terms of classification accuracy and improved possibilities to examine the properties of problem domains. Costs can be measured in terms of additional efforts of the designer, and memory and computer time costs due to additional models. It is our belief that this ratio has been radically shifted in favor of multiple knowledge by modern computer technology.

Simulated models strongly suggest that in many or even most real-life domains the improvements are possible and that they can be substantial, i.e., a couple of percents, already for 2–5 systems. For greater number of systems, simulations show all possibilities from saturation to higher increase or decrease. Since in real life costs such as time needed for programming and combining also increases, the practical advice from simulations would be to combine a couple or a couple of ten systems. Only in specific circumstances greater gains could be expected with large numbers of systems.

7.3 Formal Worst-Case Analyses

Analyses in PAC (Probably Approximately Correct) learning try to establish if the worst-case performance of the learning system achieves sufficient correctness with sufficient probability under given distribution of data. It has been shown (Littlestone, Warmuth 1991) that an algorithm using a weighted majority voting schema for combining classifications of single systems achieves at least as good worst-case performance as any single system. **These analyses have shown that multiple models enable better or equal performance as the best single model in the *worst-case*.**

7.4 Formal Average-Case Improvements

To mathematically estimate average-case improvements of the introduced models we have to determine the probability $p_{\vec{s}}$ of the occurrence of each situation $\vec{s} \in S$, and the probability of correct classification $q_{\vec{s}}$. The probability of correct classification of a combined or integrated system can be obtained as a sum over all possible situations; for two independent systems it is

$$\begin{aligned} p_M &= \sum_{\vec{s} \in S} p_{\vec{s}} q_{\vec{s}} \\ &= p_2(1-p_1)q_{FT} + p_1(1-p_2)q_{TF} + p_1 p_2 \end{aligned} \tag{1}$$

and for two dependent systems

$$\begin{aligned} p_M^* &= \sum_{\vec{s} \in S} p_{\vec{s}} q_{\vec{s}} \\ &= (1-d)p_2(1-p_1)q_{FT} + (1-d)p_1(1-p_2)q_{TF} + (1-d)p_1 p_2 + dp_1. \end{aligned} \tag{2}$$

Without any loss of generality we can assume that $p_1 \geq p_2$. Now, p_M^* can be expressed in relation to p_M

$$p_M^* = (1-d)p_M + dp_1. \tag{3}$$

For $d = 0$, we obtain the model of two independent systems and the classification accuracy of a combined system is p_M. For $d = 1$, the systems are equal and the obtained result is equal to the result of one system. For $0 < d < 1$, the classification accuracy p_M^* lies between p_1 and p_M. Therefore, it can be concluded, that

- whenever the model of integrated or combined *independent* systems indicates better classification accuracy than the best single system (or worse than the best system), the model for *dependent* systems will also indicate it, and

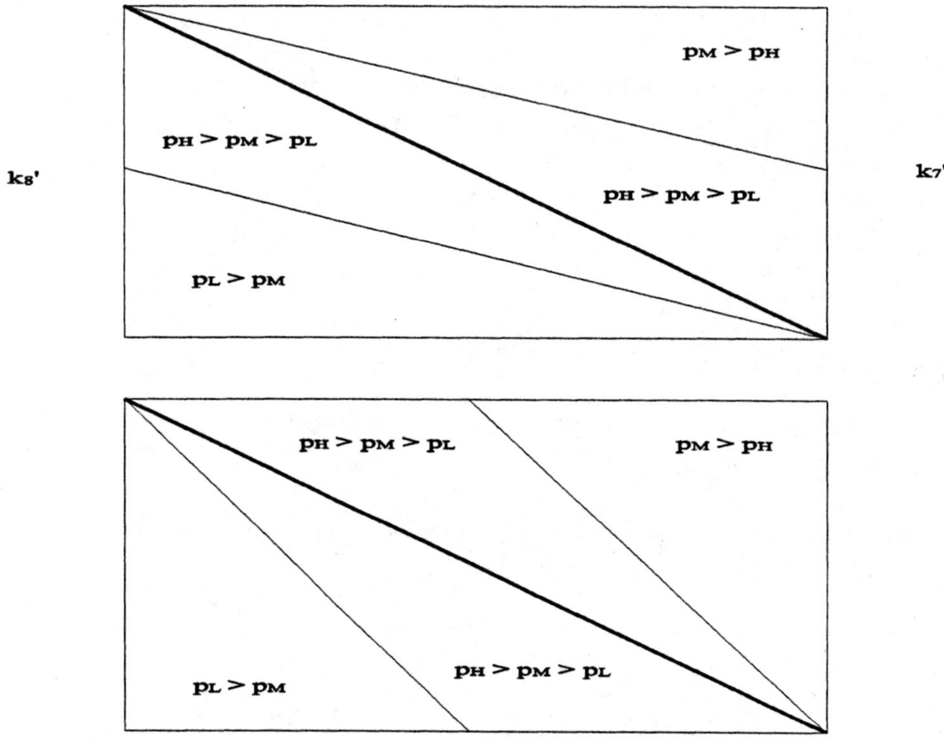

Figure 7.8: Decomposition of the q_{TF}, q_{FT} plane.

- the improvement of classification accuracy of *dependent* systems is proportional to the improvement of *independent* systems.

The last two conclusions imply that **the model of two independent systems can reveal basic conditions** in the 4-dimensional $(p_1, p_2, q_{TF}, q_{FT})$ space, under which the combined *dependent* systems are also more successful than the best single system alone. For a while, we shall study the model of two independent systems having in mind that the final classification accuracy for dependent systems can be obtained by multiplying results with $(1-d)$.

Note that whenever it holds $p_M > p_1$ it is also $p_M^* > p_1$. Similarly, $p_M \geq p_2 \Longrightarrow p_M^* \geq p_2$ and $p_M \leq p_1 \Longrightarrow p_M^* \leq p_1$. On the other hand, it can not be concluded that $p_2 \geq p_M \Longrightarrow p_2 \geq p_M^*$ since with d approaching 1, p_M^* approaches p_1. When assuming $p_2 \geq p_1$ or altering the model by introducing independent d_2 and dependent d_1^*, similar inequalities are obtained, again some of them valid only for the model of independent systems.

Whenever the model of combined independent systems indicates better classification accuracy than the best or the worst system, or worse

k_7	k_8	$p_1 : p_2 \| k_7$	$p_1 : p_2 \| k_8$	$p_M : p_H, p_L$
$0 < 1$	$1 < \infty$	$p_1 > p_2$	$p_1 < p_2$	$p_M > p_L$
1	1	$p_1 = p_2$	$p_1 = p_2$	$p_H = p_M = p_L$
$1 < \infty$	$0 < 1$	$p_1 < p_2$	$p_1 > p_2$	$p_M < p_H$

Table 7.15: Relations in the upper triangle, on the diagonal and in the lower triangle of the q_{TF}, q_{FT} plane.

than the best system, the model of dependent systems will also indicate it. Therefore, most interesting analyses of the measurement space can be performed with the simpler of the two models.

7.4.1 Conditions for Successful Classification

Typically, we shall observe performance of the model under chosen p_1, p_2, and try to find appropriate q_{TF}, q_{FT} to obtain improvements over compared system. First, classification accuracy of a combined system will be compared to p_1 (better system):

$$\frac{p_M}{p_1} = (1 - p_2)q_{TF} + \frac{p_2}{p_1}q_{FT} - p_2 q_{FT} + p_2.$$

Considering that $p_2 \leq p_1$ and subtracting 1 on both sides it can be derived

$$q_{TF} + q_{FT} \leq 1 \Longrightarrow p_M \leq p_1. \tag{4}$$

Similarly, we can compare p_M to p_2 (worse system) and obtain

$$q_{TF} + q_{FT} \geq 1 \Longrightarrow p_M \geq p_2. \tag{5}$$

Therefore, if $q_{TF} + q_{FT} \geq 1$, meaning that the combining mechanism on average estimates the correctness of combined classifications **better than at random**, again on average, **the combined system can not classify worse than the worst system**. On the other hand, if the combining mechanism estimates worse than at random, it can not classify better than the best system alone (see equation 4).

After these partial results, let us perform a little more profound analysis to obtain exact conditions under which $p_M \geq p_1$. Let us start from equation (1), but this time without a condition that $p_1 \geq p_2$.

$$p_1 \leq (1 - p_1)p_2 q_{FT} + (1 - p_2)p_1 q_{TF} + p_1 p_2 | \cdot \frac{1}{p_1 p_2} | \cdot \frac{p_2}{1 - p_2}$$

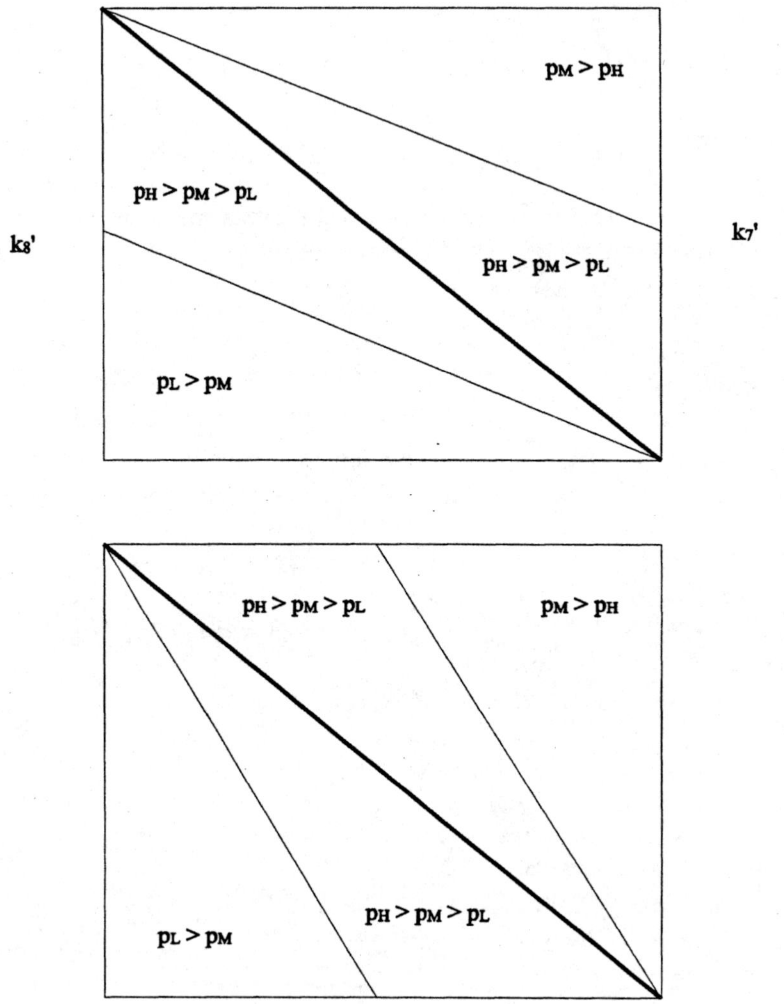

Figure 7.9: Graphical representation of relations in the upper and lower triangle of Table 7.16. The relation is obviously a symmetrical one.

k	$p_M : p_1, p_2$	$p_M : p_L, p_H$
$0 < k_7' < k_1$	$p_M > p_1$	$p_M > p_H$
$k_7' = k_1$	$p_M = p_1$	$p_M = p_H$
$k_1 < k_7' \leq 1$	$p_1 > p_M > p_2$	$p_H > p_M > p_L$
$k_1 < k_8' \leq 1$	$p_1 > p_M > p_2$	$p_H > p_M > p_L$
$k_8' = k_1$	$p_M = p_2$	$p_M = p_L$
$0 < k_8' < k_1$	$p_2 > p_M$	$p_L > p_M$
$0 < k_7' < 1$	$p_M > p_1, p_2$	$p_M > p_H$
$k_7' = k_1 = 1$	$p_M = p_1 = p_2$	$p_M = p_H = p_L$
$1 < k_7' < \infty$	$p_1, p_2 > p_M$	$p_L > p_M$
$k_1 < k_8' < \infty$	$p_M > p_2$	$p_M > p_H$
$k_1 = k_8'$	$p_M = p_2$	$p_M = p_H$
$1 \leq k_8' < k_1$	$p_2 > p_M > p_2$	$p_H > p_M > p_L$
$1 \leq k_7' < k_1$	$p_2 > p_M > p_2$	$p_H > p_M > p_L$
$k_7' = k_1$	$p_M = p_1$	$p_M = p_L$
$\infty < k_7' < k_1$	$p_1 > p_M$	$p_L > p_M$

Table 7.16: Relations $p_M : p_1, p_2$ and $p_M : p_L, p_H$ in the area of fictive k_7' and k_8' under three different relations between p_1 and p_2: $p_1 > p_2$, $p_1 = p_2$, $p_1 < p_2$.

$$1 \leq \frac{p_2(1-p_1)}{p_1(1-p_2)} q_{FT} + q_{TF}. \tag{6}$$

In order to graphically represent relations between variables p_1, p_2, q_{TF}, q_{FT}, inequality (6) will be transformed:

$$1 \leq k q_{FT} + q_{TF}, \quad k = \frac{p_2(1-p_1)}{p_1(1-p_2)}. \tag{7}$$

In a similar way, the relation between p_M and p_2 can be obtained, again without a condition that $p_1 \geq p_2$

$$p_2 \geq (1-p_1)p_2 q_{FT} + (1-p_2)p_1 q_{TF} + p_1 p_2 | \cdot \frac{1}{p_1 p_2} | \cdot \frac{p_1}{1-p_1}$$

$$1 \geq q_{FT} + \frac{1}{k} q_{TF}, \quad k = \frac{p_2(1-p_1)}{p_1(1-p_2)}. \tag{8}$$

Equations (7) and (8) determine two lines in the q_{TF}, q_{FT} plane (see Figure 7.8). The values of k for the line (7), k_7, are plotted on the right and the lower side of the q_{TF}, q_{FT} square. Symmetrically, the values of k for the line (8), k_8, are on the

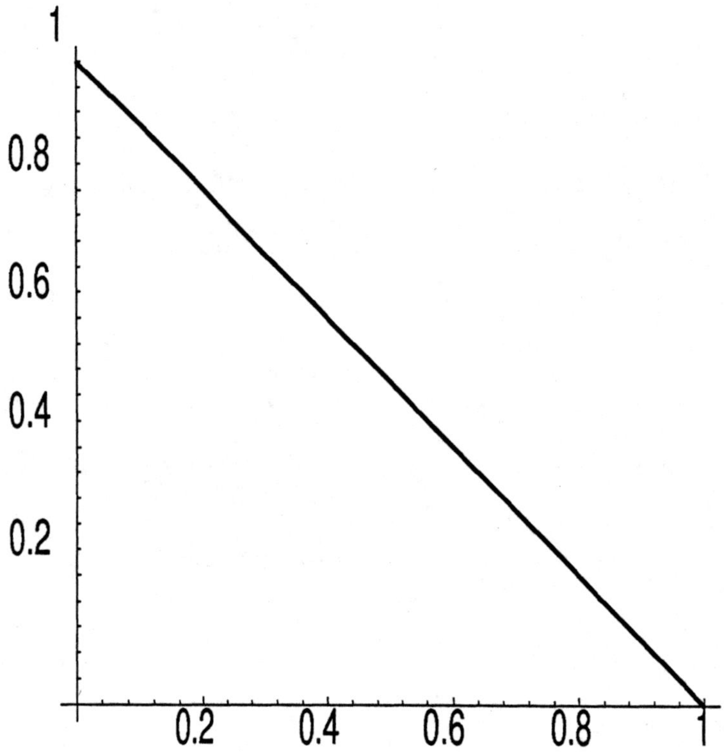

Figure 7.10: Minimal value for $q_{TF} + q_{FT}$ if $p_1 = p_2$

upper and the left side (see also Table 7.15). If $k = 1$, both lines lie on the same diagonal. Note that indexes 7 and 8 are introduced in order to distinguish between the two lines (equations) and that $k_7 = k_8$.

The q_{TF}, q_{FT} plane can be decomposed into two triangles and a diagonal (see Table 7.15). In the upper right triangle, where $q_{TF} + q_{FT} > 1$, p_M is always better than the smaller of p_1, p_2 (equation 5 with "$\geq$" changed to "$>$"). Similar relation can be observed for the left lower triangle from equation 4.

Above relations are not dependent on the value of k or, consequently, on the relation between p_1 and p_2. Therefore, let us introduce $p_H = \max\{p_1, p_2\}$ and $p_L = \min\{p_1, p_2\}$.

The three subareas of the q_{TF}, q_{FT} square correspond to the three rows in Table 7.15. The explanation of columns in Table 7.15:

- Column 1 – (k_7) can obtain values between 0 and ∞ and is continuous,
- Column 2 – (k_8) represents the same numerical expression as k_7, however, the value in the same triangle is reversed,

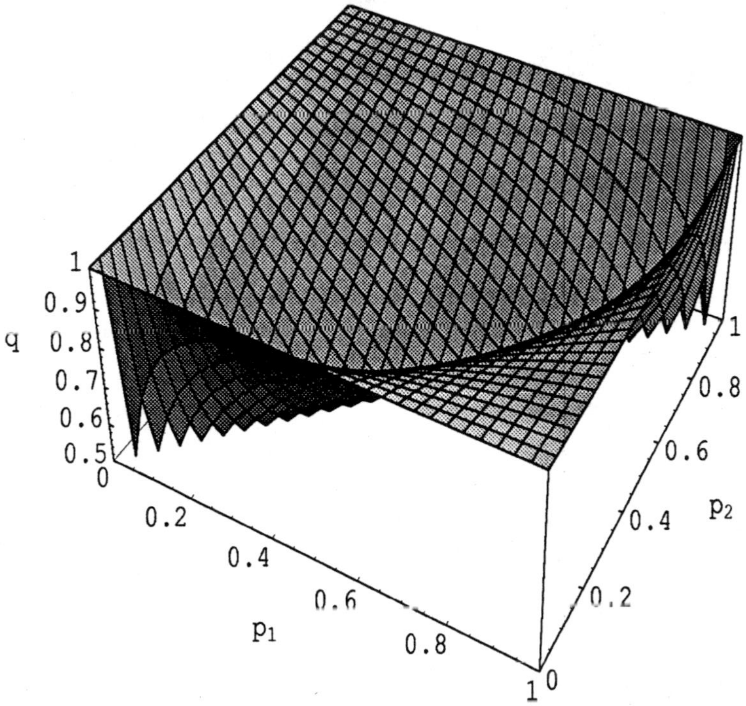

Figure 7.11: Minimal value for $q = q_{TF} = q_{FT}$ depending on p_1 and p_2. This relation is named "butterfly".

- Column 3 – $(p_1 : p_2|k_7)$ represents relation between p_1 and p_2 regarding k_7,
- Column 4 – $(p_1 : p_2|k_8)$ represents relation between p_1 and p_2 regarding k_8, and
- Column 5 – $(p_M : p_H, p_L)$ represents relations between p_M and p_H or p_L. Note that the relation $(p_M : p_H, p_L)$ is independent of the value of k.

Now, relations $p_M : p_1, p_2$ and $p_M : p_L, p_H$ can be further analysed. Namely, if the values of p_1 and p_2 are chosen, the value of k is uniquely determined and takes a certain value, e.g. k_1. It can be below 1 (upper part of Table 7.16, $p_1 > p_2$), 1 (middle part, $p_1 = p_2$) and above 1 (lower part, $p_2 > p_1$). Consequently, k_7 and k_8 take corresponding values and corresponding bordering lines can be drawn in Figure 7.9. Now, obtained areas in the q_{TF}, q_{FT} plane can be covered by lines with fictive k_7' and k_8' and relations for intervals of their values can be observed in Table 7.16. Therefore, Table 7.16 represents an extension of Table 7.15 regarding the chosen value of k. For example, if $k_1 = 1$, the area where $q_{TF} + q_{FT} > 1$ consists of points on lines with fictive k_7, $0 < k_7 < 1$, which are favourable for combined

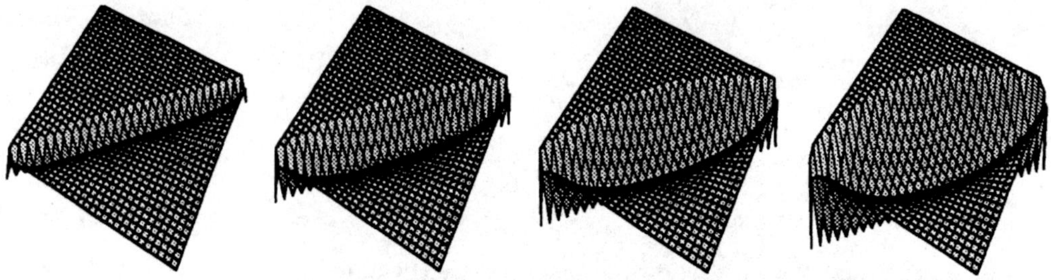

Figure 7.12: Area where combined systems perform better than the best single system with a predefined value of $q_{FT} = 0.2, 0.4, 0.6, 0.8$ from left to right.

classification. That can be observed from equation (7) and Table 7.15: $p_M > p_1$ and $p_M > p_H$. In the area where $q_{TF} + q_{FT} < 1$, the combined system is worse than the worst system (equation 8): $p_2 > p_M$ and $p_L > p_M$. If $q_{TF}+q_{FT} = 1$ and $k = k_1 = 1$, then $p_M = p_1 = p_2 = p_H = p_L$. In a similar way, relations in the upper and lower part of Table 7.16 can be obtained from equations (7) and (8) with corresponding transformations of inequality operators, and Table 7.15. Schematically, they are shown in Figure 7.9.

As a conclusion, Figure 7.9 and Table 7.16 indicate, that

- **maximal area of the q_{FT}, q_{TF} plane where $p_M > p_H$ is the upper triangle, i.e. the area where $q_{TF} + q_{FT} > 1$, and is obtained when $p_1 = p_2$,**
- **if the difference $| p_1 - p_2 |$ increases, the area where combined classification is beneficial, proportionally decreases, and**
- **if $p_1 \neq p_2$, it is more important that better system is better estimated than the worse system which has generally less effect on the successfulness of a classification.**

7.4.2 Special Cases

In previous analyses, the two variables p_1 and p_2 were determined and transformed into k. In that way, relations in partitions of the q_{FT}, q_{TF} plane were observed as a projection from a 4-dimensional space. In the following analyses, one variable is predefined and the obtained 3-dimensional space is observed in order to determine conditions under which the use of combined classification pays off, i.e. when the classification accuracy p_M is greater than the one of the best single system.

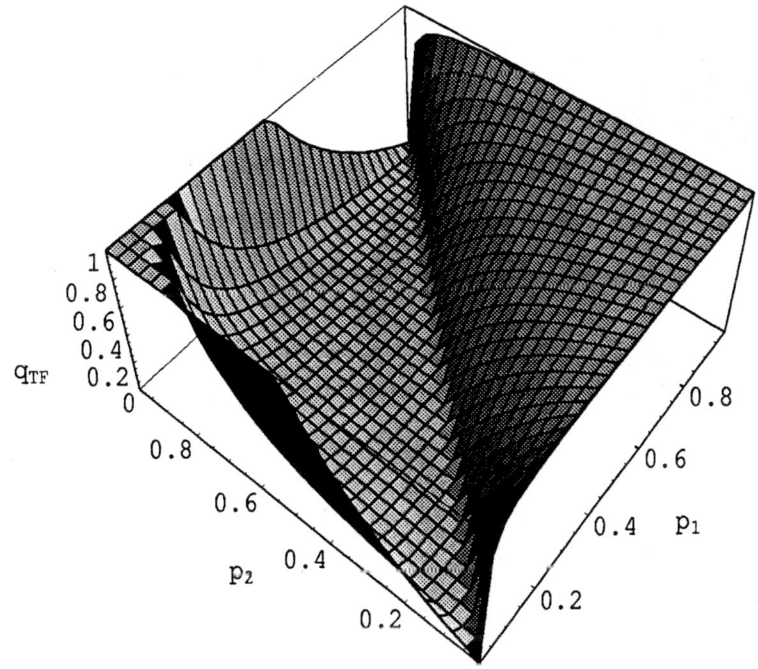

Figure 7.13: Area where combined systems perform better than the best single system with a predefined value of $q_{FT} = 0.99$.

Case 1.
First, let us consider the case where both systems have the same classification accuracy, $p_1 = p_2 = p$. Then we compare $\max\{p_1, p_2\} < p_M$ and obtain

$$1 < q_{TF} + q_{FT}.$$

This simple relation is represented in Figure 7.10.

The condition $q_{TF} + q_{FT} > 1$ means that error estimates must together behave better than randomly to obtain the improvement of classification accuracy.

Case 2.
In another simplification of equation (1) we assume that both probabilities q_{ij} are equal, $q_{TF} = q_{FT} = q$. Again we analyse under which conditions is p_M greater than $\max\{p_1, p_2\}$:

$$q > \frac{\max\{p_1, p_2\} - p_1 p_2}{p_1(1-p_2) + p_2(1-p_1)}.$$

The lower bound for q, which enables successful combined classification, depending on p_1 and p_2, is shown in Figure 7.11. The graphical relation appears similar to a

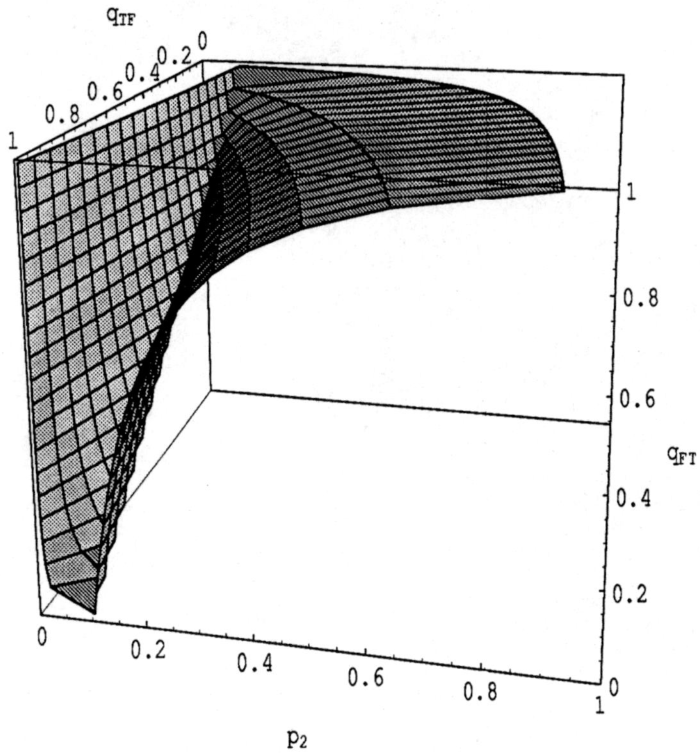

Figure 7.14: Area where combined systems perform better than the best single system with a predefined value of $p_1 = 0.1$.

butterfly. This is one of the most common relations in our formal analyses in this section. Of course, these butterflies are fatter or thinner in different figures. Remember – the space above the butterfly hyperplane is the one beneficial for multiple systems.

For $p_1 = p_2$, q must be at least $\frac{1}{2}$. This result is consistent with equations (7) and (8). From Figure 7.11, we can also see that the greater the difference between p_1 and p_2, the greater must be q to achieve the improvement over the best single system. This dependence is greater than linear around $p_1 \approx p_2$, however, the improvement is possible for all p_1, p_2 pairs.

Case 3.

Two additional special cases are obtained when one of the four variables is determined, e.g. $q_{FT} = q$ or $p_1 = p$. In the first case we obtain that the condition in equation (1) transforms into

$$q_{TF} \geq \frac{\max\{p_1, p_2\} - (1-p_1)p_2q - p_1p_2}{p_1(1-p_2)}.$$

Two cases for $q_{FT} = 0.0, 0.4, 0.6, 0.8$ and $q_{FT} = 0.99$ are presented in Figure 7.12

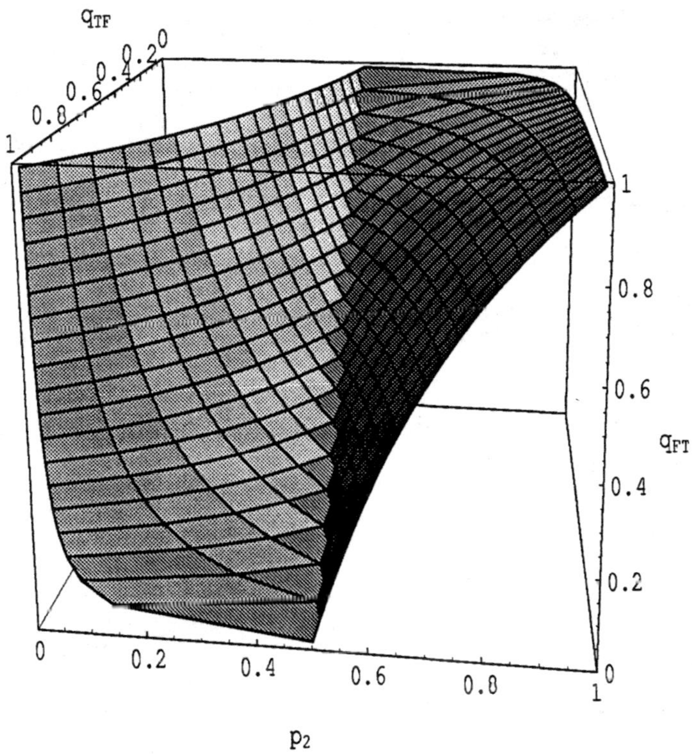

Figure 7.15: Area where combined systems perform better than the best single system with a predefined value of $p_1 = 0.5$.

and Figure 7.13. Modern mathematical packages enable showing a figure in a foor-loop thus presenting a movie on the screen. On the paper, all we can do is to show a sequence of a couple of examples. In Figure 7.12, we see that the butterfly fattens with better error estimation of q_{FT}. In certain combinations, where wings of the butterfly touch the ceiling, improvements over the best single system are not possible anymore regardless of values of the other three variables. But improvement is quite possible for reasonable q_{FT}. On the other hand, Figure 7.13 shows that even with a very good error estimation q_{FT}, improvement is not always possible. In general, as error estimate improves, the beneficial area also grows.

If $q_{FT} = 0.5$, in a large proportion of the p_1, p_2 pairs improvement is not possible. With $q_{FT} = 0.999$, in nearly the whole p_1, p_2 plane improvement is feasible. Again, good estimations of the correctness of better system play major role in determining the overall successfulness.

Case 4.
When fixing $p_1 = p$, the following condition is obtained:

$$\max\{p, p_2\} \leq p(1 - p_2)q_{TF} + (1 - p)p_2 q_{FT} + pp_2$$

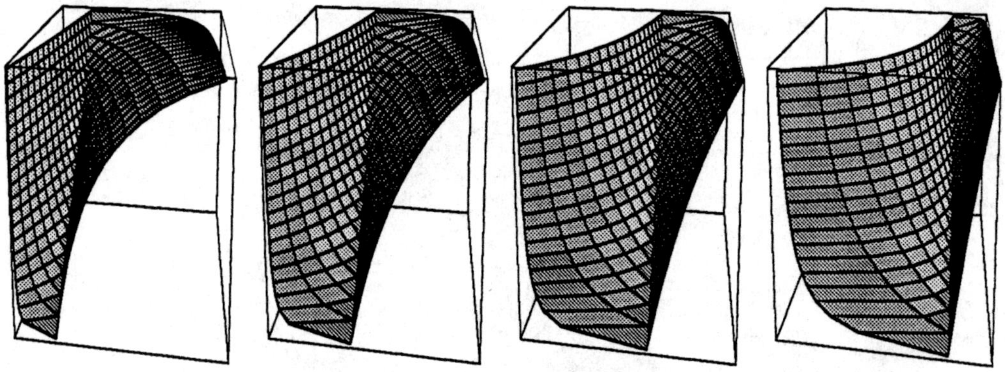

Figure 7.16: Area where combined systems perform better than the best single system with a predefined value of $p_1 = 0.2, 0.4, 0.6, 0.8$.

and two cases, $p_1 = 0.5$ and $p_1 = 0.1$ are graphically represented in Figure 7.14 and Figure 7.15.

An animated sequence is presented in Figure 7.16 for $p_1 = 0.2, 0.4, 0.6, 0.8$. Observe the influence of difference between p_1 and p_2: the greater the difference, the harder it is to obtain the improvement. The butterfly here is not totally symmetrical, though.

Therefore, it is advisable to combine two systems that are as good as possible and as independent as possible. When both systems have the same classification accuracy, the combining mechanism has to be just a little better than at random to achieve an improvement over the best single system.

7.4.3 Average Improvement of Classification Accuracy with Two Systems

In this section, an attempt is made to calculate average improvements. It is assumed that all variables q_{ij} are uniformly distributed over interval $[q_L, q_H]$. We also assume that all variables p_i are uniformly distributed over interval [0, 1]. To obtain the average gain in classification accuracy according to the better system $G_{max} = \langle p_M - \max\{p_1, p_2\}\rangle$, we have to integrate the difference in a 4-dimensional space

$$G_{max} = \frac{1}{(q_H - q_L)^2} \int_0^1 dp_1 \int_0^{p_1} dp_2 \int_{q_L}^{q_H} dq_{TF} \int_{q_L}^{q_H} dq_{FT}(p_M - p_1)$$

$$+ \frac{1}{(q_H - q_L)^2} \int_0^1 dp_2 \int_0^{p_2} dp_1 \int_{q_L}^{q_H} dq_{TF} \int_{q_L}^{q_H} dq_{FT}(p_M - p_2)$$

$$= \frac{2}{(q_H - q_L)^2} \int_0^1 dp_1 \int_0^{p_1} dp_2 \int_{q_L}^{q_H} dq_{TF} \int_{q_L}^{q_H} dq_{FT}(p_M - p_1)$$

$$= 2\int_0^1 dp_1 \int_0^{p_1} dp_2 \left(p_1(1-p_2)\frac{q_L+q_H}{2} + p_2(1-p_1)\frac{q_L+q_H}{2} + p_1p_2 - p_1\right)$$

$$= \frac{q_L+q_H}{4} - \frac{5}{12}.$$

With a similar integration, we can also find out the average gain in classification accuracy according to the worse system $G_{min} = \langle p_M - \min\{p_1, p_2\}\rangle$

$$G_{min} = \frac{1}{(q_H-q_L)^2}\int_0^1 dp_1 \int_0^{p_1} dp_2 \int_{q_L}^{q_H} dq_{TF} \int_{q_L}^{q_H} dq_{FT}(p_M - p_2)$$

$$+\frac{1}{(q_H-q_L)^2}\int_0^1 dp_2 \int_0^{p_2} dp_1 \int_{q_L}^{q_H} dq_{TF} \int_{q_L}^{q_H} dq_{FT}(p_M - p_1)$$

$$= \frac{2}{(q_H-q_L)^2}\int_0^1 dp_1 \int_0^{p_1} dp_2 \int_{q_L}^{q_H} dq_{TF} \int_{q_L}^{q_H} dq_{FT}(p_M - p_2)$$

$$= 2\int_0^1 dp_1 \int_0^{p_1} dp_2 \left(p_1(1-p_2)\frac{q_L+q_H}{2} + p_2(1-p_1)\frac{q_L+q_H}{2} + p_1p_2 - p_2\right)$$

$$= \frac{q_L+q_H}{4} - \frac{1}{12}.$$

Finally, we can also determine the average gain in classification accuracy according to the average over both systems $G_{min} = \langle p_M - \frac{p_1+p_2}{2}\rangle$

$$G_{ave} = \frac{1}{(q_H-q_L)^2}\int_0^1 dp_1 \int_0^{p_1} dp_2 \int_{q_L}^{q_H} dq_{TF} \int_{q_L}^{q_H} dq_{FT}(p_M - \frac{p_1+p_2}{2})$$

$$+\frac{1}{(q_H-q_L)^2}\int_0^1 dp_2 \int_0^{p_2} dp_1 \int_{q_L}^{q_H} dq_{TF} \int_{q_L}^{q_H} dq_{FT}(p_M - \frac{p_1+p_2}{2})$$

$$= \frac{2}{(q_H-q_L)^2}\int_0^1 dp_1 \int_0^{p_1} dp_2 \int_{q_L}^{q_H} dq_{TF} \int_{q_L}^{q_H} dq_{FT}(p_M - \frac{p_1+p_2}{2})$$

$$= 2\int_0^1 dp_1 \int_0^{p_1} dp_2 \left(p_1(1-p_2)\frac{q_L+q_H}{2} + p_2(1-p_1)\frac{q_L+q_H}{2} + p_1p_2 - \frac{p_1+p_2}{2}\right)$$

$$= \frac{q_L+q_H-1}{4}.$$

In all cases, the gain of classification accuracy linearly depends on both upper and lower integration bound. For a graphical presentation in Figure 7.17, let us take $q_H = 1$ and plot G_{max} (solid), G_{ave} (dotted) and G_{min} (dashed) vs. lower bound q_L.

No matter the value of q_L, the averages G_{min} and G_{ave} are never negative. This means that on average we can get an improvement over the worst and also the average system even if "liars" or "self-deceivers" are as probable as good self-estimators. On the other hand, G_{max} is negative for $q_L < \frac{2}{3}$, meaning that we have

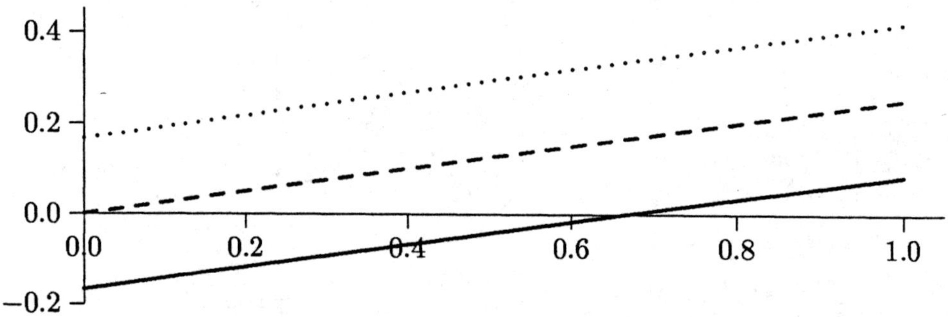

Figure 7.17: G_{max} (solid), G_{ave} (dotted) and G_{min} (dashed) vs. lower bound q_L

to be very careful when combining systems with unreliable self-error-estimates, i.e. unreliable combining mechanisms, if the goal is to achieve an improvement over the best system.

It is not very reasonable to expect that self-estimates of competent systems in real-life domains will be uniformly distributed from 0 to 1. Usually, self-estimates of systems (models) are similarly good. For example, people generally tend to be pretty sure when the case is clear and prefer to be careful when it is hard to say which possibility is the correct one. Therefore we observe performance under reasonable $\frac{q_L+q_H}{2}$. In Figure 7.18, both q_{TF} and q_{FT} are uniformly distributed over the appropriate $[q_L, q_H]$ interval, and corresponding G_{max}, G_{ave} and G_{min} are plotted vs. $\frac{q_L+q_H}{2} = 0.45 \ldots 0.95$.

When combining better than at random, i.e. when the value of $\frac{q_L+q_H}{2}$ is equal or better than 0.5, the averages G_{min} and G_{ave} are never negative. G_{max} is negative for $\frac{q_L+q_H}{2} < 0.83$, therefore, under these assumptions the improvement might not be too easy to achieve in noisy domains.

In the above reasoning, we still combined systems with their performance ranging from 0 to 1 (even those always failing and those always hitting the target). This is not very relevant (and even theoretically not possible in noisy domains!) for practical tasks. Humans typically don't combine systems which predict confidence factors worse than average, or systems with much lower accuracy than the best one. Therefore, in next analysis performed, we will integrate only over the area where $|p_1 - p_2| \leq \Delta$, where Δ is a positive constant $0 < \Delta < 1$. The integration area is shown in Figure 7.19.

The surface of integration area is calculated as

$$S = 2\left(\int_0^{\Delta} dp_1 \int_0^{p_1} dp_2 + \int_{\Delta}^{1} dp_1 \int_{p_1-\Delta}^{p_1} dp_2\right)$$

$$= \Delta(2 - \Delta).$$

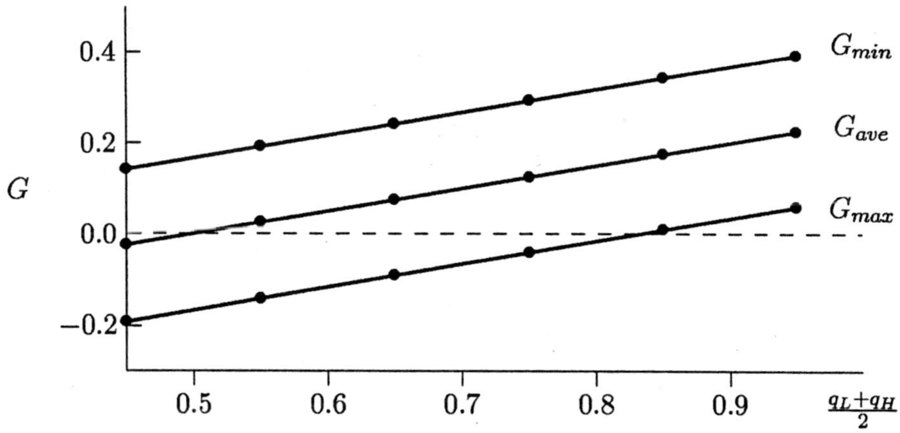

Figure 7.18: G_{min}, G_{ave} and G_{max} vs. $\frac{q_L+q_H}{2}$

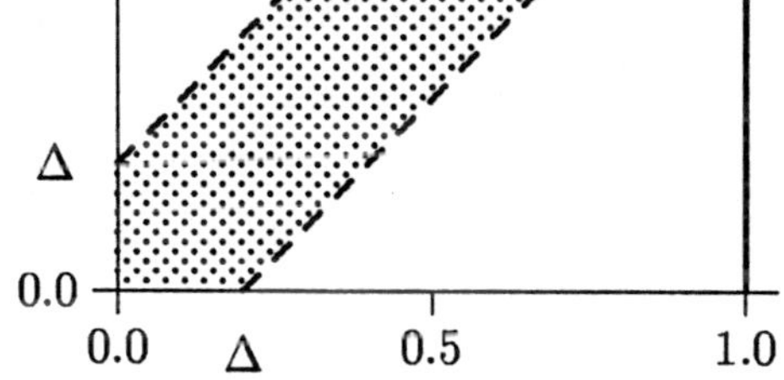

Figure 7.19: Integration area for $\Delta = 0.2$

The integration was simplified due to the symmetry over diagonal. The average gain is then

$$
\begin{aligned}
{}_{\Delta}G_{max} &= \frac{2}{S(q_H - q_L)^2}\int_0^{\Delta} dp_1 \int_0^{p_1} dp_2 \int_{q_L}^{q_H} dq_{TF} \int_{q_L}^{q_H} dq_{FT}(p_M - p_1) \\
&+ \frac{2}{S(q_H - q_L)^2}\int_{\Delta}^{1} dp_1 \int_{p_1-\Delta}^{p_1} dp_2 \int_{q_L}^{q_H} dq_{TF} \int_{q_L}^{q_H} dq_{FT}(p_M - p_1) \\
&= \frac{2}{S}\int_0^{\Delta} dp_1 \int_0^{p_1} dp_2 \left(\frac{q_L + q_H}{2}(p_1 + p_2 - 2p_1p_2) + p_1p_2 - p_1\right) \\
&+ \frac{2}{S}\int_{\Delta}^{1} dp_1 \int_{p_1-\Delta}^{p_1} dp_2 \left(\frac{q_L + q_H}{2}(p_1 + p_2 - 2p_1p_2) + p_1p_2 - p_1\right) \\
&= \frac{1}{12(2-\Delta)}\left((1 - q_L - q_H)\Delta^3 + 4\Delta^2 - 6\Delta + 4(q_L + q_H - 1)\right).
\end{aligned}
$$

As before, we can also determine the gain with respect to the worse system

$$
\begin{aligned}
{}_{\Delta}G_{min} &= \frac{2}{S(q_H - q_L)^2}\int_0^{\Delta} dp_1 \int_0^{p_1} dp_2 \int_{q_L}^{q_H} dq_{TF} \int_{q_L}^{q_H} dq_{FT}(p_M - p_2) \\
&+ \frac{2}{S(q_H - q_L)^2}\int_{\Delta}^{1} dp_1 \int_{p_1-\Delta}^{p_1} dp_2 \int_{q_L}^{q_H} dq_{TF} \int_{q_L}^{q_H} dq_{FT}(p_M - p_2) \\
&= \frac{2}{S}\int_0^{\Delta} dp_1 \int_0^{p_1} dp_2 \left(\frac{q_L + q_H}{2}(p_1 + p_2 - 2p_1p_2) + p_1p_2 - p_2\right) \\
&+ \frac{2}{S}\int_{\Delta}^{1} dp_1 \int_{p_1-\Delta}^{p_1} dp_2 \left(\frac{q_L + q_H}{2}(p_1 + p_2 - 2p_1p_2) + p_1p_2 - p_2\right) \\
&= \frac{1}{12(2-\Delta)}\left((1 - q_L - q_H)\Delta^3 - 4\Delta^2 + 6\Delta + 4(q_L + q_H - 1)\right).
\end{aligned}
$$

And finally, let us calculate the average gain in classification accuracy according to the average over both systems

$$
\begin{aligned}
{}_{\Delta}G_{ave} &= \frac{2}{S(q_H - q_L)^2}\int_0^{\Delta} dp_1 \int_0^{p_1} dp_2 \int_{q_L}^{q_H} dq_{TF} \int_{q_L}^{q_H} dq_{FT}(p_M - \frac{p_1 + p_2}{2}) \\
&+ \frac{2}{S(q_H - q_L)^2}\int_{\Delta}^{1} dp_1 \int_{p_1-\Delta}^{p_1} dp_2 \int_{q_L}^{q_H} dq_{TF} \int_{q_L}^{q_H} dq_{FT}(p_M - \frac{p_1 + p_2}{2}) \\
&= \frac{2}{S}\int_0^{\Delta} dp_1 \int_0^{p_1} dp_2 \left(\frac{q_L + q_H}{2}(p_1 + p_2 - 2p_1p_2) + p_1p_2 - \frac{p_1 + p_2}{2}\right) \\
&+ \frac{2}{S}\int_{\Delta}^{1} dp_1 \int_{p_1-\Delta}^{p_1} dp_2 \left(\frac{q_L + q_H}{2}(p_1 + p_2 - 2p_1p_2) + p_1p_2 - \frac{p_1 + p_2}{2}\right)
\end{aligned}
$$

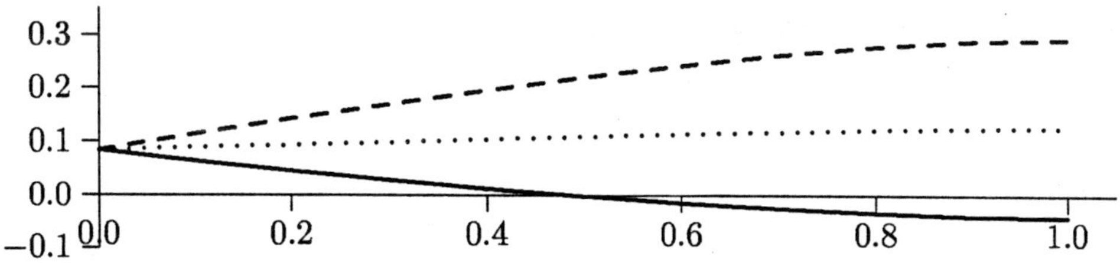

Figure 7.20: $_\Delta G_{max}$ (solid), $_\Delta G_{ave}$ (dotted) and $_\Delta G_{min}$ (dashed) vs. Δ ($q_L = \frac{1}{2}$ and $q_H = 1$)

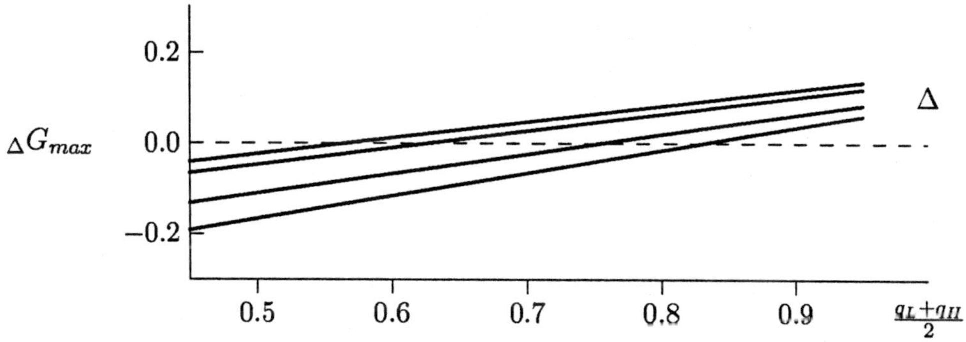

Figure 7.21: $_\Delta G_{max}$ vs. $\frac{q_L+q_H}{2}$; $\Delta = 0.1$, 0.2, 0.5 and 1.0 (from top to bottom)

$$= \frac{1}{12(2-\Delta)}\left((1 - q_L - q_H)\Delta^3 + 4(q_L + q_H - 1)\right).$$

In Figure 7.20, we can see the dependence of average gain on Δ with parameter values $q_L = \frac{1}{2}$ and $q_H = 1$.

In Figure 7.21, we can see the dependence of average gain on Δ with parameter values $\frac{q_L+q_H}{2} = 0.45 \ldots 0.95$.

For $\Delta = 1$, $_\Delta G_{max}$ is equal to G_{max} in Figure 7.18. When changing Δ, an improvement over the best system is obtained whenever $\Delta = 0.1$ and $\frac{q_L+q_H}{2} > 0.57$, $\Delta = 0.2$ and $\frac{q_L+q_H}{2} > 0.63$, and $\Delta = 0.5$ and $\frac{q_L+q_H}{2} > 0.76$.

Practical observations have shown that Δ rarely reaches 0.1.

Analyses in this section have brought the same conclusions:

- Maximal proportion of the space, where the combined system is better than the best single system, is the area where self-estimates are better than random ($q_{FT} + q_{TF} > 1$), and is obtained when both systems perform equally good ($p_1 = p_2$).
- With fixed q_{FT}, q_{TF}, increasing difference $\mid p_1 - p_2 \mid$ proportionally decreases the portion of the space where combined classification is beneficial.

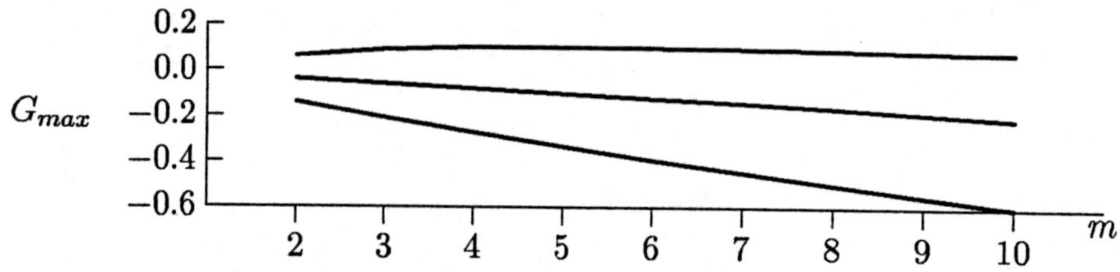

Figure 7.22: G_{max} vs. m; $\frac{q_L+q_H}{2} = 0.55, 0.75, 0.95$ (from bottom to top)

- With fixed p_1, p_2, it is more important that the combining mechanism estimates well when the better system classifies correctly than the worst system, which has generally less effect on the success of a combined classification.

7.4.4 Average Improvement of m Independent Systems

Let us evaluate the average gain in classification accuracy for combinations of more than two independent systems. It is assumed that all variables q_{ij} are uniformly distributed over the $[q_L, q_H]$ interval, and that all variables p_i are uniformly distributed over the $[p_L, p_H]$ interval. At first, $p_L = 0$ and $p_H = 1$. The average gain over the best single system is then defined as

$$\begin{aligned} G_{max} &= \langle p_M - \max\{p_1, \ldots, p_m\}\rangle \\ &= \frac{1}{V}\int_V (p_M(p1, \ldots, p_m, q_{12}, \ldots, q_{m\,m-1}) \\ &\qquad - \max\{p_1, \ldots, p_m\})dV, \end{aligned}$$

where the volume of integration is

$$V = [0,1]^m \times [q_L, q_H]^{m^2-m}.$$

It is difficult to derive G_{max} analytically for arbitrary value of m. Therefore, a Monte-Carlo method was used for integration, and results are presented in Figure 7.22.

For lower values of $\frac{q_L+q_H}{2}$ the gain is negative, and it gets even more negative with increasing m. Therefore in this model, the increasing number of systems does not automatically increase their overall performance. Substantial gains can only be achieved when the combining mechanism estimates very well.

Another series of calculations is based on previous observations that in real life good systems achieve similar classification accuracies on the same domain. Therefore, integration over $p_1, \ldots, p_m$ was performed only over the area

$$|\max\{p_1, \ldots, p_m\} - \min\{p_1, \ldots, p_m\}| \leq \Delta.$$

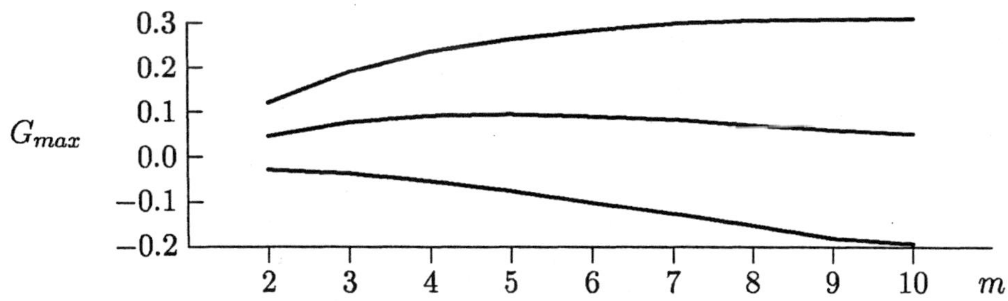

Figure 7.23: G_{max} vs. m; $\frac{q_L+q_H}{2} = 0.55, 0.75, 0.95$ (from bottom to top); $\Delta = 0.2$

For example, $\Delta = 0.3$ means that the maximal difference in classification accuracy between the best and the worst system is less than 30%. Measurements presented in Figure 7.22 were rerun, this time with $\Delta = 0.2$ instead of $\Delta = 1$.

From Figure 7.23 it can be concluded, that under favourable conditions the improvement tends to grow with the growing number of systems. Under not so favourable conditions, the improvement generally decreases with the growing number of systems especially for $m > 5$. These results may not be very reliable due to possible unrealistic assumptions.

7.4.5 Discussion – Formal vs. Real-Life Domains

These formal analyses show that when combining or integrating two or more systems, there is no improvement in an arbitrary domain with arbitrary properties. However, when assuming that cooperating systems achieve similar performance, i.e. that we do not combine very good and very bad systems, and assuming that the combining mechanism is better than random, an improvement of up to a couple percents can be expected in real-life domains.

Therefore, the catch is in special properties of real-life domains. Our first experience with the difference between formal and real-life domains is more than 15 years old. At that time, researchers were discussing about a contradictorial finding that the more thorough we search through look-ahead, the worse results we get for an average problem domain. How is it possible that mathematically correct computer analyses showed that there is no gain when searching in deeper depths while for example chess computers showed a very clear improvement with prolonged search when playing chess in reality? A clear contradiction between formal analysis and real-life experience! We (Bratko, Gams 1983) were one of the first to show that the reason lies in a simple fact that games like chess or other "interesting" games have very specific properties compared to all possible games. The important conclusion was that domains belong to different types - some are formal, other real-life, some are small and other enormous. In general, algorithms perform differently in different domains. In chess and other games, search algorithms perform better when looking further ahead. But under certain conditions in certain types of domains search algorithms perform worse with increased look-ahead depth. It is like our simulated models - under reasonable circumstances multiple models seem to be successful. Under specific conditions, multiple models can be a bad idea.

Similar results were observed in many areas. For example, it was shown that nearly all random-generated functions (99%) are not decomposable while nearly all real-life functions are decomposable (98%) – meaning that there is nearly always some law hidden in the data in real-life domains while no such thing exists in an average random-generated function.

Most of the formal analyses are assuming that there is one world, one domain, one problem, one model. No, that is not the case! **It seems that our real world and the world of truly intelligent systems are very special with very special properties.** Penrose in the "Emperor's New Mind" estimates that our world belongs to a group of similar worlds that represent only ${\frac{1}{10}}^{10^{123}}$ of all possible worlds.

7.4.6 Conclusions

- **Different analyses strongly indicate that in many real-life domains, improvements of classification accuracy can be obtained by sensibly combining two or more systems.**
- **Improvements can be expected in real-life domains where the combined system exploits different viewpoints of good systems.**
- **Systems perform significantly different in different types of domains. In formal domains with only one appropriate viewpoint, one system can achieve top performance. In real-life domains with many possible viewpoints, combined systems in most cases outperform single systems.**
- **It is reasonable to expect improvements of a couple of percents when combining systems in real-life circumstances. Note that here we are dealing with absolute percents where realistic differences between competing systems are usually within a couple of percents.**

$\vec{s}$	LYMPHOGRAPHY		PRIMARY TUMOUR	
	$p_{\vec{s}}\, measured - fitted$	$q_{\vec{s}}$	$p_{\vec{s}}\, measured - fitted$	$q_{\vec{s}}$
(*F*, *F*)	0.2600 – 0.2599	0	0.4461 – 0.4462	0
(*T*, *F*)	0.0333 – 0.0334	0.667	0.0186 – 0.0184	0.789
(*F*, *T*)	0.0311 – 0.0311	0.786	0.0128 – 0.0128	0.846
(*T*, *T*)	0.6761 – 0.6756	1	0.5226 – 0.5226	1

Table 7.17: Fitting the model for GB92**m*BAYES

7.5 Fitting the Model to Real-Life Applications

7.5.1 Combining One Statistical and One ML System

Here we try to fit our mathematical model to empirical measurements performed in previous sections (lymphography and primary tumor).

When fitting the model to empirical measurements, d and p_2 are first computed to minimize the error $\sqrt{(p_{\vec{s}}measured - p_{\vec{s}}fitted)^2}$. We choose p_1 for approximating the accuracy of the better classifier ($p_1 \geq p_2$). From practical measurements we obtain q_{FT}, q_{TF}. Finally, classification accuracy of the integrated of combined systems can be computed according to (Eq. 2) and compared to the measured accuracy. Note that the model can produce either positive or negative gains based on obtained measurements.

Measurements on our two standard sets of benchmark data were rerun, and $p_{\vec{s}}$ and q_{TF}, q_{FT} were averaged over 10 tests. In Table 7.17, results and fitting on testing data are presented for the best combination, GB92**m*BAYES.

In lymphography, the values of (d, p_2) were fitted to $(0.846, 0.694)$, and to $(0.938, 0.450)$ in the primary tumor domain. Computed classification accuracy was 0.722 (the same as measured) in lymphography, and 0.548 (measured 0.549) in primary tumor. Fitting errors are therefore very small.

Fitting the theoretical model to a real-world application indicates that our model fits well to real-life problems.

7.5.2 Integrating Four System – The Rolling Emulsion Application

During the last seven years we have been applying various artificial intelligence systems at Iron and Steel Works Jesenice (Gams, Karba, Drobnic 1996). In our first attempts, we were using first generation expert systems and ID3-like empirical learning systems. Results were quite encouraging in several domains requiring expert knowledge including steel classification, controlling the quality of the hydraulic oil and some experiments for special structural cryogenic steel. At the moment, two of our expert systems are in regular use.

While we had been quite satisfied with the first generation expert systems, we made an attempt to implement the relatively novel approach of integrating different systems in the Sendzimir rolling mill. In this case, the quality of the cold strip or cold sheet is usually acceptable if the quality of the rolling emulsion is high. For this purpose, the quality of the rolling emulsion is systematically controlled and actions are taken according to the observed parameters. Seven attributes have proven useful: mitigating number of oil, presence of Fe in oil, presence of Fe in sediment, concentration of oil, addition of oil, addition of basin oil and presence of inactive oil. Experiments with greater number of attributes have shown no improvement. For more technical details see (Karba 1994).

There are five classes according to the actions that are to be taken in order to improve the quality of the emulsion. Classes are ordered in the sense that higher class corresponds to better quality.

Measurements were performed on prestored examples (one measurement of emulsion per day). In tests, 30% of randomly chosen examples were given to classifying systems and measurements were performed 10 times to decrease statistical errors due to chance (see Table 7.18). Each learning system was each time given the remaining 70% of examples for training while KA systems (Expert System and DEX) were constructed on the basis of interviews with the expert in a classical knowledge acquisition manner.

Applied systems were:

- A – ASSISTANT PROFESSIONAL - an ID3-type algorithm with pruning mechanisms for noisy domains (Cestnik 1992);
- NN - a neural network based on Markovian algorithm;
- ES – a classical expert system with if-then rules;
- DEX – a multi-attribute decision making system for supporting multi-attribute decisions (Bohanec, Rajkovic 1991).

First, classification accuracies of single systems were measured on testing data (see Table 7.18).

Assistant Professional achieved 2.5% better accuracy than Expert System, and Expert System was 2.2% better than DEX. The accuracy of a neural network algorithm was lower than expected. Probable causes are relatively small number of examples, inappropriate domain for that type of neural network or neural networks in general, lack of a NN-expert in the team. Similarly, statistical systems did not perform well and were early on eliminated from further measurements.

In another experiment (Table 7.19), we have **combined** the four systems in various ways. The combinations of classifications were performed by rounding average

system	accuracy
A - Assistant Professional	0.791
NN - Neural Network	0.619
D - DEX	0.744
ES - Expert System	0.766

Table 7.18: Classification accuracy of single systems

class from classifications of single systems. For example, if three systems classified an object into classes 1, 2, and 5, the combined classification was 3. The approach seems reasonable when classes are ordered as in this particular case. In the first stage, the combining process was completely *automatic*. The results are presented in the second column in Table 7.19 denoted by "-E". Each row corresponds to a combination of the systems, e.g., "A + ES" in the second row denotes a combination of Assistant Professional and Expert System. Corresponding numbers in parentheses present improvements in percents over the best single system.

system	-E	+E
A+D	0.788 (–0.3%)	0.794 (+0.3%)
A+ES	0.806 (+1.5%)	0.819 (+2.8%)
D+ES	0.747 (–1.9%)	0.750 (–1.6%)
A+D+ES	0.822 (+3.1%)	0.825 (+3.4%)
A+NN+D+ES	0.825 (+3.4%)	0.829 (+3.8%)

Table 7.19: Classification accuracy of combined systems

Since an expert was involved during the whole process, his knowledge was applied also in the process of combining classifications. Namely, the expert cooperated in one round of tests thus examining classifications of each example, and his decisions were accepted as the correct one. Effectively, he corrected classifications of only four examples which were then included into further combinations only when any

system	-E	+E	I - C (-E)	I - C (+E)
A+D	0.797 (+0.6%)	0.800 (+0.9%)	+0.9%	+0.6%
A+ES	0.825 (+3.4%)	0.828 (+3.7%)	+1.9%	+0.9%
D+ES	0.753 (–1.3%)	0.763 (–0.3%)	+0.6%	+1.3%
A+D+ES	0.844 (+5.3%)	0.856 (+6.5%)	+2.2%	+3.1%
A+NN+D+ES	0.850 (+5.9%)	0.863 (+7.2%)	+2.5%	+3.4%

Table 7.20: Classification accuracy of integrated systems (see text)

of these four examples was being classified. In case of additional expert knowledge, one obtains *automated* combined classifications. The corresponding third column in Table 7.19 is denoted by "+E", and improvements over the best single systems are again in parenthesis. As observed before, the neural network didn't achieve particularly good classification accuracy, and combinations with NN were mainly deleted.

In the experiments (see Table 7.20), combined systems were integrated into one based on classifications of single systems. In Table 7.20, classification accuracies on testing data are presented in a similar way as in Table 7.19, only this time the single systems are fully integrated into one system. Experiments were again performed without "-E" and with the expert "+E". Columns 4 and 5 present improvements of integrated systems compared to combined systems. For example, "I-C (-E)" presents the difference between integrated and combined systems both without additional help from the expert.

The integrated system with additional expert knowledge achieved the best classification accuracy and was at the same time highly understandable. It has the form of a decision tree with 19 nodes and 10 leaves. This is even a little less than the tree obtained by Assistant Professional on original training data (27 nodes, 11 leaves). Most important, the classification accuracy of the final integrated system increased by very significant 7.2% compared to the performance of the best single system.

The integrative approach is in a way similar to hypothesis boosting (Schapire 1989) and knowledge integration (Brazdil, Torgo 1990). Namely, if we classify (usually learning) examples, these classifications (replacing original classes) together with descriptions of the objects represent another learning set. If an empirical learning system is trained on these data, the **integrated** system is automatically constructed. Interesting to notice, the integrating system learns on the same descriptions of objects as each single system, however, the classes are sometimes changed. In this way, the noise is somehow filtered in two passes, and corrected data represent combined views on domain properties.

Our engineering version of the integrating schema enables automatic or automated integration of arbitrary number of systems into one integrated system with one integrated knowledge base. The schema is presented in Figure 7.24. The integrated knowledge base (KB_{int}) is constructed either in a knowledge acquisition (KA) way or by machine learning (ML). Corresponding classifiers (Cl) enable classifications of new examples using corresponding knowledge bases.

Final classifications are combined from classifications of single systems and additional information such as error or probability estimates. If classifications are determined by an algorithm only, then the combining mechanism is *automatic*. The combining mechanism is *automated* if the expert (Expert knowledge) can intervene by correcting classifications of the combining function.

Combined classifications of training examples are used to change classes of training examples. In this way, a new set of training examples with identical descriptions and sometimes changed classes is obtained. The new set of data is given to an empirical learning system (ML) and the integrated knowledge base is obtained. If the number of training examples is too small or even nonexistent (e.g., there are only KA systems), new training data can be obtained by combined classifications of hypothetical examples. Descriptions of these examples can be generated by a random classifier and their classes are determined by the combining function.

In our experiments, single systems that classified all training data were then combined together (columns denoted by "C"), and finally Assistant Professional was utilized to obtain integrated systems (denoted by "I"). Improvements of the integrated system with expert's help were most successful and on average achieved around 3% better classification accuracy than the best single system.

By integrating, transparency of the whole system can substantially increase. Some of the knowledge bases, e.g., neural networks may not be transparent to humans. On the other hand, the integrated knowledge base can be fully transparent, e.g., consisting of a single decision tree or a list of rules.

system	UP	DOWN
A + E	0.741 (−8.1%)	0.853 (+3.1%)
A + D	0.791 (−3.1%)	0.828 (+0.6%)
A + M	0.794 (−2.8%)	0.819 (−0.3%)
E + D	0.672 (−9.1%)	0.841 (+6.9%)
E + M	0.703 (−6.0%)	0.765 (+0.2%)
D + M	0.741 (−0.9%)	0.746 (−0.4%)

Table 7.21: Classification accuracies of two combined systems

$\vec{s}$	$p_{\vec{s}}$ *measured* − *fitted*	$q_{\vec{s}}$ UP	$q_{\vec{s}}$ DOWN
(F, F)	0.0875 − 0.0875	0	0
(F, T)	0.1500 − 0.1500	0.1458	0.9583
(T, F)	0.0906 − 0.0906	0.5172	0.4138
(T, T)	0.6719 − 0.6720	1	1
A + E	$d = 0.809, err. = 0.01$	0.7406 − 0.7406	0.8531 − 0.8531
(F, F)	0.1156 − 0.0855	0	0
(F, T)	0.0625 − 0.626	0.9000	0.0100
(T, F)	0.1344 − 0.1346	0.3488	1.0000
(T, T)	0.6875 − 0.6873	1	1
A + D	$d = 0.485, err. = 0.01$	0.7906 − 0.7905	0.8281 − 0.8282
(F, F)	0.1406 − 0.1405	0	0
(F, T)	0.0375 − 0.0376	0.2500	0.0000
(T, F)	0.2594 − 0.2595	0.8554	0.9880
(T, T)	0.5625 − 0.5624	1	1
A + M	$d = 0.473, err. = 0.02$	0.7938 − 0.7938	0.8188 − 0.8188
(F, F)	0.0938 − 0.0938	0	0
(F, T)	0.1563 − 0.1563	0.2200	0.7200
(T, F)	0.1438 − 0.1437	0.2174	0.8478
(T, T)	0.6063 − 0.6062	1	1
E + D	$d = 0.190, err. = 0.01$	0.6719 − 0.6719	0.8406 − 0.8406
(F, F)	0.0750 − 0.0990	0	0
(F, T)	0.3250 − 0.3180	0.7788	1.0000
(T, F)	0.1625 − 0.1385	0.0792	0.0000
(T, T)	0.4375 − 0.4445	1	1
E + M	$d = 0.000, err. = 3.54$	0.7031 − 0.7031	0.7652 − 0.7625
(F, F)	0.1781 − 0.1781	0	0
(F, T)	0.2219 − 0.2217	0.9437	0.9857
(T, F)	0.0719 − 0.0719	0.0435	0.0000
(T, T)	0.5281 − 0.5283	1	1
D + M	$d = 0.417, err. = 0.00$	0.7406 − 0.7407	0.7462 − 0.7468

Table 7.22: Fitting the model for combinations of two systems

Different combinations and approaches were further analyzed. First, various combinations of all 6 combinations of 2 systems were performed. The combined classification had to be the same as one of the two classifications proposed by the two single systems. The combinations of two different classes (e.g., 1 and 2) was once rounded UP (2), and once DOWN (1). When two systems classified 2 or more classes apart (e.g., 1 and 3), the classification of previously assumed better system was chosen. Obtained classification accuracies and differences to the best single classifier are presented in Table 7.21.

In Table 7.21, combining DOWN (average +1.1%) is more successful than combining UP (average -3.0%). Altogether, combining yields 1.9% decrease in classification accuracy. "Blind" combining has not been beneficial in this case.

Fitting the model to the six combinations of two systems (see Table 3) are presented in Table 7.22. In each combination of two systems, the measured and fitted probabilities of the four cases are presented (The same for UP and DOWN). In the third and the fourth column the successfulness of combining mechanism is presented for UP and DOWN, respectively. In the fifth row for each combination, dependence between both systems is denoted by "*d*". Standard error of $p_{\bar{s}}$ in percents is denoted by "err". In the last two columns of this row, measured and computed accuracy are presented for UP and DOWN.

Except for the fifth combination (E+M) the error is well bellow 0.1%.

The final integrated programming system has a couple of thousands of lines. However, it integrates single programs with altogether around 100.000 lines of code (e.g., Assistant, DEX etc.). The system is most often used when the expert is not present (weekends, holidays). In very complicated cases the expert is contacted through a pager. The expert estimates the system as successful although it does not achieve 100% accuracy (as claimed by the expert when classifying himself). The observed differences were typically bordering cases when it does not make much difference which action one starts with. Furthermore, the expert found integrated decision trees very transparent and reasonable. In some cases, integrated knowledge bases showed relations between attributes which were new and interesting to the expert. Altogether, the system was in use for seven years. Each year, the machine produced 100.000 tons of steel of a little better quality than if using any single system.

In summary, **several combinations and integrations achieved significantly better classification accuracy than the best single system.** The integrated combination with additional expert knowledge achieved the best average classification accuracy and was at the same time highly understandable.

7.5.3 Conclusions

When fitting the formal schema to the application, the fitting error was generally small indicating that formal models are a good approximation of

real-life events. The above statement was confirmed with fitting in two oncological domains and in the rolling emulsion domain.

Fitting also indicates that "blind" combining mechanisms may not be very successful. The obvious disadvantage of the introduced combining mechanism is a lack of error estimates. An expert or appropriate cross-validation technique may be needed for successful combining or integrating.

We have also presented a general integrating schema which enables integration of an arbitrary number of systems as black boxes into a transparent knowledge base. The schema can be iterated arbitrary number of times. In further extension, each system can be treated as a neuron in a neural network, and algorithms for neural networks can be applied. The integrating schema also enables transformation of knowledge representations from nontransparent forms into a transparent one, e.g., from a neural network into a decision tree.

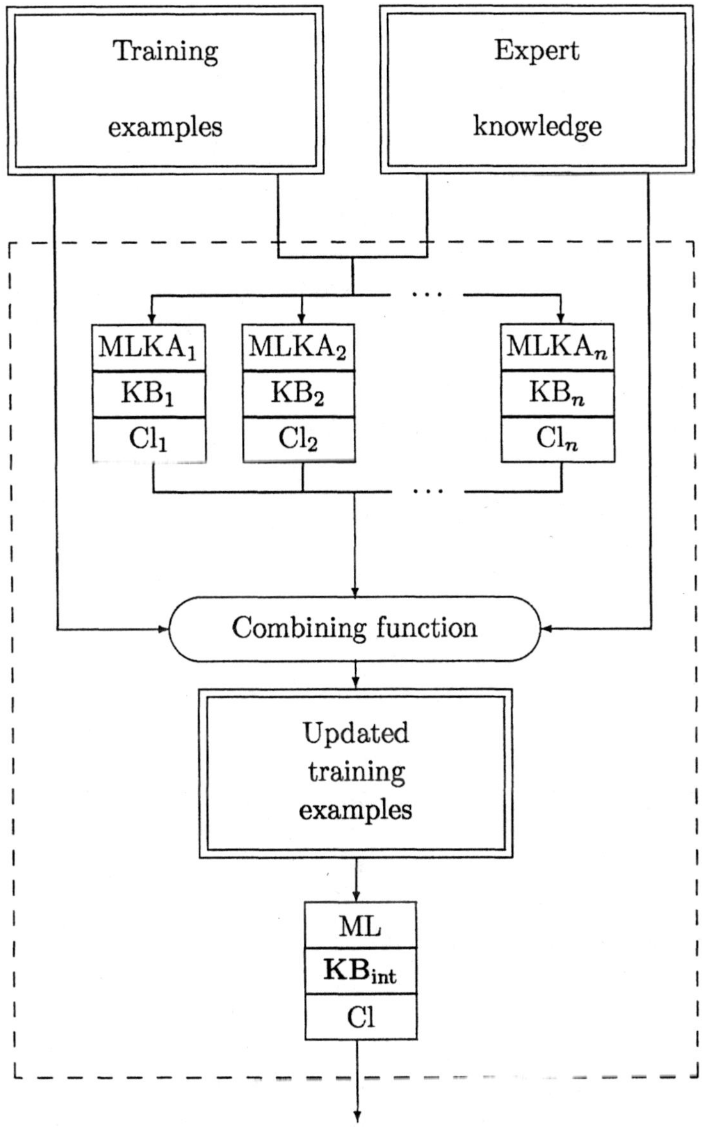

Figure 7.24: A general integrating schema.

7.6 Human Multiple Reasoning

Human multiple reasoning is observed at two levels: (1) in a group of experts, and (2) at the human brain level.

7.6.1 Expert groups

Forming the group of experts has long been a common matter for humans when difficult questions were raised. First such groups probably date back to the cave man and were conditioned by speech abilities and social life. Psychologists are studying different forms of cooperation in groups, their behaviour and performance. A group can malfunction because of many reasons, but **it is a general practice that a group performs better than any of the individuals.** In certain branches such as medicine, the performance increase of expert groups is especially characteristic due to the fact that diagnostic tasks can be rather objectively performed on unseen patients. Therefore, classification accuracy can be precisely evaluated and compared on difficult real-life domains. These measurements show that the average improvement of the group performance over the performance of the best expert alone is typically from 1 to 5 %.

7.6.2 The Human Brain

Lately, several studies have been performed by different scanning and other nondestructive techniques. Generally, they confirm older conclusions of the research on the asymmetry and lateralization of human brain (SCI-AM-92).

Although anatomically there are no great differences between both hemispheres, they process information in quite contrasting ways. Typically, the left hemisphere controls the right-hand side of the body and the right hemisphere controls the left-hand side. The left thinks analytically, discreetly, rationally and reductively, is aware of temporal sequences and linearity and is heavily involved in language and mathematics. The right hemisphere thinks holistically, intuitively, synthetically, diffusely, processes inputs simultaneously and visuo-spatially, and recognizes patterns and faces.

Since **both hemispheres process information quite differently**, as a result different ways of thinking emerge: vertical and lateral thinking or convergent and divergent thinking. On the other hand, both hemispheres show some activity almost all the time, and they intensively cooperate and communicate through the corpus callosum. For example, vertical thinking typically develops the best alternative under given classes and categories while lateral thinking generates other alternatives by reformulating and elaborating the problem. Similarly, the process of creative thinking consists of two sequential stages of processing information: divergent thinking followed by convergent thinking. Mind is conceived as constantly branching out in cyclical patterns.

In the last decade, the multiplicity of human brain became widely accepted. Says Gazzaniga (1989): "What was thought to be the product of an integrated system **is actually the product of the interaction of at least two systems with discrete neural localisation**". It seems that brain consists not only of two hemispheres but also of several specialized hardware (e.g. sensors) and software subsystems. Similarly, psychologists discuss about the multiplicity of human thought processes. In the AI field, Minsky (1987) introduced a large-scale model of the mind with the thesis that the human brain performs its great variety of functions by exploiting the advantages of many different knowledge representations.

Particularly interesting is the split brain research which is concerned with damages caused by the splitting of corpus callosum and thus by severely disrupting the inter-hemispheric communication. One of the questions is, why there are so small consequences regarding so major damage in the centre of the human brain. One possible answer is that long-term effects are related not only to the amount of physical damage but also to the ability of brain self-adaptation. Indeed, a small infant can lose an entire hemisphere and grow up normally. Only after the age of about two or more increasingly serious impairments result from loosing either hemisphere. Furthermore, different studies imply that the corpus callosum becomes mature after the age of ten. Therefore, the smaller and earlier the damage is done the fewer long term effects.

On the other hand, it still seems unreasonable that evolution would be so uneconomical that a surgical cut of a couple of centimeters in the centre of the brain would cause only a small difference in performance. The hypothesis at hand, in analogy with the principle of multiple knowledge would be, that the performance would generally decrease by a couple of percents if multiplicity is severely declined but basic knowledge bases remain intact. Such a small decrease is very difficult to measure because human performances vary a lot be it at the level of individuals or groups. For example, females for the most part have a more symmetrical brain than males, their corpus callosum is proportionally bigger and more often used. Nevertheless, the general pattern seems reasonably reliable: more advanced inter-hemisphere cooperation exploiting different processing approaches, and by this more advanced multiple knowledge is strongly linked to more advanced human performance.

True hemisphere specialization and multiple cooperation appears to be an endowment that is unique to human maturity. **Only traces of asymmetry can be found in other animals, but much more in early man. Multiple thinking is highly related to the most advanced human thinking, be it a necessity or a by-product. Humans intensively utilized multiple strategies roughly a million to 100.000 years ago.**

7.7 Cognitive Sciences and Common Sense

Regarding the debate whether computers can think at all, we shall refer to the now classical work presented by Hauser and Rapaport (1993). Hauser proposes his arguments for the claim that his pocket calculator Cal or at least his personal computer Sparky thinks. There are four basic evaluation properties/criteria for his claim: **consciousness, autonomy, intentionality and unity**. If any machine can meet them, then it thinks. Hauser points out that autonomy and self-consciousness are both subjective categories and that humans can be easily judged out by the standards of computing machines. Intentionality provides more difficult line of reasoning, yet, it is claimed that computers have intentionality when performing the calculations and the limit between computers and humans is again subjective.

Regarding the **multiplicity** subject, the most interesting is the fourth Hauser's argument: "The Unity Objection, rather than claiming that some specific mental ability is necessary for thought or calculation, claims what is essential to something's thinking, or even calculating, is having *enough* interconnected mental abilities of various sorts. Even if we stop short of the strong Cartesian demand that thought must be 'a universal instrument which can serve for all kinds of situations' (Descartes 1673: 140), perhaps we can at least require that would-be thought processes should be *flexible* instruments that serve for *various* situation. This seems sufficient to exclude Cal without excluding me or you or Helen Keller." Further on, Hauser claims that the same criterion might not exclude personal computers, i.e., his Sparky.

In a response, Rapaport suggest that mere calculating is not thinking on a strong view of thinking. However, on a weak and unexciting sense of thinking calculators do think, i.e., compute. Regarding the argument from unity, it is claimed that "The more mental things a computer can do, the more it can (be said to) think, the more maximal its thinking is." And about the argument that Sparky is an indissoluble highly-interconnected unit: "the different programs that Sparky runs are unrelated and unconnected to each other. Suppose, however, that they *were* all suitably connected. Suppose Sparky is running 'Lotus 1-2-3-∞', which treats as a single humongous unit a simultaneously running calculator, word-processor, spreadsheet, database, e-mail program, etc., Sparky could be said to think - but this is far different from arbitrary computation and far different from ordinary PCs."

In my opinion, the last couple of sentences in the last paragraph directly correspond to the strong version of the principle of multiple knowledge. Therefore, **in cognitive sciences the Principle is already known for years, although in an intuitive form**, and not technically presented as in this book.

In the same discussion, both Hauser and Rapaport discuss subject which is strongly related to the paradox of multiple knowledge, and to the universality of Turing machines. Hauser himself proposes a paradox - if any computer (say, Sparky) is accepted as capable of thinking (in relation to the unity criterion), and any computer can simulate other in the sense of Turing machines, than, how can it be that one is thinking and the other not? This is in a way similar to the Searle's paradox.

Rapaport replies: "perhaps all mental abilities are at the bottom the *same*. For example, if thinking is computing, then all different kinds of thinking are ultimately expressible in terms of the primitives and constructs of, say, a Turing Machine."

In terms of the paradox of multiple knowledge, it is possible that knowledge (and intelligence) can be storable and executable on simple digital machines. Some remarks were already presented: First, practical feasibility of such simulation remains very questionable in real time due to different hardware. Second, one should not mix syntax with semantics. In a black box one integrated system performs like a single system, yet they do differ from the semantic point of view like a black room of humans differs from a black room with one human. A simple automaton, i.e., the Turing machine, can (theoretically) simulate complex behavior of the intelligent systems, but it is not its general inherent property at semantic level. An appropriate version of the Turing test can differentiate between a room with one human and a room with many people, and between a human and a computer.

Another interesting aspect emerges when analyzing the Turing test. Michie (1993) observes that "In earlier generations students of intelligent behavior generally ignored the phenomenon of consciousness", that (quoting Popper) "possibly the right hemisphere is conscious but not self-conscious, and that the left hemisphere is both conscious and self-conscious", further (quoting Trevarthen) "The brain is adapted to create and maintain human society and culture by two complementary conscious systems.", (by quoting James) "We see that the mind is at every stage a theatre of simultaneous possibilities. Consciousness consists in comparison of these with each other, the selection of some, and the suppression of others, of the rest by the reinforcing and inhibiting agency of attention."

Michie also mentions the work which is one of the earliest explicit introductions of multiplicity – Dennett's 'Consciousness Explained' (1991), where model of conscious recollection is proposed as the writer's 'Multiple Drafts'. O'Rourke (1993) sees Dennet's multiple drafts as a model "in which all mental activity consists of intertwining parallel skeins of processes of interpretation and elaboration. His claim is that there is no need to re-represent the data, no need to move it to a center." And in conclusions: "Dennett is one of the few philosophers to take AI seriously, and those in AI should consider returning the favor."

Indeed, **it is surprising, that (strong) AI has for so long taken so little interest in related, e.g., cognitive sciences.** The difference in approaches is astonishing. One just has to compare the CYC project (Stefik and Smoliar 1993) and the OSCAR project (Pollock 1989). Says Pollock (1989): "OSCAR represents the dream of AI since its infancy, but it is a dream that has faded in much of the AI community. This is because researchers in AI have made less progress than anticipated in achieving the dream. My claim in this book is that the failure is not intrinsic to the task, but stems from the fact that many of the problems involved are essentially philosophical, while researchers in AI have not usually been trained in philosophy."

In summary, **cognitive scientists have for long thought that there is an essential difference between computers and humans often based on multiplicity arguments, but were rejected by formal scientists who accept arguments only in the technical form of formal equations.** It was claimed that the cause for wrong interpretations of cognitive scientists was based on a) the lack of knowledge of basic scientific concepts like the Turing machine and Church thesis, and b) the lack of knowledge about computers. But times have changed and **scientists in general are more open to ideas that there must indeed be something in/out there.**

Chapter 8

Consequences

The principles of multiple knowledge derives several consequences, among them in relation to:

- Occam's principle,
- statistics, and
- properties of knowledge.

8.1 Occam's Razor Vs. Multiple Knowledge

In early 1300th William of Occam declared his Razor as disagreement with the superfluous elaborations of Scholastic school. Basically he stated that if two models (or two expressions) are constructed with the same classification accuracy, then the simpler is preferable. Consequently, Razor is applied to eliminate too complex expressions.

His principle had great impact on theory and practice. For example, since than it has been known that it is always possible to find a sufficiently complex model which is able to optimally explain the observed events. But the quality of the constructed knowledge is measured on the events which were not available to the system during the learning phase. Models that achieve very good classification accuracy on learning data are typically too complex because they overfit noise in learning data and as a result achieve worse classification accuracy on test data. For example, in (Blumer *et al.* 1986) it has been shown that under very general assumptions Occam's razor prefers models with higher classification accuracy on test data. If models of minimal or near minimal complexity can be produced in polynomial time from learning data, by applying Occam's razor a polynomial learning algorithm can be designed (Valiant 1984).

Extensive theoretical and practical analyses have confirmed the validity of Occam's razor within the scope of one classifier, e.g., when constructing and pruning one decision tree (Breiman et. al. 1984; Niblett and Bratko 1986; Mingers 1989; Holder 1991).

But blindly applying Occam's razor might sometimes be Counterproductive (Ali, Pazzani 1994). The following example considers rules which were actually constructed by our system GINESYS (Gams *et al.* 1991) when trying to diagnose a location of primary tumour:

if (axilliar = yes) and (degree of diff = fairly) and (lung = no)
then breast (100%)

if (axilliar = yes) and (degree of diff = fairly) and (lung = no)
and (sex = female)
then breast (100%)

The consequences of both rules represent class prediction and are exactly the same - a 100% probability that primary tumour is in breasts. The antecedents differ only in the "sex" attribute. Strictly applying Occam's razor, the second rule could be deleted. Now, imagine a computer program diagnosing a male patient with characteristics matching the first antecedent. Not only medically educated people would find this situation suspicious since it is well known that a vast majority of breast cancers are found in a female population. Furthermore, if the second rule is chosen as the more correct, it would not match the male patient with serious indications for breast cancer. Such cases, although very rare, do happen. Only with both rules a possible conflict can be identified which is solved in GINESYS by applying naive Bayes which evaluates additional attributes and sends an additional warning.

Deleting the more complex of the two rules with the same class probability distribution is in contradiction with empirical observations of different authors. Indeed, simple domains can be generated (Gams *et al.* 1991) to show that combinations of simple multiple rules can represent the essential law of the domain.

Another aspect is the cost of searching, storing and using multiple models. In the days of William of Occam such efforts had to be done manually and were proportional to the number of models. Therefore, they represented an important percentage of the whole effort. The reduction in storage and computing may be important for people, but is much less important for computers. For example, if an algorithm is designed which produces one model in the form of one decision tree, simple modifications are necessary to construct one tree per one class or to force different attributes at the top of several different trees. Modern computer technology significantly changed the cost/benefit ratio in favour of multiple models.

Occam's razor promotes a cybernetic approach that is in specific circumstances consistent with the principle of multiple knowledge, and globally different. The Razor should be applied with great precaution if the goal is to construct the best approximation of a real-life problem (where a combination of submodels enables top performance) instead of finding the best model alone. However, regarding all possible combinations of all submodels or each of the submodels itself, Occam's principle may be useful again.

8.2 Bayes' Classifier and Multiple Knowledge

Bayes' inductive procedure for constructing the optimal model consists of the following basic steps (Cheeseman 1989):
1. Define the whole space of possible models.
2. Assign prior probabilities to the models.
3. Use Bayes' theorem to obtain posterior probabilities of models.
4. Choose a search algorithm for finding the optimal model in the whole space.
5. Stop the search when the optimal model is found.

Except for very simple domains or domains with special properties it is usually not possible to find the optimal model because the computation is too expensive and probabilities can not be set with sufficient certainty. Bayes' inductive algorithm is therefore mainly a declarative algorithm which enables the construction of a model with the best expected accuracy according to the given data, domain knowledge and the chosen space of models.

An important addition to this procedure is known (Cheeseman 1989): "It might seem obvious that finding the most probable model is the goal of scientific discovery, but this assumption is questionable. The standard scientific method is to base all predictions on the most probable model alone. However, if **the goal is to make as accurate predictions as possible about future data, then taking a weighted average over possible models is optimal by the Bayes' criterion**. Basing all predictions on a single model is jumping to conclusions, and is especially dangerous when alternative high-probability models make radically different predictions." This resembles the general Principle of multiple knowledge, however, in our experiments taking a weighted average over possible models was not always as perspective as other ways of combining. For example, best-one voting schema typically achieved better overall classification accuracy in a great majority of our simulations and was especially better for smaller number of models (Gams *et al.* 1993).

Future research will hopefully give better indications how to combine different models and how to estimate the number and properties of the set of models which achieve the optimal cost/benefit ratio. However, at this point a modification of the inductive Bayes' procedure can be proposed in steps 4 and 5:

4. Choose a search algorithm for finding the optimal set of models in the whole space.
5. Stop the search when the optimal set of models is found.

8.3 Properties Of Knowledge

Principles of multiple knowledge offer several conclusions regarding the properties of knowledge including answers to the following questions:

- Can knowledge be stored?
- Is knowledge predictable?
- Is knowledge understandable?
- What is the form of knowledge?

8.3.1 Can Knowledge Be Stored?

This question is relevant because of a thesis that knowledge stored in a computer can not capture the meaning because it consists of strings of meaningless symbols (Searle 1980). For example, so far we have been able to store descriptions of only relatively simple sequential domains while for complex real-life domains storing the knowledge in existing knowledge representations is beyond our existing capabilities and knowledge. Said Clancey (1989): "Machine learning will never progress beyond its current state until people realise that knowledge is not a substance that can be stored."

To summarise previous debates: since the days of Gödel, Turing, Church and Shannon it has been more or less accepted that anything describable can be in principle stored in a string of symbols. One possibility left is that thinking is not describable at all. On the other hand, theoretical confirmation may not mean much for practical feasibility. It may be that although theoretically possible, the process of transforming the knowledge of one human into the fastest possible digital computer would take, say, 10.000 years. Therefore, there are many options opened for further study.

The principle of multiple knowledge can enhance our understanding – problems could emerge due to the inappropriateness of existing ways of describing knowledge. Currently, formal science and computers can handle well simple sequential (or parallel) implementations of formal knowledge. But, the principle of multiple knowledge implies that **storing (human) knowledge in a simple sequential way is not feasible. If storing of knowledge is feasible, it must be multiple, i.e., more complex than previously thought. This is not a minor difference** since we are talking about several orders of magnitude more difficult problems and more capable solving mechanisms which, on the other hand, can not solve better formal problems appropriate for formal systems. Multiple systems enable only a couple of percents better performance in real-life problems at the price of more powerful computing mechanisms. Intelligence and consciousness therefore might seem redundant or a by-product of human evolution. But according to the principle, this is not so. **Essential human processing properties are part of the superior computing mechanism.**

At the very end, statical transformation from multiple systems into sequential ones seem feasible, given sufficient time and space. However, the future performance is lost.

In analogy with human brain, one has to store several types, forms and representations of knowledge. At the top, there is a clear distinction between two types of thinking that are performed by the brain hemispheres. It is quite possible that any computer system emulating human intelligence would have to have similar top-level architecture consisting of modules with different computing approaches.

8.3.2 Is Knowledge Predictable?

Can we predict the behavior of stored knowledge, i.e., a computer model of a real-world domain? In most artificial domains a positive answer is a common case. For example, theoretically we can predict the behavior of a computer program on the bases of its listing. On the other hand, it is commonly known that the Turing halting problem is unsolvable on the Turing machine. The halting problem can be solved by other, more powerful computing mechanisms, however, each so far known computing mechanism has its own unsolvable questions. Therefore, it is theoretically impossible to predict all future behavior of digital computers. Even simple random generators based on system clock and the contents of a random page on Internet produce unpredictable numbers. Introducing multiple knowledge makes things only worse. Complex real-world models consist of several levels of submodels, each potentially similar to the Turing halting problem. **Realistical predictability in detail seems unfeasible in general.**

But for most formal and real-life domains, much can be predicted in normal circumstances because only rational performance is evolutionally rewarded. In addition, it is often possible to execute, i.e., to simulate knowledge models, and observe the performance.

8.3.3 Is Knowledge Understandable?

The famous "Feigenbaum's Bottleneck" (Feigenbaum 1985) was based on observations in the process of acquisition of expert's knowledge. Experts were able to achieve very good performances and at the same time they were able to explain specific solutions in a human understandable and meaningful way. But when trying to formalize or even only to describe their knowledge in the form of rules or trees they found it very difficult and even frustrating. As if expert knowledge would not be appropriate for transparent single knowledge models.

Accepting the principle we can see why it is so difficult to put the knowledge on a paper. Not only that submodules are changing over the time, the possible combinatorial explosion (remember Figure 1) in the

combining mechanism makes knowledge very difficult to understand at the top integrated level. But after each specific conclusion is made, it can be easily explained. This makes the combining mechanism that utilizes knowledge one of the core secrets of human thinking. Quite probably, it is at least partially hardware/brain coded. Maybe, it is not executable with formal mechanisms after all.

Research in animal orientation can be taken as another example (Long 1991). Several ten years ago researchers in that area discovered major patterns: ants follow their scented tracks produced by a marking ant, pigeons orient according to the sun at day and stars at night, bees can even communicate to others the direction of food according to the position of the sun. More detailed observations revealed that major patterns alone can not explain why ants do not get lost without their tracks and why pigeons do not get lost even if the sky is full of clouds at night. Later it was discovered that animals use several navigation methods, e.g., pigeons can detect magnetic fields and also use smell. Again it was thought that exact algorithms for animal orientation were discovered. Only for a while, because certain puzzles attracted further attention. For example, pigeons at Illinois, USA, systematically got lost in an area with magnetic disturbance only if raised there and not if brought there. This behavior could not be simply explained by a single model of knowledge since most indications were more likely to be familiar to local pigeons. Experiments revealed that pigeons not only use multiple methods for navigation but also learn the best combination according to their surroundings. Suddenly, when researchers actually achieved a step further in understanding of pigeon orientation, they were not any more able to describe it in the form of a simple procedural algorithm. Then, **how can it be expected to explain human knowledge with one (huge) decision tree?**

Constructing a set of multiple models seems better (although not the ultimate) idea and in our experiments they enabled much better possibilities to analyze the laws of the domain. Unfortunately, it is more difficult to explain solutions with multiple models than with one model alone.

At this stage it seems that expert's knowledge can not be simply transformed into one model (i.e. knowledge base) through knowledge acquisition or learning without loosing performance in the sense of top performance and consistency with expert's knowledge.

In another thought, it is only a rather common myth that knowledge stored in computers is fully understandable. And, that a formal computer program cannot be intelligent because it can be fully explained (which we argue as unfeasible).

8.3.4 What is the Form of Knowledge?

Undoubtfully, parts of knowledge can be stored, can be consistent, and can be stored in a string of symbols. On the other hand, **it is argued that complex real-life knowledge can not be (easily) stored in a consistent, compact** and sequential form. Real-life knowledge has different properties than knowledge describing formal domains. As declared by the principle of multiple knowledge, the form of knowledge in real-life domains must be truly multiple.

Chapter 9

Many-Worlds Theory and Quantum Computing

This section could be one of the "Confirmation" subsections since **the hypothesis at hand is that the many-worlds theory represents an ideal physical-theory background for the principle of multiple knowledge.** However, this hypothesis seems less confirmed by empirical evidence than the cases with human multiple thinking or by computer multiple models. Furthermore, this subject needs much more attention and space than presented here.

9.1 Paradoxes of Modern Physics

The mystery of quantum physics is well studied and published. Here we shortly refresh the basic phenomena.

In the real world around us we see, feel, learn about it as children and later as adults. Most of humankind history we were unaware of any other world, except maybe the mystical ones. The real world around us also determined our evolutionary progress. The stuff around us behaves like consisting of specific objects, e.g., a computer, a book, a pencil. These objects behave according to the laws of macro particles. It is always possible to measure or calculate the speed and location of objects.

Experiments in quantum physics have showed that the world of atomic particles behaves according to a different set of rules. An object, e.g. an electron, can not be described with the same characteristic values as big objects. Instead of having one position and speed, an atomic particle has several possible states, a superposition of simple states. Each atomic particle behaves as a particle and as a wave at the same time. The good thing is that it is possible to compute quite well with large amounts of particles despite the fact that properties of one single particle can not be as strictly determined as properties of objects in the macro world. According to Penrose (1989), quantum mechanics is computable as well as mechanics of big objects.

The most basic law in the atomic world is the Schrödinger equation. It is something like Newtonian equations for classical physics, something that holds without doubt. It describes how the wave function of a system evolves. An important property of the Schrödinger equation is that it tends to increase the space of possible superpositions with increasing time. At an atomic level, there is no problem – in time we have less and less determined information about a wave-particle. But that is not what we see in our world of big objects.

Quantum mechanics is not part of our experience we have learned during childhood. Our common sense does not help us. Several phenomena are counter intuitive.

9.2 Interpretations Of Quantum Physics

Although unaware of it, we constantly depend on quantum effects. For example, seeing is a process of counting atomic particles - photons that hit our retina. Other quantum connections are less investigated. E.g., many researchers hypothesize that consciousness is connected to quantum physics (Penrose 1989; Chalmers 1996).

How are the world of atomic particles and our macroscopic world binded together? There are a couple of major interpretations:

- classical interpretation or the GRW interpretation
- Bohm's interpretation
- multiple-worlds interpretation.

Classical interpretation assumes that a collapse of a vector space of possible superimposed states into one macroscopic state occurs from time to time.

Bohm's interpretation assumes that the basic particle is always determined also in the microscopic world, we are just not able to determine it more precisely as by the Schrödinger equation.

The *multiple-worlds interpretation* assumes that the Schrödinger equation just holds also in the macroscopic world.

All the three interpretations have their own advantages and problems. Since we are dealing with the principle of multiple knowledge one might by now guess that the multiple-worlds theory is the one most relevant for our research thesis.

9.3 The Many-Worlds Theory

The multiple-worlds theory was introduced by Everett (1957), Wheeler (1957), DeWitt (1970; 1973) and Deutch (1991). As written before, the backbone of this theory is the Schrödinger equation, the basic law for atomic particles. It is well verified by all scientific means, e.g. verified by millions of experiments. But each equation has also its meaning, the framework that ascribes physical meaning to the theoretical symbols. This is - of course - the interpretation.

There is no mathematical transition from the Schrödinger equation into macroscopic world. Other theories such as the classical or Copenhagen theory assert that the equation holds until some event, e.g. when a measurement occurs. When it happens, the equation is not valid any more, and the name of the game changes.

The multiple-worlds theory assumes that there is no collapse of the vector state, that there is no way a particle has just one state, one position and one speed (momentum). In other words – the strange world of atomic particles is also the world of macro objects we live in. **In the world of big objects, all properties of the Schrödinger equation are just as valid as in the world of atomic particles.**

This interpretation is far the most elegant, universal, and powerful. For example, it enables travel in time (Deutch, Lockwood 1994). It also easily provides solutions to several dilemmas of quantum physics, e.g. the Schrödinger's cat. In this mental experiment, a cat is inside a box where a truly random quantum event determines whether the cat lives or dies. Outside the box, there is no way one can predict the outcome of the experiment. The atomic world (quantum event) and the macroscopic world (the cat) interacted, but unlike in real-life, none of the interpretations can give good prediction of the outcome. The multi-world theory replies that since the event is related to the transition according to the Schrödinger equation in the atomic world, our universe will also become superimposed. In simple words - there will be two universes, in one the cat will live and in the other not. Since each quantum event produces transposition of states, the number of all universes must be huge.

In real life we experience just one world, one universe. Where are these additional universes?

Everett proposed that different universes are just in our minds. Since the whole process is highly dependent on the observers (measurements), our minds are crucial for the process.

Other researchers propose that these multiple universes exist in reality. That we are just aware of only one universe. One of the possibilities is that all these universes we see are in a bigger universe which has at least one dimension more than the one we see (see Figure 9.1).

9.4 Objections to the Multiple-World Interpretation

This section is similar to the one presented by Chalmers (1996):

- physical splitting of universes is not reasonable
- why is there a preferred basis for multiple minds

- are superimposed minds associated
- why do we perceive only one mind as ourselves
- where are all possibilities for split universes.

Chalmers concentrated on a modification of Everett's original representation, the one that sees different universes in the human mind. Therefore, there are no physical multiple universes to which several objections apply. Chalmers sees all quantum interpretations as "crazy", and "Everett's the most". Still, he finds Everett's interpretation "easily the most intellectually appealing .. Maybe it is simply too strange to belive."

The problem with multiple universes is besides the common-sense observation the following: With each quantum event, the universe is supposed to split and there are several problems including the energy consumption, i.e. violation of the mass-energy conservation. One possible reply to these critics is that in $N > 3$ dimensions these problems are not relevant. To show analogy in a three-dimensional world where inhabitants live in two dimensions – if a quantum event in two dimensions produces two universes, these two universes are just two planes in the 3-dimensional space (Figure 9.1). Since the number of planes in a three-dimensional is huge, i.e. infinite, there is no problem with sufficient number of universes. Still, the problem with multiple-worlds theory is that what we experience is happening in our three-dimensional world with additional time running in one direction.

9.5 Quantum Computing

Quantum computation is interesting because (Spector 1999):

- Moore's law about exponential growth of computer power will hit limits in a couple of decades while quantum computing enables a significant step ahead in miniaturization.
- Quantum computation is often more powerful than classical computing - for several families of problems more can be computed in less time because they have different time complexity. Some problems with exponential complexity can be computed in much shorter time.

The Church-Turing thesis (i.e. principle) interpreted through the Turing machine says that any computational task that can be performed by any physical object can also be programmed on a universal Turing machine (Deutch 1992). However, the Turing machine computes only with 0's and 1's while quantum computers deal with a vector of superimposed states. **While Turing proposed a universal computing model for classical computation, Deutch in 1985 described a universal quantum computer.** Other researchers like Benioff (1982), Feynman (1986), Albert (1992), Lloyd (1996) also presented important contributions.

Here is a short list of interesting tasks that quantum computers might perform better than classical computers (Deutch 1992):

- Find at least one solution that satisfies given input conditions. Quantum computers (QC) can perform this much faster.
- Confirm that a statement is true. QC can sometimes prove a statement without producing the proof.
- Create random events with given preconditions. QC can produce truly unpredictable random numbers.
- Provide cryptography services. QC can provide truly secure unbreakable types of cryptography.
- Mimic a specific physical event. QC can be much faster for specific physical domains.
- Create human-like performance like consciousness. QC have several interesting properties that make them potential candidates for artificial-intelligence computing mechanisms.

However, quantum computers can not

- compute an average function significantly better than the universal Turing machine
- compute any function that a universal Turing machine can not.

In other words, quantum computers are just as strong as classical digital computers or Turing machines (Deutch 1992). Still, practical differences are essential.

The interesting question is where do the differences in computing come from. According to Deutch, **quantum computations rely on the many-worlds inference phenomena.** When the world splits in two, the inhabitants of one world cannot perceive the other world anymore and vice versa. But they are indirectly influenced. When a quantum computer performs computation, it can perform several tasks simultaneously in different parallel universes. In this way the quantum computer delegates sub-tasks to copies of itself in different worlds (universes) and uses inference to construct the final answer. Since only one world is finally observable by the computer and us, only one solution can be found. Still, that one solution can be found in a time needed to find just one solution, in a parallel way not needing parallel simulation.

We should be aware that only prototypes of quantum computers exist today, and that they can compute only the simplest tasks with a couple of logic gates. But their mathematical concept is quite neatly defined. The Turing machine was defined years before actual electronic computers were constructed, yet all the properties were as predicted. Similar case seems to be valid for quantum computers. We don't know yet when and how difficult, but quantum computers are obviously constructable.

9.6 From Many Worlds To The Principle Of Multiple Knowledge

Before blindly jumping to a conclusion that the Multiple-World theory is the physical background to the principle of multiple knowledge we should apply serious scientific experiments to verify the hypothesis. The major problem with interpretations of quantum physics is that serious scientists, physicians included, don't actually put much trust in these metaphysical interpretations. Specific scientific fields are just too elusive at a particular time to be sure what to believe in. The interpretations we mentioned here are at the moment just possible scientific hypothesis without sufficient scientific confirmation till now. The theory of multiple knowledge assumes that there are multiple models in the brain, in the mind, in successful computing mechanisms. These multiple mechanisms are more successful that single-model mechanisms, and human multiple thinking is more successful than single straight forward thinking of non-intelligent beings. We have developed our theory of multiple knowledge first by observing single and multiple computational models. This part of the theory seems confirmed beyond doubt. Then we have extended the theory to human thinking. Again, human multiple thinking is confirmed beyond doubt. But it is not confirmed beyond doubt that multiple thinking is a necessary condition for intelligence. We infer a hypothesis that it is, but are unable to prove it beyond doubt. We just give reasonable argumentation as to why that is so.

Where does multiple processing in the human brain and also in quantum computers come from? We present a hypothesis that it comes from the multiple-worlds theory. Similarities seem strikingly big. If there is a relation between multiple worlds and multiple knowledge as we hypothesize, that very strongly confirmed our principle.

Fair to say, most physicians currently object the multiple-world idea. But even if they are right, our principle of multiple knowledge does not get devastated. The principle still remains valid, just the physical background changes. Maybe groups of neurons competing for success produce multiple models in the human brain and thus result in multiple thinking. If that is so, neuroscience will have big troubles decoding these processes.

Still, **the multiple-worlds theory is too similar to the principle of multiple knowledge** that our minds would not be eager to connect the two phenomena. If our brain is indeed capable of somehow thinking in more dimensions in many worlds or in the many-minds-observations version by Everett and Chalmers, then it explains the seemingly additional power of humans over computers. As with quantum computers, maybe both computing mechanisms are indeed basically capable of solving similar problems, but **the way of thinking is significantly different and in specific categories like intelligence and consciousness maybe out of reach of classical digital computers. While our brains are not capable of performing very fast and very delicate algebraic calculations, maybe clas-**

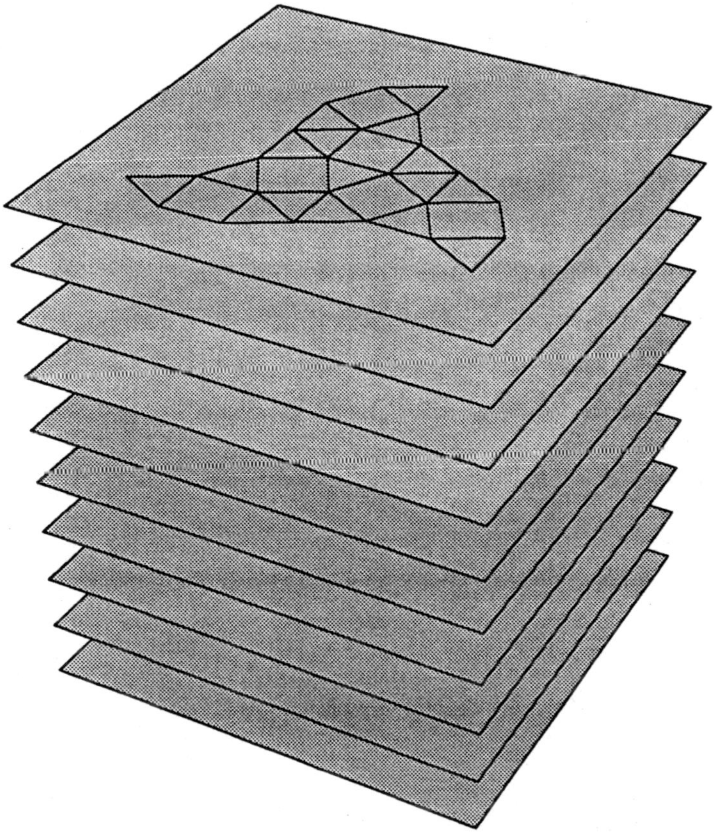

Figure 9.1: What if multiple universes are hidden in another dimension? Semantically, inhabitants of a 2-dimensional universe live and observe only one universe although there are plenty around in 3 dimensions. Maybe we live in a 4-dimensional world being able to perceive just 3 dimensions. This is one possible scenario for the multiple-world theory.

sical computers are not capable of thinking and being conscious. Mother Nature gives some beings speed and others power. None is dominant in all categories.

Chapter 10

Strong AI Fights Back

In the last ten years strong AI has finished attacking weak AI and cognitive sciences as a research field in general. Instead, new scientific discoveries from these newer subfields are in theory welcome. At the same time, several basic criticisms of strong AI were thoroughly analyzed and - rejected.

Penrose's analyses of the Gödel's statement are intensively analyzed in several publication, and nearly always rejected. For example, LaForte et al. (1998) show that Penrose's arguments are flawed because Penrose uses ambiguities between precise and imprecise senses of key terms.

The Searle's Chinese-room argument was fairly demolished by Hauser (1997). He showed that Searle's argument, despite "its rhetorical flash, is logically and scientifically a dud". Searle's argument is presented as:

1. A program is a formal syntactic system.
2. Minds necessarily have semantics.
3. Formal properties don't necessarily suffice for semantics.
4. Programs don't necessarily suffice for mind.

The Church thesis as argumented by strong AI is as follows:

1. Thinking is a way of computation.
2. Turing machines can compute any computable function.
3. Digital computers are Turing machines.
4. Digital computers can think.

Unlike Minsky who presented similar opinion about falsity of the Chinese room argument without formal analyses, Hauser examines Searle's line of reasoning and shows ambiguities that make logical conclusions invalid.

Schapiro (1995) reviews several main thesis such as Luca's and Penrose's argument about Gödel's statement, Searle's Chinese room, and embodiedness. In Schapiro's opinion his own refutations to some well-known weak-AI alleged refutations of computationalism are well argumented. His two main arguments are that

- people are more limited than often recognized, and that
- computer are much more complicated than generally thought.

His basic idea is that from computing point of view, humans and computers have the same limitations, e.g. Gödel's theorem. To show that a computer can think, Schapiro constructs a cognitive agent that has theoretically all the needed properties for intelligence and consciousness.

It is unfair to say that the above weak-AI refutations are false. On the contrary, formally they seem more valid than the refutations of strong AI. But the key question here is what is the set of basic truths, i.e. the name of the game that one accepts as a backbone for further derivations.

In this book it was often claimed that by designing a single-model single-formalism computing mechanism one could not design anything intelligent. Furthermore, we claim that such a system will not achieve as good computing performance as the multiple one. Therefore, differences between strong and weak AI still exist. In our assertion, these **differences are formally cleanly defined through the principle of multiple knowledge and with Wegner's interactive Turing machines.**

Furthermore, even in this section we will show that the semantical criticism of weak AI is not grounded. It is possible to show that attacks on weak AI are not (fully?) grounded even without the principle of multiple knowledge. One just has to start thinking in terms of real life around us.

Take for example the Gödel's statement. In a (too naive but still illustrative) simplification it says about itself that "*I am a liar.*" Now, according to critics of weak AI, nobody, humans or computers, can conclude that the above statement is true. But, an average human will very likely conclude that such a person is quite probably a liar and that the statement is therefore true. People who don't lie don't talk such things around! In real life there is no point formally thinking that if one is a liar then one can not say such a true statement telling the truth and so on. We humans know that formal thinking is useless in such cases. The problem with formal systems is that they can not do the same trick because their formal mechanism which makes them powerful would crack. As easy as that.

In reality, we know that when one says that he/she is a liar, there are still many possible scenarios. We know that usually a person is not either a liar or not. Therefore, multiple thinking and common sense enable us to see that refutations of weak AI are not valid in general. They are valid in the world of specific, often formal domains, but they are not valid in our real world.

Despite some grounded criticism of the weak AI approaches this does not mean that the weak-AI scientific field is not relevant. It just means that the weak AI field is a new progressing field where lots of hypotheses still have to be modified. In general, it could be said that the new weak AI field is progressing and that e.g. the number of books is growing. For example, Pfeifer and Scheier (1999) in "Understanding intelligence" write about an "exciting new field, new AI". And later: "This book provides a systematic introduction to this new way of thinking", which is named "behavior-based AI". In "Cambrian intelligence; The Early History of the New AI" (1999) Brooks writes about "bottom-up approach at the fore-front of current research in not only AI but all of cognitive science".

Chapter 11

Conclusion

Several empirical measurements by different authors strongly indicate that the benefits of multiple reasoning are observed not only in noisy, incomplete domains with insufficient number of examples, but in most domains with at least one of these three properties. A typical improvement of classification accuracy is from 1 to 5% and, although it might seem small, it is important due to the Bayes limit. In the last couple of years, this approach is getting generally accepted thus corresponding to the general version of the principle of multiple knowledge.

From practical point of view, it seems nearly certain that in general no single-strategy algorithm can achieve the performances of algorithms using multiple knowledge. For example, no single decision tree can cope with multiple decision trees in practical domains. Although each application of multiple knowledge is domain dependent, at the same time in most real-life domains there is a wide range of successful applications which enable important improvements over single knowledge representations.

Another conclusion is that single-strategy algorithms will quite probably never achieve the level of intelligence admitted by humans. In other words – **if anybody wants to construct truly intelligent programs one must build multiple systems from the start. Humans not only invented multiple knowledge, they also intensively use it at various levels from groups of experts to the architecture of human brain and mind processes.** Compared to humans, computer multiple knowledge representations have been developed only in recent years and are still at a rather unsofisticated level. Further more, computer science is largely devoted to copying vertical thinking while large proportion of human activities, e.g., divergent thinking are practically neglected. Since there is a strong correlation between multiple knowledge and the advanced performance of the human brain it could be argued that **multiple reasoning is an essential ability that has to be mastered before human-level intelligence can be approached.**

Both phenomena, the principle and the paradox of multiple knowledge were observed before, e.g., in the analyses of the human brain and cognitive sciences.

Our contribution is seen as an attempt to explicitly point out the importance of multiple knowledge for computer applications, to try to bring together conclusions from different sciences, and to make a risky step towards definitions of properties of intelligence.

What are the new comprehensions for the readers of this book? Those who believe that formal science can sufficiently cope with real life around us and inside of us including the mind and consciousness, should reconsider their position. **Formal sciences are not wrong or irrelevant for real life, but there seem to exist more complex mechanisms which are essential for top performance in real-life domains.** This is first of all good for science since it enables further progress.

For those who always believed that there is an essential difference between computers and humans, this book represents a confirmation at more advanced technical level then before.

Consider again the differences between the macro physical world we live in and the strange world of atomic particles. One might say that quantum physics is irrelevant for the world we live in since we are generally unaware of it. But now some researchers claim that quantum physics is actually the essence of all our worlds and the macro world is only one of its derivations. Our hypothesis is that **the multiple world of our knowledge and thinking is a prime candidate for analogy with multiple worlds in physics,** especially the many-worlds Everett-Wheeler-DeWitt interpretation.

We are usually aware of ourselves only as of "oneness" as Penrose claims (1989). But the observable "one" comes from many nonobservable submodels which are combined in the exponential way. Multiple reasoning enables integration into one "I think therefore I am." It means: "I can reasonably and meaningfully combine multiple meanings from single meanings and observations."

To summarise: The world of intelligent creatures differs substantially from Turing machines. The world of intelligent machines, when constructed, will also substantially differ from the Turing machines. The boarder line between these worlds is the principle of multiple knowledge. Similar to physics, atomic particles were for a long time thought to behave as very small balls. After the introduction of the Heisenberg principle, atomic particles are seen as wave-patterns. After the introduction of the principle of multiple knowledge, **knowledge enabling intelligent functions is not seen as a tape or a book, but as many multidimensional models enabling several ways of cooperation, integration and competition.** The principle needs some mathematical polishing, however, already enables another step in human evolution.

If our principle of multiple knowledge is valid as we claim, it means that we humans are actually much more complex and smarter than thought before. It means that **our minds hide much deeper secrets than we possibly comprehend at this moment.**

It also means that humans and computers are and will not be competitors like humans and cars are not since they are functionally compatible and not competitive.

From a technical point of view, new comprehensions constructed by the help of weak AI will enable construction of better computers and thus another step in scientific and technical revolution.

Bibliography

[1] Abrahamson J.R. (1994a), Mind, Evolution, and Computers, *AI magazine*, pp. 19-22.

[2] Abrahamson J.R. (1994b), A Reply to Mind, Evolution, and Computers, *AI magazine*, pp. 8-9.

[3] Ali K., Pazzani M. (1994), Error reduction through multiple learning descriptions, Report, Irvine, pp. 37.

[4] Alpaydin E. (1998), Techniques for combining multiple learners, Proc. Of Engineering of Int. Systems'98, pp. 7.

[5] Agre P.E., Rosenchein S.J. (eds.) (1995), Computational Research on Interaction and Agency, *Artificial Intelligence*, **73**, pp. 1-2.

[6] AIM-15-3 (1994), Consenting Agents, *AI magazine*, **15**.

[7] Albert D. (1992), *Quantum mechanics and experience*, Cambridge Press.

[8] Ammon K. (1993), An Authomatic Proof of Gödel's Incompleteness Theorem, *Artificial Intelligence*, **61**, pp. 291-307.

[9] Angell I.O. (1993), Intelligence: Logical of Biological, *Communications of the ACM*, **36**, pp. 15-16.

[10] Baffes P.T., Mooney R.J. (1993), Extending Theory Refinement to M-of-N Rules, *Informatica*, **17**, pp. 387-399.

[11] Baldi L. (1991), Microelectronic trends, *Future Generation Computer Systems* **7**.

[12] Baran N. (1992), Operating systems now and beyond, *Byte*, Special issue, January.

[13] Barnett J.A. (1984), How Much is Control Knowledge Worth? A Primitive Example, *Artificial Intelligence*, **22**.

[14] Bauer E., Kohavi R. (1999), An Empirical Comparison of Voting Classification Algorithms: Bagging, Boosting and Variants, *Machine Learning*, **36**, 1/2, pp. 105-139.

[15] Benioff P. (1982), Quantum-Mechanical models of Turing machines that dissipate no energy, *Physical Review Letters* 28, 32, pp. 1581-1585.

[16] Birnbaum L. (1992), Rigor Mortis: a Response to Nilsson's 'Logic and Artificial Intelligence', *Foundations of Artificial Intelligence*, pp. 57-79, (ed.) D. Kirsh, MIT/Elsevier.

[17] Blumer A., Ehrenfeucht A., Haussler D., M. K. Warmuth (1986), Occam's Razor, Technical Report USCS-CRK-86-2.

[18] Boden M.A. (1991), *The Creative Mind: Myths and Mechanisms*, Basic Books.

[19] Boden M.A. (1995), AI's Half-Century, *AI magazine*, Winter 1995, pp. 96-99.

[20] Bohanec M., Rajkovič V. (1991), DEX : an Expert System Shell for Decision Support, *Sistemica*, **1**, pp. 145-157.

[21] Bojadžiev D. (1995), Sloman's View of Gödel's Sentence, *Artificial Intelligence*, **74**, pp. 389-393.

[22] Boolos G. (1990), On 'Seeing' the Truth of the Gödel's Sentence, *Behavioral and Brain Sciences*, **13**, pp. 655-656.

[23] Boolos G.S., Jeffrey R.C. (1980), *Computability and Logic*, Cambridge University Press.

[24] Boose J., Bradshaw J., Kitto C., Shema D. (1989), From ETS to Aquinas : Six Years of Knowledge AcquisitioTon ol Development, *Proc. of EKAW 89*.

[25] Boyle, F. (1990), Algorithms and Physical Laws, *Behavioral and Brain Sciences*, **13**, pp. 656-657.

[26] Bratko I. (1986), *Prolog Programming for Artificial Intelligence*, Addison-Wesley.

[27] Bratko I., Dzeroski S. (1999), *Machine Learning ICML'99*, Morgan Kaufmann.

[28] Bratko I., Muggleton S. (1995), Applications of Inductive Logic Programming, *Communications of the ACM*, **38**, pp. 65-70.

[29] Breiman L. (1996), Bagging predictors, *Machine Learning*, **36**, pp. 123-140.

[30] Breiman L. (1997), Arching the edge, Tech. Report 486 Berkeley University.

[31] Breiman L. (1999), Pasting Small Votes for Classification in Large Databases and On/Line, *Machine Learning*, **36**, 1/2, pp. 85-104.

[32] Brazdil P., Gama J., Henery B. (1994), Characterizing the Applicability of Classification Algorithms Using Meta-Level Learning, *Proc. of ECML-94*, Italy.

[33] Brazdil P., Gams M., Sian L., Torgo L., van de Velde W. (1991), Learning in Distributed Systems and Multi-Agent Environments, *Proc. of EWSL-91*, Porto, Portugal.

[34] Brazdil P., Torgo L. (1990), Knowledge Acquisition via Knowledge Integration, *Proc. of EKAW-90.*

[35] Breiman L., Friedman J.H., Olshen R.A., Stone C.J. (1984), *Classification and Regression Trees*, Wadsworth International Group.

[36] Breuel T.M. (1990), AI and the Turing Model of Computation, *Behavioral and Brain Sciences*, **13**, p. 657.

[37] Brooks R.A. (1991), Intelligence without Representation, *Artificial Intelligence*, **47**, pp. 139-160.

[38] Brooks R.A. (1999), *Cambrian intelligence; The Early History of the New AI*, a Bradford book.

[39] Buntine W. (1989), Learning Classification Rules Using Bayes, *Proc. of the 6th International Workshop on Machine Learning*, Ithaca, New York, USA, pp. 94-98.

[40] Buntine W. (1990), *A Theory of Learning Classification Rules*, Ph.D. thesis, Sydney, Australia.

[41] Butterfield J. (1990), Lucac revived? An Undefended Flank, *Behavioral and Brain Sciences*, **13**, p. 658.

[42] CACM-36-3 (1993), The Fifth Generation Project, *Communications of the ACM*, **36**.

[43] Campbell G.A. (1990), Inventing the PC's future, *Byte*, Extra issue, January 20.

[44] Carbonell J. (1991), Scaling up Knowledge-based Systems via Machine Learning, key-note presentation, *Proc. of EWSL-91*, Porto, Portugal.

[45] Cestnik B. (1992), *Probability Estimations in Automatic Learning*, Ph.D. Dissertation.

[46] Cestnik B., Bratko I. (1988), Learning Redundant Rules in Noisy Domains, *Proc. of ECAI*, Munich, Germany.

[47] Cestnik B., Bratko I. (1991), On Estimating Probabilities in Tree Pruning, *Proc. of EWSL-91*, Porto, Portugal, pp. 138-150.

[48] Chalmers D.J. (1990), Computing the Thinkable, *Behavioral and Brain Sciences*, **13**, pp. 658-659.

[49] Chalmers D.J. (1996), *The consciousness mind*, Oxford Press.

[50] Chan P.K., Stolfo S.J., Wolpert D. (ed.)(1999), Special issue on Integrating Multiple Learned Models for Improving and Scaling Machine Learning Algorithms, *Machine Learning*, **36**, 1/2.

[51] Cheeseman P. (1991), On Finding the Most Probable Model, *Computational Models of Scientific Discovery and Theory Formation*, (ed.) Shrager, J., Langley, P., Morgan Kaufmann.

[52] Churchland P.M., Churchland P.S. (1990), Could Machine Think?, *Scientific American*, **262**, pp. 32-37.

[53] Clancey W.J. (1989), The Knowledge Level Reinterpreted: Modeling How Systems Interact, *Machine Learning*, **4**, pp. 255-257.

[54] Clancey W.J. (1993), The biology of consciousness, *Artificial Intelligence*, **60**, pp. 313-356.

[55] Clark P. (1990), Representing Knowledge as Arguments for Judgmental Problem Solving, *Proc. of Expert Systems 90*, London.

[56] Clark P., Niblett P. (1989), The CN2 Induction Algorithm, *Machine Learning*, **3**, Kluwer Academic Press.

[57] Clark P., Boswell R. (1991), Rule Induction with CN2: Some Recent Improvements, *Proc. of EWSL-91*, Porto, Portugal, pp. 151-163.

[58] Collins H.M. (1996), Embedded or embodied? a review of Hubert Dreyfus' What Computer Still Can't Do, *Artificial Intelligence*, **80**, pp. 99-117.

[59] Crick F. (1994), *The Astonishing Hypothesis, The Scientific Search for the Soul*, New York.

[60] Cromer A. (1994), *The Heretical Nature of Science*, Oxford Press, 240 p.

[61] Cronin M.R. (1994), A Reply to Mind, Evolution, and Computers, *AI magazine*, pp. 6.

[62] Davis M. (1990), Is Mathematical Insight Algoritmic? *Behavioral and Brain Sciences*, **13**, pp. 659-660.

[63] Dennett D.C. (1981), *Brainstorms: Phylosophical Essays on Mind and Psychology*, MIT Press, Cambridge.

[64] Dennett D.C. (1990), Betting your Life on an Algorithm, *Behavioral and Brain Sciences*, **13**, pp. 660-661.

[65] Dennett D.C. (1991), *Consciousness Explained*, Little Brown.

[66] Deutch D. (1985), Quantum Theory, the Church-Turing Principle and the Universal Quantum Computer, *Proceedings of Royal Society*, pp. 97-117.

[67] Deutch D. (1991), Quantum mechanics near closed timelike lines, *Physical Review* 44, 10, pp. 3197-3217.

[68] Deutch D. (1992), Quantum Computation, *Physics Word*, pp. 57-61.

[69] Deutch D., Lockwood M. (1994), The quantum physics of time travel, *Scientific American*, March 1994, pp. 50-56.

[70] DeWitt B.S. (1970), Quantum mechanics and reality, *Physics today* 23, 9, pp. 30-35.

[71] DeWitt B.S. (1973), *The many-worlds interpretation of quantum mechanics*, Princenton University Press.

[72] Dietterich T.G. (1997), Machine-learning research, Four current directions, *AI Magazine*, Winter 1997, pp. 97-136.

[73] Domingos P. (1997), Knowledge acquisition from examples via multiple models, in Fischer D. (ed.), Machine Learning: Proceedings of the 14th Internal conference, pp. 107-115.

[74] Doyle J. (1990), Perceptive questions about Computation and Cognition, *Behavioral and Brain Sciences*, **13**, p. 661.

[75] Drescher G.L. (1991), *Made-Up Minds: A Constructivist Approach to Artificial Intelligence*, MIT Press.

[76] Dreyfus H.L. (1979), *What Computers Can't Do*, Harper and Row.

[77] Dreyfus H.L., Dreyfus S. (1986), *Mind Over Machine*, Free Press.

[78] Drucker H. (1997), Improving regressors using boosting techniques, in Fischer D. (ed.), Machine Learning: Proceedings of the 14th Internal conference, pp. 107-115.

[79] Duby J.J. (1991), The evolution of information technologies in the 90s and its impact on applications, *Future Generation Computer Systems* **7**.

[80] Dyer M.G. (1991), Book Review, *Artificial Intelligence*, **48**, pp. 321-334.

[81] Eagelson R. (1990), Computations over Abstract Categories of Representations, *Behavioral and Brain Sciences*, **13**, pp. 661-662.

[82] Eccles J.C. (1990), Physics of Brain-Mind Interaction, *Behavioral and Brain Sciences*, **13**, pp. 662-663.

[83] Edelman G. (1987), *Neural Darwinism: The Theory of Neuronal Group Selection*, New York, Basic Books.

[84] Edelman G. (1989), *The Remembered Present: A Biological Theory of Consciousness*, New York, Basic Books.

[85] Edelman G. (1992), *Bright Air, Brilliant Fire, On the Matter of the Mind*, Penguin Books.

[86] Epstein R. (1992), The Quest for the Thinking Computer, *AI magazine*, **13**, pp. 81-95.

[87] Epstein R. (1996), *Cognition, Creativity, and Behavior*, Praeger.

[88] Etzioni O. (1993), Intelligence without Robots: A Reply to Brooks, *AI Magazine*, pp. 7-13.

[89] Etzioni O., Weld D.S. (1995), Intelligent Agents on the Internet: Fact, Fiction, and Forecast, *IEEE EXPERT, Intelligent Systems & Their Applications*, Vol. 10, No. 4, pp. 44-49.

[90] Everett H. (1957), Relative state formulation of quantum mechanics, *Reviews of modern physics*, 29, 3, pp. 454-462.

[91] Feigenbaum E.A. (1985), Themes and Case Studies of Knowledge Engineering, *Expert Systems in the Microelectronic Age*, ed. Michie D., Edinburgh University Press.

[92] Feynman R. (1986), Quantum mechanical computers, *Foundations of physics*, 16, pp. 507-531.

[93] FGCS (1993), The Fifth Generation Project, *Communications of the ACM*, **36**, pp. 46-100.

[94] Foltz P.W., Dumais S.T. (1992), Personalized Information Delivery: An Analysis of Information Filtering Methods, *Communications of the ACM* **35**, pp. 51-60.

[95] Fox M.S. (1990), AI and Expert System Myths, Legends, and Facts, *IEEE Expert*, February 1990, pp. 8-19.

[96] Franklin S. (1995), *Artificial Minds*, Bradford.

[97] Freund Z., Schapire R. (1996) Experiments with a new boosting algorithm, Proc. of the 13th Conference on Machine Learning, pp. 148-156.

[98] Furukawa K. (1993), Fifth Generation Computer Systems (FGCS) Project in Japan, *Japan Computer Quaterly* **93**, pp. 1-33.

[99] Gams M. (1973/74), Ant Orientation, *Proteus*, **9/10**, pp. 426-427.

[100] Gams M. (1988), *Unifying Principles in Automatic Learning*, Ph.D. thesis, Ljubljana.

[101] Gams M. (1989), New Measurements Highlight the Importance of Redundant Knowledge, *Proc. of EWSL-89*, Montpellier, France, pp. 71-79.

[102] Gams M. (1995), Strong vs. Weak AI, *Informatica*, **19**, pp. 479-483.

[103] Gams M., Bohanec M., Cestnik B. (1994), A Schema for Using Multiple Knowledge, *Computational Learning Theory and Natural Learning Systems*, Vol. 2, MIT Press, pp. 157-171.

[104] Gams M., Bojadziev D., Knap Z. (1995), Is Intelligence Multiple?, *Communication and Cognition – Artificial Intelligence*, **12**, pp. 285-310.

[105] Gams M., Cestnik B., Sluga L., Butala P. (1986), OPEX - an Expert System for CAPP, *Proc. of the 6th International Workshop on Expert Systems & Their Applications*, Avignon, France.

[106] Gams M., Drobnič M. (1988), Approaching the Limit of Classification Accuracy, *Informatica, 12*, pp. 12-17.

[107] Gams M., Drobnič M., Petkovšek M. (1991), Learning from Examples – a Uniform View, *International Journal of Man-Machine Studies*, **34**, pp. 49-68.

[108] Gams M., Hribovsek B. (1996), An Intelligent-Personal-Agent Interface for Operating Systems, *Applied Artificial Intelligence*, **10**, pp. 353-383.

[109] Gams M., Karalič A. (1989), New Empirical Learning Mechanisms Perform Significantly Better in Real Life Domains, *Proc. of the International Workshop on Machine Learning*, Ithaca, New York.

[110] Gams M., Karba N., Drobnič M. (1993), Average-Case Improvements when Integrating ML and KA, *Applied Intelligence*, Vol. 6, No. 2, pp. 87-99, and *Proc. of IJCAI'93 Workshop: Machine Learning and Knowledge Acquisition*, France, pp. 79-95.

[111] Gams M., Krizman V. (1991), The Principle of Multiple Knowledge, *Informatica*, **15**, pp. 23-28.

[112] Gams M., Lavrač N. (1987), Review of Five Empirical Leaning Systems Within a Proposed Schemata, in *Progress in Machine Learning*, (ed.) Bratko I., Lavrač N., Sigma Press.

[113] Gams M., Žitnik K. (1990), Trends of computer progress, *Informatica* 11, pp. 45-48.

[114] Garnham A. (1990), Don't Ask Plato About the Emperor's Mind, *Behavioral and Brain Sciences*, **13**, pp. 663-664.

[115] Gazzaniga M.S. (1989), Organization of the Human Brain, *Science* **245**, pp. 947-952.

[116] Gigerenzer G. (1990), Strong AI and the Problem of Second-order Algorithms, *Behavioral and Brain Sciences*, **13**, pp. 663-664.

[117] Gilden D.L., Lappin J.S. (1990), Where is the Material of the Emperor's Mind?, *Behavioral and Brain Sciences*, **13**, pp. 665-666.

[118] Ginsberg M. (1991), Book Review, *Artificial Intelligence*, **48**, pp. 335-339.

[119] Glymour C., Kelly K. (1990), Why You'll never Know whwther Rorer Penrose is a Computer, *Behavioral and Brain Sciences*, **13**, pp. 666-667.

[120] Good I.J. (1950), *Probability and the Weighting of Evidence*, Charles Griffing & Co. Limited, London.

[121] Goodstein D. (1995), Ethics and Peer Review, *Biotechnology*, **13**, June, p. 618.

[122] Harmon P., Maus R., Morrisey W. (1988), *Expert Systems, Tools and Applications*, John Wiley & sons.

[123] Hauser L., Rapaport W.J. (1993), Why Isn't My Pocket Calculator a Thinking Thing?, *Minds and Machines*, **3**, pp. 1-29.

[124] Hauser L. (1997), Searle's Chinese box: debunking the Chinese room argument, *Minds and machines* 7, pp. 199-226.

[125] Hayes-Roth F., Fikes R. (1991), Interview, *IEEE Expert*, 6, 5, pp. 3-14.

[126] Hayes P.J., Novak G.S., Lehnert W.G. (1992), ACM Forum – In Defence of Artificial Intelligence, *Communications of the ACM*, **35**, 12, pp. 13-14.

[127] Hendler J., Bobrow D., Gasser L., Hewit C., Minsky M. (1991), Multiple Approaches to Multiple Agent Problem Solving, *Proceedings of IJCAI'91*, Sydney, Australia.

[128] Hertzberger L.O. (1991), Trends in parallel and distributed computing, *Future Generation Computer Systems,* **7**.

[129] Higginbotham J. (1990), Penrose's Platonism, *Behavioral and Brain Sciences,* **13**, pp. 667-668.

[130] Hodgkin D., Houston A.I. (1990), Selecting for the Con in Consciousness, *Behavioral and Brain Sciences,* **13**, pp. 668-669.

[131] Hofstadter D.R. (1979), *Gödel, Escher, Bach: An External Golden Braid*, Basic Books, New York.

[132] Holder L.B. (1991), Maintaining the Utility of Learned Knowledge Using Model-Based Adaptive Control, Ph.D. thesis, University of Illinois, USA.

[133] Hopcroft J.E., Ullman J.D. (1979), *Introduction to Automata Theory, Languages, and Computation*, Addison-Wesley.

[134] Hribovsek B. (1994), Intelligent Interface for VAX/VMS, M. Sc. Thesis.

[135] Hunter G. (1971), *Metalogic - An Introduction to the Metatheory of Standard First Order Logic*, University of California Press.

[136] I.C.E. Report (1990): Mid-term 1990 status and forecast of the IC industry.

[137] INF-17-4 (1993), Special Issue: Multistrategy Learning, *Informatica,* **4**.

[138] Intelligent Agents to the Rescue; Can They Put AI Back On Its Feet? (1996), *IEEE EXPERT, Intelligent Systems & Their Applications*, Vol. 11, No. 6, pp. 2-88.

[139] Jennings N.R., Wooldridge M. (1995), Intelligent Agents and Multi-Agent Systems, *Applied Artificial Intelligence, An International Journal*, Vol. 9, No. 4, pp. 357-369.

[140] Johnson J.L., Ettinger R.H., Hubbard T.L. (1990), A long time ago in a Computing Lab far, far away ..., *Behavioral and Brain Sciences,* **13**, p. 670.

[141] Kalbfleish J. (1979), *Probability and Statistical Inference II*, Springer-Verlag.

[142] Karba N. (1994), *Integrating Knowledge Bases According to the Principle of Multiple Knowledge*, Ph.D. thesis, Kranj, Slovenia.

[143] Karba N., Gams M. (1991), Knowledge-Based Model for Constructing Integrated Knowledge Base, *Proc. of the World Congress on Expert Systems*, Orlando, Florida, USA.

[144] Karba N., Gams M., Drobnic M. (1994), A General Integrating Schema Applied at Iron & Steel Works, *Electrotechnical Review, Special Issue on Applications of Artificial Intelligence in Control Systems*, **62**, pp. 206-212.

[145] Kentridge R.W. (1990), Parallelism and Patterns of Thought, *Behavioral and Brain Sciences*, **13**, pp. 670-671.

[146] Keyes J. (1989), Why Expert Systems Fail, *AI Expert*, **4**, No. 11.

[147] Kitano H. (1993), Challenges of Massive Parallelism, *Proc. of the 13th Int. Joint Conf. on Art. Int.*, pp. 813-834, France.

[148] Kitano H., Hendler J. (1994), *Massively Parallel Artificial Intelligence* (Kitano and Hendler, Eds.), AAAI Press/The MIT Press.

[149] Kohavi R. (1995), A study of cross-validation and bootstrap for accuracy estimation and model selection, in Mellish (Ed.), Machine Learning: Proceedings of the 14th Internal conference, pp. 1137-1143.

[150] Kononenko I. (1985), ASSISTANT: A System for Inductive Learning, *M.Sc. thesis*, Ljubljana.

[151] Kononenko I. (1992), Combining Decisions of Multiple Rules, *Artificial Intelligence V*, (ed.) B. de Boulay and V. Sgurev, North-Holland, pp. 87-96.

[152] Kosslyn S.M., Koenig O. (1992), *Wet Mind: The New Cognitive Neuroscience*, Free Press.

[153] Kovačič M. (1991), Markovian Neural Networks, *Biological Cybernetics*, **64**.

[154] Koza J. (1995), *Codes 5510/5514*, Distributed ad the Sixt Int. Conf. on Genetic Algorithms, Pittsburgh, A Booklet.

[155] Kwok S.W., Carter C. (1990), Multiple Decision Trees, *Uncertainty in Artificial Intelligence*, **4**, pp. 327-335.

[156] LaForte G., Hayes P.J., Ford K.M. (1998), Why Gödel's theorem cannot refute computationalism, *Artificial Intelligence 104*, pp. 265-286.

[157] Laird J.E., Newell A., Rosenbloom P.S. (1987), SOAR: An Architecture for General Intelligence, *Artificial Intelligence*, **33**, pp. 11-64.

[158] Lakoff G. (1987), *Women, Fire, and Dangerous Things: What Categories Reveal about the Mind*, University of Chicago Press.

[159] Leitch R.R, Wiegand M.E., Quek H.C. (1990), Coping with Complexity in Physical System Modelling, *AI Communications*, Vol. 3, No. 2.

[160] Lenat D.B. (1989), When Will Machines Learn?, *Machine Intelligence*, **4**, 255-257.

[161] Lenat D.B. (1995), CYC: A Large-Scale Investment in Konwledge Infrastructure, *Communications of the ACM,* **38**, pp. 33-38.

[162] Lenat D.B., Guha R.V. (1990), *Building Large knowledge-Based Systems: Representations and Inference in the Cyc Project*, Addison-Wesley.

[163] Libet B. (1990), Time-delays in Conscious Processes, *Behavioral and Brain Sciences*, **13**, p. 672.

[164] Littlestone N., Warmuth M.K. (1991), The Weighted Majority Algorithm, Technical Report UCSC-CRL-91-28, USA.

[165] Lloyd S. (1996), Universal Quantum Simulators, *Science*, 273, pp. 1073-1078.

[166] Loebner H.G. (1994), *Communications of the ACM*, **37**, pp. 79-82.

[167] Long M.E. (1991), Secrets of Animal Navigation, *National Geographic*, pp. 70-99.

[168] Lutz R. (1990), Quantum AI, *Behavioral and Brain Sciences*, **13**, pp. 672-673.

[169] Maclennan B. (1990), The Discomforts of Dualism, *Behavioral and Brain Sciences*, **13**, pp. 673-674.

[170] Madsen M.S. (1990), Uncertainty about Quantum Mechanics, *Behavioral and Brain Sciences*, **13**, pp. 674-675.

[171] Maes P. (1994), Agents that Reduce Work and Information Overload, *Communications of the ACM*, **37**, pp. 31-40.

[172] Manago M.V., Kodratoff Y. (1987), Noise and Knowledge Acquisition, *Proc. of IJCAI*, Milano, Italy.

[173] Manaster-Ramer A., Savitch W.J. (1990), Gödel Redux, *Behavioral and Brain Sciences*, **13**, pp. 675-676.

[174] McDermott D. (1990), Computation and Consciousness, *Behavioral and Brain Sciences*, **13**, pp. 676-678.

[175] Merz C.J. (1999), Using Correspondence Analzsis to Combine Classifiers, *Machine Learning*, **36**, 1/2, pp. 33-58.

[176] Merz C.J., Pazzani M.J. (1999), A Principal Components Approach to Combining Regression Estimates, *Machine Learning*, **36**, 1/2, pp. 9-32.

[177] Mettrey W. (1992), Expert Systems and Tools: Myths and Realities. *IEEE Expert*, 7, 1, pp. 4-12.

[178] Michalski R. (1994), Inferential Theory of Learning: Developing Foundations of Multistrategy Learning, in Michalski, Tecuci (ed.), *Machine Learning, A Multistrategy Approach*, Vol. IV, Morgan Kaufmann.

[179] Michalski R.S., Larson J.B. (1983), *Incremental Generation of VL1 Hypotheses: The Underlying Methodology and Description of the Program AQ11*, Technical Report ISG 83-5, Urbana: University of Illinois, USA.

[180] Michalski R.S., Mozetič I., Hong J., Lavrač N. (1986), The Multi-purpose Incremental Learning System AQ15 and its Testing Application to three Medical Domains, *Proc. of AAAI 86*, Philadelphia, USA.

[181] Michalski R.S., Tecuci G. (ed.) (1993), *Proceedings of the Second International Workshop on Multistrategy Learning*, Harpers Ferry, USA.

[182] Michalski R.S., Tecuci G. (1993b), Multistrategy Learning, *IJCAI-93 Tutorial T15*, Chambery, France.

[183] Michalski R., Tecuci G. (ed.) (1994), *Machine Learning, A Multistrategy Approach*, Vol. IV, Morgan Kaufmann.

[184] Michie D. (1991), Methodologies from Machine Learning in Data Analysis and Software, *Computer Journal*, **34**, pp. 559-565.

[185] Michie D. (1993a), Turing's test and conscious thought, *Artificial Intelligence*, **60**, pp. 1-22.

[186] Michie D. (1993b), Methodologies from Machine Learning in Data Analysis and Software, *Informatica*, **17**, pp. 3-13.

[187] Millikan R.G. (1984), *Language, Thought, and other Biological Categories: New Foundations of Realism*, MIT Press.

[188] Mind and Brain, *Scientific American*, **267** (September, Special issue, 1993).

[189] Mingers J. (1989), An Empirical Comparison of Pruning Methods for Decision Tree Induction, *Machine Learning*, **3**, pp. 319-343.

[190] Minsky M. (1987), *The Society of Mind*, Simon and Schuster, New York.

[191] Minsky M. (1991a), Society of mind: a response to four reviews, *Artificial Intelligence*, **48**, pp. 371-396.

[192] Minsky M. (1991b), Logical versus Analogical or Symbolic versus Connectionist or Neat versus Scruffy, *AI magazine*, **12**, pp. 45-51.

[193] Minsky M. (1994), Will Robots Inherit the Earth?, *Scientific Magazine*, October 1994, pp. 87-91.

[194] Minsky M., Papert S. (1969), *Perceptrons: An Introduction to Computational Geometry*, MIT Press, Cambridge.

[195] ML-93 (1993), 'Special Issue on Multistrategy Learning', *Machine Learning,* **11**, No. 2/3.

[196] Moore G.E. (1975), Progress in digital integrated electronics, Technical Digest of 1975, International Electronic Devices Meeting 11.

[197] Moor J.H. (1987), Turing Test, in Shapiro S. C. (ed.), *Encyclopedia of Artificial Intelligence*, John Wiley & Sons.

[198] Moravec H. (1988), *Mind Children: The Future of Robot and Human Intelligence*, Harvard University Press.

[199] Morik K., Wrobel S., Kietz J. U., Emde W. (1993), *Knowledge Acquisition and Machine Learning - Theory, Methods and Applications*, Academic Press.

[200] Mortensen C. (1990), The Power of Machines and Minds, *Behavioral and Brain Sciences*, **13**, pp. 678-679.

[201] MTCM (1992), The Machine that Changed the Word, TV series, ACM.

[202] Murphy P.M., Pazzani M.J. (1994), Exploring the decision forest: an empirical investigation of Occam's razor in decision tree induction, Journal of AI research 1, pp. 257-275.

[203] Nagao M. (1984), A Framework of a Mechanical Translation between Japanese and English by Analogy Principle, in *Artificial and Human Intelligence*, eds. Elithorn, Banerji, Elsevier Science Publishers.

[204] Nance B. (1992), The future of software technology, *Byte*, Special issue, January 15.

[205] Negroponte N. (1970), *The Architecture Machine; Towards a more Human Environment*, MIT Press.

[206] Neufeld E. (1994), Here's the AI (Guest Editor's Introduction), *Computational Intelligence*, **10**, pp. 1-2.

[207] Niall K.K. (1990), Steadfast Intentions, *Behavioral and Brain Sciences*, **13**, pp. 679-680.

[208] Niblett T., Bratko I. (1986), Learning Decision Rules in Noisy Domains, *Expert Systems*, Brighton, UK.

[209] Nilsson N.N. (1980), *Principles of Artificial Intelligence*, Tioga Publishing.

[210] Nilsson N.N. (1991), Logic and Artificial Intelligence, *Artificial Intelligence*, **47**, pp. 31-56.

[211] Ornstein R. (1991), *The Evolution of Consciousness: Of Darwin, Freud, and Cranial Fire: The Origins of the Way We Think*, Prentice Hall.

[212] O'Rourke J. (1993), Triple Book Review, *Artificial Intelligence*, **60**, pp. 303-312.

[213] Otsu N. (1993), Toward Flexible Intelligence: MITI's New Program of Real World Computing, *Proc. of the 13th Int. Joint Conf. on Art. Int.*, pp. 786-791.

[214] Pazzani M. (ed.) (1995), *Machine Learning List*, **7.14**, Electronic journal.

[215] Pearl J. (1978), On the Connection Between the Complexity and Credibility of Inferred Models, *International Journal of General Systems*, **4**.

[216] Penrose R. (1989), *The Emperor's New Mind: Concerning computers, minds, and the laws of physics*, Oxford University Press.

[217] Penrose R. (1990), Precis of the Emperor's New Mind: Concerning computers, minds, and the laws of physics, *Behavioral and Brain Sciences*, **13**, pp. 643-705.

[218] Penrose R. (1994), *Shadows of the Mind, A Search for the Missing Science of Consciousness*, Oxford University Press.

[219] Perlis D. (1990), The Emperor's Old Hat, *Behavioral and Brain Sciences*, **13**, pp. 680-681.

[220] Pfeifer R., Scheier C. (1999), *Understanding Intelligence*, A Bradford Book.

[221] Pinker S. (1984), *Language Learnability ad Language Development*, MIT Press.

[222] Pollock J.L. (1989), *How to Build a Person: A Prolegomenon*, MIT Press.

[223] Putnam H. (1988), *Representation and Reality*, MIT Press.

[224] Quinlan R.J. (1983), Learning Efficient Classification Procedures and Their Application to Chess End Games, (ed.) Michalski R.S., Carbonell J.G., Mitchell T.M., *Machine Learning: an Artificial Intelligence Approach*, Tioga Publishing, pp. 463-482.

[225] Quinlan J.R. (1986), Induction of Decision Trees, *Machine Learning,* **1**, Kluwer Academic Publishers.

[226] Quinlan J.R. (1987), Generating Production Rules From Decision Trees, *Proc. of IJCAI*, Milano.

[227] Reeke G.N. (1991), Book Review, *Artificial Intelligence*, **48**, pp. 335-339.

[228] Rendell L., Powell B., Cho H., Seshu R. (1988), Improving the Design of Rule-Learning Systems, *Proc. of The 8th International Workshop on Expert Systems & Their Applications*, Avignon, France.

[229] Rendell L., Seshu R., Tcheng D. (1987), Layered Concept-Learning and Dynamically-Variable Bias Management, *Proc. of IJCAI*, Milano.

[230] Robbin J.W. (1969), *Mathematical Logic – A First Course*, Benjamin.

[231] Robinson P. (1990), The four multimedia gospels, *Byte*, February.

[232] Roeper T. (1990), Systematic, Unconscious Thought is the Place to Anchor Quantum Mechanics in the Mind, *Behavioral and Brain Sciences*, **13**, pp. 681-682.

[233] Rosenblat F. (1962), *Principles of neurodynamics*, Spartan Books.

[234] Rosenfield I. (1992), *The Strange, Familiar and Forgotten: An Anatomy of Consciousness*, A. A. Knopf.

[235] Roskies A. (1990), Seeing Truth or just Seeming True? *Behavioral and Brain Sciences*, **13**, pp. 682-683.

[236] Ryan B. (1990), The once and future king, *Byte*, November.

[237] Schank R. (1991), Where's the AI?, *AI magazine*, **12**, pp. 38-49.

[238] Schapire R. (1989), The strength of weak learnability, *Proc. of 21st ACM Symp. of Computing*, pp. 28-33.

[239] Schlimmer J.C. (1987), Learning and Representation Change, *Proc. of AAAI 87*.

[240] SCI-AM-93 (1993), Mind and Brain, *Scientific American*, **267**, (September, Special issue).

[241] Seager W. (1991), *Metaphysics of Consciousness*, Routlidge, London.

[242] Searle J.R. (1982), The Chinese Room Revisited, *Behavioral and Brain Sciences*, **8**, pp. 345-348.

[243] Searle J.R. (1990), Is the Brain's Mind a Computer Program?, *Scientific American*, **262**, (January), pp. 26-31.

[244] Searle J.R. (1992), *The Rediscovery of the Mind*, MIT Press.

[245] Shannon C.E., Weaver W. (1964), *The Mathematical Theory of Communications*, Urbana, Illinois, University of Illinois Press.

[246] Schapire R.E. (1997), Using output codes to boost multiclass learning problems, in Fischer D. (ed.), Machine Learning: Proceedings of the 14th Internal conference, pp. 313-321.

[247] Schapire R.E., Freund Y., Bartlett P., Lee W.S. (1997), Boosting the margin: a new explanation for the effectiveness of voting methods, in Fischer D. (ed.), Machine Learning: Proceedings of the 14th Internal conference, pp. 322-330.

[248] Schapiro S. (1995), Computationalism, *Minds and machines* 5, pp. 517-524.

[249] Shapiro S.C. (ed.) (1990), *Encyclopedia of Artificial Intelligence*, John Wiley & Sons.

[250] Shapiro L.G. (1987), *Structural Induction in Expert Systems*, TI Press, Addison-Wesley Publishing.

[251] Shieber S.M. (1994), Lessons From a Restricted Turing Test, *Communications of the ACM*, **37**, pp. 70-78, pp. 83-84.

[252] Shortliffe E.H. (1976), *Computer-Based Medical Consultations: MYCIN*, American Elsevier Publishing.

[253] Sloman A. (1992), The emperor's real mind: review of the Roger Penrose's The Emperor's New Mind: Concerning Computers, Minds and the Laws of Physics, *Artificial Intelligence*, **56**, pp. 335-396.

[254] Sluga A., Butala P., Lavrač N., Gams M. (1988), An attempt to implement expert system techniques in CAPP, *Robotics & Computer-Integrated Manufacturing*, 4, 1/2, p. 77-82.

[255] Smyth P., Wolpert D. (1999), Linearly Combining Density Estimators via Stacking, *Machine Learning*, **36**, 1/2, pp. 59-84.

[256] Smithers T. (1990), The Pretender's New Clothes, *Behavioral and Brain Sciences*, **13**, pp. 683-684.

[257] Smoliar S. W. (1991), Book Review, *Artificial Intelligence*, **48**, pp. 349-370.

[258] Soucek B., Paradigm / Problem Matching, in *Dynamic, Genetic and Chaotic Programming*, Wiley, New York, (1992).

[259] Soucek B, Soucek M. (1988), *Neural and Massivelly Parallel Computers*, Wiley, New York.

[260] Special Issue on Multistrategy Learning (1993), *Machine Learning*, **11**.

[261] Spector L. (1999), Quantum computation, Tutorial, GECCO conference, July 14.

[262] Stanfil C., Waltz D. (1988), The Memory-Based Reasoning Paradigm, *Communications of the ACM.*

[263] Stanovich K.E. (1990), And then a Miracle Happens ..., *Behavioral and Brain Sciences*, **13**, pp. 684-685.

[264] Steels L., Van de Velde W. (1985), Learning in Second Generation Expert Systems, *Knowledge Based Problem Solving*, ed. Kowalik J.S., Prentice Hall Inc., New Jersey.

[265] Stefik M.J., Smoliar S.W. (ed.) (1993), The commonsense reviews, *Artificial Intelligence*, **61**, pp. 37-181.

[266] Taylor M.M. (1990), The Thinker Dreams of Being an Emperor, *Behavioral and Brain Sciences*, **13**, pp. 685-686.

[267] Tecuci G. (1991), Learning as Understanding the External World, *Proc. of the First International Workshop on Multistrategy Learning*, Harpers Ferry, USA, pp. 49-65.

[268] Tecuci G. (ed.) (1993), Special Issue: Multistrategy Learning, *Informatica*, **4**.

[269] Tecuci G., Kedar S., Kodratoff, Y. (ed.) (1993), *Proc. of IJCAI-93 Workshop Machine Learning and Knowledge Acquisition*, France.

[270] Tsotsos J.K. (1990), Exactly Which Emperor is Penrose Talking About?, *Behavioral and Brain Sciences*, **13**, pp. 686-687.

[271] Turing A.M. (1937), On Computable Numbers with an Application to the Entscheidungsproblem, *Proc. of the London Mathematics Society*, pp. 230-265.

[272] Turing A.M. (1950), Computing Machinery and Intelligence, *Mind*, **59**, pp. 433-460.

[273] Urbančič, T., Kononenko I. Križman V. (1991), *AI applications in Slovenia*, Technical report IJS DP-6183, Jozef Stefan Institute.

[274] Utgoff P.E. (1986), *Machine Learning of Inductive Bias*, Kluwer Academic Publishers.

[275] Valiant L.G. (1984), A Theory of the learnable, *Communications of ACM* **27**, pp. 1134-1142.

[276] Valiant L.G. (1990), General purpose parallel architecture, in Handbook of Theoretical Computer Science, ed. Leeuween, North-Holland.

[277] Varela F.J. (1990), Between Turing and Quantum Mechanics there is Body to be Found, *Behavioral and Brain Sciences*, **13**, pp. 687-688.

[278] Varga M. (1990), Gödel wusste sehr wohl, was er meinte, *Ethik und Sozialwissenschaften*, **1**, pp. 145-148.

[279] Wallace M. (1996), Constraint Logic Programming - Status and Prospects, *Proc. of the Third World Congress on Expert Systems*, pp. 13-23, Seoul, Korea.

[280] Waltz D., Pustejovsky J. (1990), Prenrose's Grand Unified Mystery, *Behavioral and Brain Sciences*, **13**, pp. 688-690.

[281] Wandschneider D. (1975), Zur Eliminierung des Gödelschen Unvollständigkeitsproblems im Zusammenhang dem Antinomienproblem, *Zeitschrift für ellgemeine Wissenschaftstheorie VI-1*, pp. 65-81.

[282] Wandschneider D. (1990), Die Gödeltheorie und das Problem Künsticher Intelligenz, *Ethik und Sozialwissenschaften*, pp. 107-159 (with replies).

[283] Weisenbaum J. (1986), *Computer Power and Human Reason: From Judgment to Calculation*, Freeman.

[284] Wheeler J.A. (1957), Assessment of Everett's Relative state formulation of quantum theory, *Reviews of modern physics*, 29, 3, pp. 463-465.

[285] Wilensky R. (1990), Computability, Consciousness, and Algorithms, *Behavioral and Brain Sciences*, **13**, pp. 690-691.

[286] Wilkes M.W. (1992), Artificial Intelligence as the Year 2000 Approaches, *Communications of the ACM*, **35**, pp. 17-20.

[287] Winograd T., Flores F. (1986), *Understanding Computers and Cognition: A New Foundation for Design*, Norwood New Jersey: Ablex.

[288] Winograd T. (1991), Thinking Machines: Can There Be? Are We?, in Sheehan J, Sosna M., eds., *The Boundaries of Humanity: Humans, Animals, Machines*, University of Berkeley, pp. 198-223.

[289] Winston P.H. (1992), *Artificial Intelligence*, Addison-Wesley.

[290] Wittgenstein L. (1974), *Philosophical Investigations*, Oxford, UK.

[291] Xu L., Krzyzak A., Suen C.Y. (1992), Methods of Combining Multiple Classifiers and Their Applications to Handwrite Recognition, *IEEE Transaction on Systems, Man, and Cybernetics*, **22**, 418-435.

[292] Zhang B., Zhang L. (1990): Hierarchy and Statistical Heuristic Search, *Future Generation Computer Systems*, **6**.

[293] Zytkow J.M. (1990), Minds Beyond Brains and Algorithms, *Behavioral and Brain Sciences*, **13**, pp. 691-692.

Index